Discourse Features
of Ten Languages of
West-Central Africa

Summer Institute of Linguistics and
The University of Texas at Arlington
Publications in Linguistics

Publication 119

Editor

Donald A. Burquest
University of Texas at Arlington

Consulting Editors

Doris A. Bartholomew
Pamela M. Bendor-Samuel
Desmond C. Derbyshire
Robert A. Dooley
Jerold A. Edmondson

Austin Hale
Robert E. Longacre
Eugene E. Loos
Kenneth L. Pike
Viola G. Waterhouse

Discourse Features of Ten Languages of West-Central Africa

Stephen H. Levinsohn, Editor

A Publication of
The Summer Institute of Linguistics
and
The University of Texas at Arlington
1994

©1994 by the Summer Institute of Linguistics, Inc.

Library of Congress Catalog No: 94–67160

ISBN: 0–88312–619–2

ISSN: 1040–0850

Printed in the United States of America

Cover design by Hazel Shorey

Copies of this and other publications of the Summer Institute of Linguistics may be obtained from

International Academic Bookstore
7500 W. Camp Wisdom Road
Dallas, TX 75236

Contents

Section Three: Semantic Constraints on
Relevance and Prominence Devices

Preface

Stephen H. Levinsohn

The Niger-Congo and Chadic languages of Cameroon and surrounding countries are a goldmine of linguistic features whose meaning and contextual effects can only be elucidated by taking into account domains larger than the sentence. The topics covered in this volume scarcely scratch the surface of this vast area of study.

The three papers of the first section concentrate on how coherence is maintained in a well-formed text when the author introduces a local discontinuity of reference (involving a change in the topic of the text and its participants), of situation (a change in its spatiotemporal setting), and of action (an interruption in its chronological or logical progression). The Levinsohn paper which begins the section provides an overview of Givón's (1983, 1990) work on coherence and discontinuities. It then outlines three devices that are associated with discontinuities in languages of Cameroon: (a) topicalization; (b) the presence, rather than absence, of tense-aspect markers; and (c) the employment of particular (generally, increased) forms of participant reference encoding. Heath and Heath describe topicalization in Makaa, and then move to a fourth device—the use of the focus-presupposition construction. In Makaa, this construction interrupts the flow of an argument as prominence is given to the assertions with which it is associated. In Nɔmaandɛ, the same construction is employed in connection with summary statements (see the Wilkendorf paper).

Any work on participant reference encoding must also build on Givón's insights, particularly those encapsulated in his "iconicity principle" (1983:18). The three papers of the second section of this volume identify different factors which affect the amount of encoding that is used as a speaker refers to participants throughout a discourse. Pohlig and Levinsohn concentrate on two sets of demonstratives which qualify nouns in Mofu-Gudur; one indicates whether the referent is or is not the current center of attention; the other marks, among other things, the status of a known referent as locally salient or non-salient. Taylor, after describing how five categories of participants are introduced in Nɔmaandɛ narratives, presents the system of participant reference encoding at points of discontinuity and in connection with highlighted or backgrounded information in the language. Finally, Levinsohn outlines eight steps in a methodology of field procedures for the analysis of participant reference encoding in monologue.

Regina Blass' application of insights from Relevance Theory to particles which "facilitate the interpretation process" (1990:126) has been of great value in the study of morphemes which provide "semantic constraints on relevance" (Blakemore 1987) in languages represented in this volume. Section 3 of the volume begins with Morgan's study of three such particles in the Lobala language of N.W. Zaïre: indicators of addition, countering, and exclusion. Mfonyam also describes an additive marker in Bafut. In addition, he discusses what Levinsohn calls a "developmental marker" (1992:32–37). Such a marker indicates that the information concerned "is relevant in its own right" (Blass 1990:256–57) because it represents a new development in the discourse, as far as the author's purpose is concerned. Pohlig and Pohlig present a set of four particles in Mandara: developmental, additive (strengthening a previous expectation), countering a previous expectation, and strengthening a counter-expectation. Finally, a further dimension to the topic of constraining particles is provided by Spreda's notes on three Meta' markers which indicate parallelism between actions or situations.

Several papers discuss prominence and backgrounding. Taylor and Mfonyam both describe how the functions of indirect and direct reported speech differ. Taylor finds that, in Nɔmaandɛ, direct speech is the norm, while indirect speech is used when the speech concerned is the 'trigger' to a new development in the story. Mfonyam recognizes three types of reported speeches in Bafut; the norm is direct speech in which a logophoric pronoun refers to the speaker; indirect speech is restricted to information of a background nature, while direct speech which uses a first person pronoun spotlights the speaker. Another way in which a known participant may be spotlighted in Bafut is by omitting the article, when referring to him or her with a proper name.

Follingstad notes a strong correlation between the presence of a particular conjunction in Tyap and foreground information. Iconically related conjunctions convey focus or emphasis on the proposition concerned.

Mfonyam's paper also outlines devices which portray emphasis in Bafut. In addition, he discusses the use of repeated information in order to highlight following assertions. Heath and Heath report a similar device in Makaa. The volume concludes with Perrin's description of how the rheme (most important piece of new information) of a Mambila sentence may be distinguished from a focused constituent, even though, typically, both are placed at the end of the sentence.

The papers in this collection were produced during a discourse analysis workshop held during the first quarter of 1993 in Yaoundé, Cameroon. The research was undertaken at the training center of the Société Internationale de Linguistique, under a cooperative agreement with the Ministry of Scientific and Technical Research of the Republic of Cameroon. I am very grateful to all those who were involved in any way in the workshop. I particularly want to thank my fellow-consultants, Miss Mona Perrin, Dr. James Roberts, and Dr. Keith Snider, for their input and their dedication to the production of the papers. The last two named, together with Miss Terri Scruggs, also assisted the workshop participants in the polishing of the papers.

Stephen H. Levinsohn
Yaoundé, March 1993

References

Blakemore, Diana. 1987. Semantic constraints on relevance. Oxford: Basil Blackwell.

Blass, Regina. 1990. Relevance relations in discourse: A study with special reference to Sissala. Cambridge: Cambridge University Press.

Givón, Talmy, ed. 1983. Topic continuity in discourse. Philadelphia: Benjamins.

————. 1990. Syntax: A functional-typological introduction 2. Philadelphia: Benjamins.

Levinsohn, Stephen H. 1992. Discourse features of New Testament Greek. Dallas: Summer Institute of Linguistics.

Section One

Cohesion and Discontinuities

Discontinuities in Coherent Texts

Stephen H. Levinsohn

Abstract

Coherent texts display local discontinuities of reference (involving changes in the topic of the text and its participants), of situation (involving changes in the time and location of the events of the text), and of action (most commonly, when the actions are not in chronological sequence). Devices associated with such discontinuities in the languages represented in this article include topicalization, the presence of tense-aspect markers, and increased coding material when refering to participants.

Résumé

Les textes cohérents se distinguent par des discontinuités locales de référence, de situation et d'action. Ces discontinuités impliquent, dans le cas des discontinuités de référence, des changements au niveau du topique du texte et des participants présentés dans celui-ci et, dans le cas des discontinuités de situation, des changements au niveau du cadre temporel et physique dans lequel se produisent les événements décrits dans le texte. Enfin, des discontinuités d'action se dégagent le plus souvent lorsque les actions ne se présentent pas par ordre chronologique. Dans le cas des langues représentées dans le présent volume, des mécanismes associés à ces discontinuités sont les suivants : la topicalisation ; la présence des marqueurs temporo-aspectuels ; et, enfin, le recours à un encodage plus important dans les références aux participants.

What makes a well-told story or a well-written newspaper article cohere?[1] Why is it, for example, that the following sentences belong together, even though the way the main participant and the places are referred to differs?

> For the second time in one month, the Prime Minister was in the North-West province over the weekend for what has become a copyright grassroots style of interacting with the people. Mr. Simon Achidi Achu was in Boyo and Menchum Division to preach appeasement and national reconciliation... (Cameroon Tribune of 26 January 1993, p. 1)

Talmy Givón says (1990:896–97) that "coherent discourse tends to maintain, over a span of several propositions, respectively:

(a) the same referent ('topic')
(b) the same or contiguous time
(c) the same or contiguous location
(d) sequential action."

Such coherence is at least partially illustrated in the passage cited above. It has the same referent; "the Prime Minister" and "Mr. Simon Achidi Achu" refer to the same person. It is located in the same place; "Boyo and Menchum Division" are found in the "North-West province." Furthermore, the two sentences are assumed to refer to the same occasion in time.

Nevertheless, examination of the internal structure of a coherent monologue that extends over more than two or three sentences reveals that the sentences do not form a simple string. Rather, the text naturally segments into sub-units, which may be referred to as paragraphs or chapters.

Such segmentation results from LOCAL DISCONTINUITIES of the same parameters that Givón listed, namely:

> discontinuities of reference (topic, participants);
> discontinuities of situation (time, location);
> discontinuities of action.

---

[1]An earlier version of this paper was given at the University of Yaoundé in February 1993. It was prepared during a discourse analysis workshop hosted by the Société Internationale de Linguistique and attended by linguists studying various languages of Cameroon, Chad, Nigeria, and Zaïre. Thanks is due to them for allowing the citation of the examples which appear in the paper.

One thing this paper seeks to bring out is that the devices employed by speakers and writers to indicate discontinuities in a coherent monologue also maintain the overall unity and continuity of the text by guiding the listener or reader across the discontinuity.

The paper looks briefly, first of all, at what constitutes discontinuities of reference, situation, and action. It then turns to some devices employed in various languages of Cameroon that mark such discontinuities and at the same time preserve the overall continuity of the text in which they occur.

Discontinuities of REFERENCE concern changes in the topic of the text and in the participants involved. Expressions such as 'the second reason' or 'other speakers' may mark such changes.

Discontinuities of SITUATION concern changes in the time and location of the contents of the text. Expressions such as 'the next day' or 'back at the house' may mark such changes.

Discontinuities of ACTION are perhaps less obvious. Givón (1983:8) defines action continuity as follows:

> ACTION continuity pertains primarily to *temporal sequentiality* within [a] thematic paragraph, but also to temporal *adjacency* therein . . . actions are given primarily in the natural sequential order in which they actually occurred, and most commonly there is small if any temporal gap . . . between one action and the next.

It follows that common action discontinuities occur, inter alia, (a) when actions are not given in natural sequential order (including when a narrative is interrupted by a background comment or a flashback to an earlier event) and (b) when a significant temporal gap occurs between the actions, even though a new temporal setting is not given.

What, then, are the types of devices associated with these discontinuities? This paper considers three which are exemplified in languages of Cameroon: topicalization devices, tense-aspect markers, and participant reference encoding. (A fourth device, the use of a focus-presupposition construction in connection with an action discontinuity, is described in this volume for Makaa (Heath and Heath's paper) and for Nɔmaandɛ (Wilkendorf's paper).)

Topicalization

To discuss the concept of topicalization, it is first necessary to distinguish between different sentence "articulations" (Andrews 1985:77–80). Andrews recognizes three principal types of articulation: topic-comment, focus-presupposition, and presentational.

An example of topic-comment articulation, in which there is a topic (usually a pronoun or noun phrase) and a comment giving (new) information about the topic, is in (1). An example of focus-presupposition articulation, in which the presupposition ('someone went to cock's house') is known to the hearer and the focus is on WHO went, is in (2). An example of presentational articulation, in which a participant is introduced to the text, is in (3).

(1) Squirrel / went to cock's house.

(2) (It was) SQUIRREL (who) went to cock's house.

(3) Once upon a time there was a squirrel.

This paper concentrates on sentences with topic-comment articulation. In a single sentence with such an articulation as in (1), the author wishes to talk about something—the topic—and to make a comment about that topic.

In addition to topic and comment, however, a sentence may have an adverbial phrase or clause (or, more rarely, some other constituent) which has been topicalized as in (4).[2]

(4) On another day / squirrel / went to cock's house.

Topicalized constituents occur at the beginning of the sentence and in many languages are associated with a marker. For example, in Guɗe (Chadic),[3] *má* introduces a topicalized constituent as shown in (5).

(5) *má* on another day / squirrel / went to cock's house.

The first claim of this paper is that topicalized constituents occur at points of discontinuity. This is illustrated in the Guɗe text which appears in the appendix. Topicalized constituents occur as follows:

---

[2]To avoid potential confusion between the terms TOPICALIZED CONSTITUENT and TOPIC, Dik (1981:141) labels them respectively "theme" and "topic." Beneš (1962) calls them "basis" and "theme" (see also Levinsohn 1987). Levinsohn (1992a) calls them "point of departure" and "sentence topic."

[3]Guɗe is a Chadic language of the Margi-Gbwata group (Dieu and Renaud 1983:357), spoken in the Mayo Tsanaga Division, Northern Province, Republic of Cameroon, and also in Nigeria (Hoskison 1983).

—at the beginning of the story (7a), in connection with the change of situation from real time to story time;

—in (7d), in connection with the change of location from Goat's house to that of Squirrel's in-laws;

—in (7h), in connection with the change of time to when Goat returned; in addition, the main clause of (7h) is a flashback, describing what had happened before Goat returned (an example of an action discontinuity);

—in (7m), in connection with the change of time to another day; and

—in (7o), in connection with the background comment about Cock being clever (another example of an action discontinuity).

Furthermore, in the body of the story (ignoring summary sentences (7y) and (7z)), there is CONTINUITY of reference, situation, and participants when a topicalized constituent does not occur.

The above discussion does not deal with the topicalized constituent in (7g). This is of a special type known as TAIL-HEAD LINKAGE, because information from the end of the previous sentence (the tail) is repeated at the beginning (head) of the next. The effect of repeating information like this is to slow the story down. Such repetition typically occurs immediately before especially important information like the climax of a paragraph. As for the use of the topicalization marker, it may be thought of as artificially introducing a discontinuity, so that the climactic event itself can be set off from those that led up to it.

It has already been suggested that devices such as topicalization which are used to indicate discontinuities in a coherent text also maintain the overall unity and continuity of that text by guiding the listener or reader across the discontinuity. This is because topicalized constituents have a BIDIRECTIONAL function: (a) they serve as a POINT OF DEPARTURE for what follows and (b) they indicate the primary BASIS for linking what follows to its context (see Beneš 1962, Givón 1990:846–47).

In (7a) of the Gude text, for instance, the topicalization of 'on another day' provides the temporal point of departure for what follows—it sets the time for subsequent events. In addition, it indicates that this event is to be related to earlier ones primarily on the basis of time, by a "switch" (Andrews 1985:78) from the previous temporal setting (in this case, implicit) to the new one.

Similarly, in (7o), the topicalization of 'Cock' provides the referential point of departure for what follows: it indicates that the next assertions concern Cock. It also indicates that what follows is to be related to what precedes by a switch of attention from Squirrel to Cock.

In addition to adverbial constituents of time and noun phrases describing the subject of a clause (or the object as in (6)), many other constituents can be topicalized. Most commonly they are adverbials of location, condition, purpose, or reason. In each case, they mark a discontinuity in the text, while at the same time maintaining its overall continuity by indicating the primary basis for linking what follows to the context.[4]

Chadic languages tend to have specific markers of topicalization (see Hollingsworth and Peck 1992). In Niger-Congo languages of Cameroon, however, topicalized constituents generally carry no marker. Rather, they are recognized primarily by their position at the beginnning of the sentence (see Heath and Heath, this volume).

Tense-aspect markers

Many of the languages of Cameroon employ verb forms without overt tense-aspect markers to present the main events of a narrative which is set in the past. Hoskison (1983:88) calls such forms "neutral aspect"; Perrin (1983:6) refers to them as having a "temps narratif." (See also Longacre 1990:109.)

The conditions for using forms which contain tense-aspect markers vary from one group of languages to another. In Grassfields Bantu languages, for instance Bafut and Meta', the presence in a narrative of the appropriate past tense marker indicates that the information concerned is of a background nature (Mfonyam, this volume; Spreda, p.c.).

In Chadic languages like Gude, by way of contrast, the presence of such a marker is associated with certain types of action discontinuity. In particular, it occurs when actions are not given in natural sequential order.[5]

---

[4]See Levinsohn 1992b for references to articles discussing the functions of preposed and postposed adverbials in English.

[5]Nevertheless, sentences containing a tense-aspect marker in Chadic languages may still present information of a background nature. Thus, Hollingsworth (1989–90:134) claims for Mofu-Gudur "verbs marked for tense/aspect are off the event line and provide background information." In Gude, however, a more general indicator of background information in narrative appears to be verb-subject order (an order which sentences containing a tense-aspect marker must follow) and sentences with neutral aspect-narrative tense have subject-verb order (Hoskison 1983:88).

In the text which appears in the appendix, for instance, the tense-aspect marker $k\acute{\sigma}$[6] (labelled T/A) occurs in independent clauses in the following places:

— in the first sentence of the story, in connection with the switch from real time to story time;
— in the main clause of (7h), which is a flashback, occurring prior to the event described in the topicalized clause of that sentence;
— in (7v), which is a background comment on how Squirrel felt about being outwitted by Cock, not the result of him eating;
— in (7y), which is a summary of what happened in the previous sentences, not the next event in sequence (7x); and
— in (7z), which refers to an event prior to that of (7y).

In contrast, the tense marker does not appear in any independent clause which describes an event in chronological sequence with the one presented in the previous clause or sentence. Even when the sentence concerned is introduced with a topicalized constituent, the tense marker does not occur. This last observation is at variance with Hoskison's claim (1983:88):

In narrative discourse, the first sentence in a paragraph (logically coherent sequence of sentences) normally has explicit aspectual marking... This first sentence has the effect of establishing the temporal and aspectual setting for the whole paragraph. All of the subsequent sentences in that paragraph will be in the neutral aspect.

Were Hoskison's claim true, sentence (7m) of the text would certainly have had "explicit aspectual marking."

Thus, the presence versus absence of tense-aspect markers in a language like Guɗe is closely related to the presence versus absence of action discontinuities.

---

[6]Perrin (1983:6) calls this marker "temps passé"; Hoskison (1983:83) calls it "completive aspect." $k\acute{\sigma}$ is generally accompanied by some form of palatalization of the verb and associated constituents (Hoskison). An apparently related marker, $t\acute{\sigma}$, occurs in those topicalized constituents which refer to actions that took place prior to those of the clause to which they are subordinated, namely, in sentences (10), (14), and (19) (this last perhaps being a verbless clause). In the Guɗe dialect studied by Hoskison, this marker appears to be realized as $k\acute{\sigma}$ (see the examples cited on pp. 129–30).

Participant reference encoding

Linguists have long recognized that, following a discontinuity in a text, "more coding material" (Givón 1983:18) must be used to refer to a topic or participant than if no discontinuity is present. Thus, if the normal way to refer to the same subject in successive clauses or sentences is with an unstressed pronoun, then, following a discontinuity, a stressed pronoun or even a full noun phrase may be used. For examples of this phenomenon, see Taylor's paper in this volume.

An interesting example of this "iconicity principle," as Givón (1983) calls it, occurs in a number of Niger-Congo languages. In Makaa, for instance, speakers who wish to refer to the same class 1 third-person singular subject as in the previous clause or sentence must choose between two pronouns: *à* and *nyà*.

At first sight, the selection of one or other of these pronouns in a narrative appears to be determined phonologically—*à* precedes consonants, *nyà* precedes vowels—whether the subject is the same as or different from that of the preceding clause or sentence. However, *nyà* is found in verbless clauses introducing reported speech, even though the pronoun is always followed by the particle *nà*. This is shown in (6).

(6)   pronoun   next morpheme

Ant	*nyà*	*á* [PAST]	comes leaves on a journey
that	*à*	*kà* [goes]	proposing to ...,
			walks until now goes arrives
			at intersection of a road,
	à	*mú* [then]	goes stops
	à	*njúl* [waits]	there
and	*à*	*ŋgà* [PROGRESSIVE]	rests
and	*nyá**	*ka* [now]	comes moves goes to his goal
dog			then arrives finds *nyà* [him]
	nyà	*nà* [that]	'Dog, where are you going?'
	nyà	*nà* [that]	'I'm going ...'
			...
Ant, woman			then sends *nyà* [him] water
	à	*shin* [finishes]	goes washes

*The high tone on the pronoun indicates that the clause concerned is subordinated.

The illusion of phonological conditioning for *à* and *nyà* is created by the fact that verb roots in Makaa always begin with a consonant, whereas some tense markers consist only of a vowel. Tense markers typically occur only at points of discontinuity in a narrative, whereas, at points of continuity, the pronoun is always followed immediately by a verb root or by one of a set of particles which also happen to begin with a consonant, hence the illusion!

As already hinted above, the distribution of *à* and *nyə̀* in Makaa is best described in terms of the absence or presence of a discontinuity. *à* is used when there is continuity, whether or not the subjects of successive clauses remain the same. *nyə̀* is employed at points of discontinuity.[7]

Partial confirmation of the association of *à* with continuity and of *nyə̀* with discontinuities is found from listening to tape recordings of oral Makaa texts. Sentences containing *nyə̀* most frequently are preceded by a general declination of pitch (sometimes called downdrift) plus resetting of the tonal register. These characteristics are frequently absent before sentences containing *à*. It must be emphasized, though, that the correlation between the presence versus absence of these characteristics and the use of *nyə̀* versus *à* is only partial.

To summarize the distribution of the two class 1 third-person singular pronouns in Makaa: (a) *nyə̀* is employed at points of discontinuity and (b) *à* is used when there is continuity.

A similar distribution of two class 1 third-person singular pronouns is found also in Tyap, a Plateau Niger-Congo language spoken in the middle belt of the Federal Republic of Nigeria (Follingstad this volume).

Finally, by way of review, this paper started from the position that coherent texts contain discontinuities of action, situation, and reference. It has then shown that the presence versus absence of discontinuities influences the use versus non-use of topicalization devices and of tense-aspect markers, as well as the employment of different forms of participant reference encoding.

Appendix

The following is a simplified, free translation of a text told in Gudᶒ by Mr. Wouyardiya Timothée which was written down, analyzed, and translated by Miss Catherine Menetrey and Miss Mona Perrin. T/A represents a tense-aspect marker.

---

[7]Nevertheless, the use of *nyə̀* in verbless clauses which introduce a reported speech appears to be formulaic, since the referent of *nyə̀* may be the same as that of the subject of the preceding clause. Furthermore, *à* is never employed in such clauses, however devoid of discontinuities the context seems to be.

(7)   Squirrel, Goat, and Cock

a.	*má* once upon a time,	Squirrel	T/A	got up.
b.		He		went to look for Goat in order that they go to his in-laws.
c.		They		got up and left.
d.	*má* they arrived,	people		brought them fufu.
e.		Squirrel		tasted and said to Goat, 'No salt in this sauce! Go to the house and get some for us!'
f.		Goat		got up and left.
g.	*má* he left to look for salt in the house,	Squirrel		took and ate all the fufu.
h.	*má* Goat returned with the salt,	Squirrel	T/A	ate (had eaten) the fufu.
i.		He (Goat)		said to him, 'Where's the fufu?'
j.		He		said, '[explanation]'
k.		They		got up and left for home.
l.		Goat		was angry coming to the house.
m.	*má* on another day	he (Squirrel)		went to Cock's house.
n.		He		said to him, 'Let's go to my in-laws.'
o.	Now, *má* Cock,	he		truly clever.
p.		He		took salt and put it under his wing.
q.		They		left and arrived.
r.		People		brought them fufu, as before.
s.		He (Squirrel)		tasted and said to Cock, 'No salt!'
t.		Cock		brought out the salt.
u.		They		put it in and ate.
v.		Squirrel's stomach	T/A	spoilt.
w.		They		got up and left for home.
x.		Cock		came mocking him.
y.	Thus,	he (Squirrel)	T/A	failed to fool Cock.
z.	However,	he	T/A	fooled Goat.

References

Andrews, Avery. 1985. The major functions of the noun phrase. In Timothy Shopen (ed.), Language typology and syntactic description, 1:62–154. Cambridge: Cambridge University Press.

Beneš, Eduard. 1962. Die Verbstellung im Deutschen, von der Mitteilungsperspektive her betrachtet. Phililogica Pragensia 5:6–19.

Dieu, Michel and Patrick Renaud, eds. 1983. Situation linguistique en Afrique Centrale : inventaire préliminaire: le Cameroun. Paris/Yaoundé: ACCT CERDOTOLA Délégation Générale à la Recherche Scientifique et Technique.

Dik, Simon C. 1981. Functional grammar. Dordrecht: Foris Publications.

Gerhardt, Ludwig. 1989. Kainji and Platoid. In John Bendor-Samuel and Rhonda L. Hartell (eds.), The Niger-Congo languages: A classification and description of Africa's largest language family, 359–76. Lanham, MD: University Press of America.

Givón, Talmy, ed. 1983. Topic continuity in discourse. Philadelphia: Benjamins.

———. 1990. Syntax: A functional-typological introduction 2. Philadelphia: Benjamins.

Guthrie, Malcolm. 1971. Comparative Bantu 2. Farnborough, England: Gregg International Publishers.

Hollingsworth, Kenneth R. 1989–90. Mofu-Gudur grammar: Clause, sentence, paragraph, and discourse levels. Yaoundé: Société Internationale de Linguistique. ms.

——— and Charles Peck. 1992. Topics in Mofu-Gudur. In Shin Ja J. Hwang and William R. Merrifield (eds.), Language in context: Essays for Robert E. Longacre, 109–23. Dallas: Summer Institute of Linguistics and the University of Texas at Arlington.

Hoskison, James T. 1983. A grammar and dictionary of the Guɗe language. Ph.D. dissertation. Ohio State University.

Levinsohn, Stephen H. 1987. Textual connections in Acts. Atlanta: Scholars Press.

———. 1992a. Discourse features of New Testament Greek. Dallas: Summer Institute of Linguistics.

———. 1992b. Preposed and postposed adverbials in English. Workpapers of the Summer Institute of Linguistics, University of North Dakota XXXVI:19–30. Grand Forks.

Longacre, Robert E. 1990. Storyline concerns and word order typology in East and West Africa. Studies in African Linguistics, Supplement 10. Los Angeles: University of California.

Perrin, Mona. 1983. Bilan des recherches entreprises entre novembre 1982 et janvier 1983 en langue gudѐ. Yaoundé: Société Internationale de Linguistique.

Cohesion and Discontinuities in Nɔmaandɛ Expository Discourse

Patricia L. Wilkendorf

Abstract

This paper examines the devices which function as markers of cohesion and discontinuities in Nɔmaandɛ expository discourse. Topicalization has a bidirectional function to mark both cohesion between paragraphs and points of discontinuity within the overall discourse. In addition, focus constructions play a role in marking the end boundaries of some paragraphs. These function as summary statements to conclude a paragraph, but they do not occur at the end of a text. Cohesion within paragraphs is maintained primarily through the type of encoding of participant reference and the use of subordinate clauses.

Résumé

Le présent article examine les mécanismes servant de marqueurs de cohésion et de discontinuités dans les textes démonstratifs en nɔmaandɛ. La topicalisation a une fonction bidirectionnelle qui permet de signaler tant la cohésion liant des paragraphes que les points de discontinuité parsemés à travers le texte dans son ensemble. Par ailleurs, les constructions de focalisation permettent de marquer la fin de certains paragraphes. Ces constructions peuvent servir à résumer le contenu d'un paragraphe, sans pour autant apparaître à la fin d'un texte. A l'intérieur des paragraphes, la cohésion se maintient essentiellement de deux façons : grâce au type d'encodage choisi pour les références aux participants, et grâce également à l'emploi des propositions subordonnées.

In their opening sentence, Brown and Yule (1983:1) correctly state that "the analysis of **discourse** is, necessarily, the analysis of language in use." The present study,[1] therefore, explores how speakers of Nɔmaandɛ, a Narrow Bantu language spoken in Central Cameroon, use their language in expository discourse.[2] In particular, it concentrates on the devices which function as markers of cohesion and discontinuity in expository discourse. These markers facilitate the maintenance of thematic continuity within the discourse. Every text is divided into coherent subunits which are referred to as paragraphs, and within which a certain degree of cohesion must be maintained. Forster (1976:3–6), in speaking of different text genres, describes expository discourse as relating to a goal or an object. If the object is a person, that person is treated as a topic about which one wishes to say something. The unifying factor in expository discourse is therefore the TOPIC rather than TIME, which narrative texts have as their unifying factor.

1 Discontinuities

As Levinsohn states in the first article of this volume, languages employ various devices which mark discontinuities within a given coherent discourse. These same devices "also maintain the overall unity and continuity of the text by guiding the listener or reader across the discontinuity." Givón (1990:896–97) lists three parameters which are involved in producing a coherent discourse. These are coherence of reference (participants and topics), situation (time and location), and

---

[1]Four major expository texts were used for this study.

Text A Likes and dislikes of women's fieldwork

Text B Where court cases are judged

Text C When to go to the doctor versus going to the traditional healer

Text D Political parties in Cameroon

Texts A and B appear in the appendix.

The orthography used in the text examples is based on the General Alphabet of Cameroon Languages, and is currently being used to write all literature in Nɔmaandɛ. High tone is marked with an accent over the vowel while low tone is unmarked.

[2]Studies have already been conducted on propositional relations (Taylor 1985) and paragraph markers in Nɔmaandɛ narrative discourse (Wilkendorf 1985). In addition, this volume contains a further study by Taylor on participant reference on Nɔmaandɛ narratives.

action. Applying this then to Nɔmaandɛ expository discourse, this section identifies those devices used in Nɔmaandɛ to mark referential, situational, and action discontinuities.[3]

1.1 Discontinuities of reference

When a new paragraph, due to a referential discontinuity, is required in Nɔmaandɛ, the paragraph is marked by one of the following two devices: (a) reiteration of a complete noun phrase or (b) topicalization of a subject or direct object by means of left-dislocation.

Text A contains repeated examples of device (a), in which the restated complete noun phrase 'women' marks referential discontinuities—in this case changes in topic. An example of this (in the context of a discussion of work women do not like to do) appears in (1).[4]

(1) *beénju ŋe bú léne ɔnyiɔ beébe bímuóci buóli háyɛ buenu*
     women PR 3p like to^work them alone work like rework

    onyuke anyía a kɛlá wé hiite bɔsɔɔkɔ bé ŋe búlu o
    yams because 3s make 3s take others 3p F1 HAB -

    yoomisi bíɔnyía ɔkɔ bé áŋa o oloosi
    injure yams if 3p are LOC produce
Women like to work the reworking of yams on their own because if she takes others, they will tend to injure the yams if they are already growing.

    ta ananyía bɔmɔté bá bɔŋa na yaáká bé ŋeé túme o
    even that some they are with jealousy 3p PR start INF

    hulu fúnúne
    around pull^out
Or even others are jealous, they begin to pull out (the yams).

---

[3]The discussion of discontinuities (§1) precedes that of cohesion or continuity (§2) because it is much easier to discuss how paragraphs cohere to one another after they are identified, or defined, in connection with discontinuities.

[4]The abbreviations in this paper are: DEM demonstrative pronoun, EMP emphatic pronoun, F1 near future, HAB habitual, INF infinitive, LOC locative marker, NEG negative marker, P3 distant past, PERF perfect, PL plural, PR present, REL relative pronoun, SG singular, 1s, 2s, 3s first-, second-, third-person singular, 3p third-person plural.

beénju ŋeé léne tɔ́naá ɔbényiɔnɔ buóli beébe bímuóci buóli
women PR like also to^work work them alone   work

háyɛ okuline bɛɔbɔ
like rework taros
Women also like to work alone a job like reworking taros.

In (1), the topic changes from work which women do not like to do to
work which women like to do alone.[5] The second occurrence of 'women'
begins a new topic of a second kind of work they like to do alone.

The second device Nɔmaandɛ uses to denote a referential discontinuity
is topicalization of a subject or direct object. When a subject is topicalized,
left-dislocation is obligatory. Left-dislocation involves the fronting of a
grammatical constituent in the clause, while leaving a pronominal trace in
the slot that the constituent would normally fill. Left-dislocation is
obligatory when the subject is topicalized because, if the pronominal trace
were not present in the case of a subject, it would be impossible to tell
whether or not fronting had occurred. An example of a topicalized subject
(in bold) is given in (2).

(2)   *búmɔté bé ŋe bú léne ɔnyiɔ   ɛmbáséké*
      some   3p PR 3p like to^work corn
      Some (they) like to work corn.

Referential discontinuity is indicated in (2) by both the fronting of the
subject 'some', which denotes a subclass of the main subject of the preceding paragraph ('women'), and by the change in topic from the work of
tending cucumbers to the work of tending corn. Example (3) illustrates a
topicalized subject (in bold), in this case 'the work of clearing grass', which
does not occur at the beginning of the sentence.

(3)   *ananyía buóli bú ɔwaasa   bú áŋa na   makénda buéŋí*
      because work of clear^grass 3s is with strength much
      (Sometimes women like to clear grass with others) because the
      work of clearing grass is very hard.

Even though this topicalized subject is not occurring sentence initially, it
does occur in the first sentence of the paragraph and, therefore, qualifies

---

[5]Restating the complete noun phrase in order to mark referential discontinuity is an
example of its default use in Nɔmaandɛ EXPOSITORY texts. For a discussion of how this
device functions in Nɔmaandɛ NARRATIVE texts, see Taylor (this volume).

as a marker of a paragraph boundary. The topicalized element 'work of clearing grass' is a change of topic from the preceding paragraph.

Topicalization of the direct object in order to denote a referential discontinuity is illustrated in (4).

(4)   *asana háyɛ buébi bé ŋeé yiíye kála   a   búnɔ́ŋɔ*
       case   like   theft 3p PR it   judge LOC village
       A case like theft one judges in the village.

That this example involves left-dislocation can be seen by the presence of a pronominal trace (in bold) following the fronted direct object. Left-dislocation functions as a means of marking a pronounced discontinuity.

Example (5) illustrates a topicalized direct object, in this case 'corn', which does not occur in the sentence initial position.

(5)   *ananyía ɛmbáséké ciíci   u ŋaá nyia afényɛ*
       because corn   it^EMP 3s PR   eat fufu
       (Some like to work corn) because by using corn, she is able to eat fufu.

As in (3), the topicalized element (in bold) also occurs in a reason clause following a paragraph-initial clause. The emphatic pronoun is being used to highlight the importance of corn in the preparation of fufu, but it is not a pronominal trace. The noun 'fufu' is in the default direct object position. Left-dislocation does not occur at a paragraph boundary if the topicalized element is found in a clause which does not occur sentence initially.

Markers that signal referential discontinuity are also found at the end of units in Nɔmaandɛ expository texts. The device of left-dislocation of either the subject or the direct object, which can mark the beginning of a paragraph, can also be used to mark the end. The sentence in (6) illustrates a topicalized subject used to mark an end boundary in the context of whom to go to locally if murder occurs, i.e., the police.

(6)   *biíbí   bíá nyɛmána na   nyɛnamá nyé asana eényi aana*
       them^EMP 3p suffice   with kind   of   case DEM   then
       Them, they are able to handle such a case.

Here, the emphatic pronoun replaces the complete noun phrase 'police', which is stated in the preceding clause. This pronoun occurs in a fronted position with a pronominal trace (in bold) in the normal subject position.

The sentence in (7) illustrates a topicalized direct object which marks the end boundary of a paragraph.

(7)   *buŋaŋa bú búnɔ́ŋɔ ɔɔcɔ ɔmɔté tí*   **buúbu** *békéléna háyɛ*
      riches   of country man one   NEG them use   like

        búáyá bú bémuáta
        his   of own
        The country's riches, one man should not use them as if they were
        his own . . .

Although two clauses follow (7) in the paragraph, both are subordinate to this clause. It should also be noted that fronting of the direct object as a means of marking an end boundary is achieved by left-dislocation (the pronominal trace is once again in bold). Since it is marking a major discontinuity in the text, this type of direct-object topicalization is what is expected.

1.2 Discontinuities of situation

Changes in time and location within a text also denote paragraph breaks in Nɔmaandɛ discourse. These situational discontinuities are marked in expository texts by the topicalizing of either an adverbial clause or a locative phrase. The clauses in (8) illustrate both types.

(8)   *a*   *búásɔ́ búnɔ́ŋɔ bú Kámerun*   *buá yáaŋa*   *ɔ*   *ɔcɔ́ba*
      LOC our   country of Cameroon 3s   is^already LOC go

        hoóhi tuɔŋɔ́ túfendí atɔ́ éŋɔ́ŋɔ cí ɔ́mbána cí mo   yóofine
        nearly years two   REL parties of many   3p PERF enter

        buáyá   *bunɔŋɔ ŋaá bá búe líhéke hú   na   ɛŋɔŋɔ ɛmɔté*
        long^ago country P3 be 3s   live   only with party one
        In our country of Cameroon, it has already been close to two years
        that a multitude of political parties have entered the scene. Long
        ago the country had only one party.

The phrase 'in our country of Cameroon' is fronted, and the following subject pronoun agrees in noun class with *bunɔŋɔ* 'country'. This suggests left-dislocation once again, even for a locative phrase. The fact that this left-dislocation occurs at the very beginning of a text supports the claim that left-dislocation functions as a marker of pronounced discontinuity. In this case, the discontinuity of situation involves a switch from real time and location to that of the expository text. *buáyá* 'long ago' also appears to mark a situational discontinuity while background information is being given for the current political situation in Cameroon.

A topicalized temporal clause can also function as a boundary marker at the end of units as in (9).

(9)   *ekúlú eéye mbá bekélísi á*   *háma a*   *nɔ́haátɛ bá*
       time DEM then judges (having) leave LOC outside 3p

       kaámbaka buhúnyi bú ɔ́sɔ́mbɔ́tɔ́na asana
       look^for   word   of to^decide   case
       At that time then the judges, once they have gone out, are going to look for a decision.

The conjunction *mbá* 'then' in Nɔmaandɛ functions as a 'spacer' (Dooley 1990:477) when it is placed between the topicalized temporal clause and the main clause. Its purpose is to give further backgrounding to the topicalized element in order to highlight what follows.

1.3 Discontinuities of action

Although action discontinuities are less plentiful than the other types of discontinuities, they do occur in Nɔmaandɛ expository texts. They are marked using three devices: preposed temporal clauses, positive-negative switch, and focus constructions.

Preposed temporal clauses. Preposed temporal clauses can be used to refer to either a continuation of the time previously mentioned or a change of time. The use of these temporal clauses to mark a change in time causes an action discontinuity in the text, as shown in (10), taken from text B.

(10)   *buátá kána buɔ́sé á kaáháma*
      that   same day   3s arrive
      That same day having arrived ...

This clause marks a significant time gap between the preceding action and those that follow. In addition, the clause gives background information to the actions that follow.

Example (11) provides two clauses which are separated in the text by an entire paragraph.

(11) *ɔkɔɔ́háma ahá   ú ŋaá nyíána butéŋí   yó bíhulínyi sɔ́ɔ́kɔ́*
      until   when 3s P3 leave governing 3s entrust   other

      wɔ ɔláta
      of to^follow
      until he left power, entrusting (it) to the successor

      ahá   butéŋí   ŋaá kuá né otéŋí wɔ ɔláta
      when governing P3 fall to chief of to^follow
      When the right to govern fell to the following leader ...

The last clause of (11) is an example of a special type of topicalization
called tail-head linkage. This linkage is necessary in order to reintroduce
an action from earlier in the text that was interrupted by an explanation
of the goals of a certain political party. Tail-head linkage, while marking a
discontinuity with the immediately preceding unit, also functions as a
cohesive device which picks up the original theme line of the text.

Positive-negative switch. Another device used to mark discontinuity of
action in Nɔmaandɛ expository discourse is a positive-negative "switch"
(Andrews 1985:79). A positive-negative switch involves action that is the
negative of the initial verb in the preceding paragraph (with the topic
remaining constant for both paragraphs). The example in (12), which states
what women don't like to do, is preceded in the expository texts by two
paragraphs which refer to work that women like to do.

(12) *beénju ti   ŋé bú léne ɔnyiɔ   moólí be bisíéne bé*
      women NEG PR 3p like to^work jobs of fields of

      maatɛ
      plantations
      Women do not like to work in the plantations.

In (12), the discontinuity in the text is also marked by restating the
complete noun phrase 'women'.
   Another example of a positive-negative switch is given in (13). The
speaker introduces the kind of cases which are not judged in the village.
The preceding paragraph in the text refers to the kind of cases which are
judged in the village.

(13)   *asana ayé bá tɛ   ŋáa kála   a   búnɔ́ŋɔ yá aŋɛna asana ayé*
      case   REL 3p NEG PR judge LOC village 3s is   case   REL
      A case that one does not judge in the village is a case that...

In addition to the switch to a negative, (13) illustrates topicalization of the subject (marked by the noun class agreement of the pronoun in bold in the main clause).

After the negative paragraph in text B (beginning with (13) = (25i)), the paragraph which follows it switches back in (25m) to positive, i.e., to the action of the initial paragraph of the text. This negative-positive switch is marked by topicalization of the direct object (see (4)).

Focus constructions. Focus constructions in Nɔmaandɛ expository discourse tend to be used to conclude a paragraph. All of the examples found in the four texts studied occur at the end of paragraphs within the discourse, but none occurs at the end of the entire text. Typically, such constructions are marked by an initial word or phrase in the sentence, such as *aáha* 'there, here', *ɛɛhɛ́* 'that's why', *buáté bɔkɔ* or *yaáté asana* 'for that reason'. They tend to function as summary statements, and may show the relationship between what has just been said (the reason) and the presupposition (a result) which is stated previously in the text. As such they mark a clear break in the flow of the argument, a disruption which Givón (1983:8) considers a discontinuity of action.

The sentence in (14) illustrates the use of *aáha* as a focus marker.

(14)   **aáha** *u ŋa cɔ́cɔba ɔ   ɔ́   mɛ ɔ́ŋɔ́kɛ́na nyɛnamá nyɛ́*
      there 3s F1 go   LOC INF me write   kind   of

      mákanyɛ anyɛ́ yamɛ nyɛmana wo óhiiteke
      medicine REL 1s   need   SG to^take
      Then he is going to write for me the kind of medicine that I need to take.

In this example, the construction with *aáha* functions as a way to tell the hearer or reader that now is when an anticipated event is going to occur in the procedure under discussion.

Example (15) illustrates the use of *ɛɛhɛ́* as a focus marker in Nɔmaandɛ.

(15) *ɛɛhɛ bé ti   ŋé bú lene ɔnyiɔ   buólí háyɛ ɔtáma ɔ*
      then 3p NEG PR 3p like to^work work like   clear   LOC

      bétualɔ́   anyía   bú áŋa na   makénda
      savannas because 3s is   with strength
      That is why they do not like to work the work of clearing the
      savannas, because it is very hard.

In (15), *ɛɛhɛ* 'that's why' functions as a marker of new information. It
focuses on the fact that women do not like to clear the savannas, and then
provides a reason for this.

The clause in (16) illustrates the use of *buáté bɔkɔ* as a focus marker in
Nɔmaandɛ.

(16) **buáté bɔkɔ** *i ŋeé mi léne hɛtɔké hí UPC*
      DEM thing 1s PR 1s   like group of UPC
      For that reason I like the UPC party...

The focus construction in (16) is followed by other clauses in the paragraph, but they are all grammatically subordinate to it. *buáté bɔkɔ* 'for that
reason' also functions as a marker of new information, with the goals of
the UPC party being given as the reason (i.e., the new information) for
the speaker's preferring that party. (His party preference was known
information to the hearer at the time this discourse was originally given.)

One instance of a focus construction (which begins with *aáha* 'here') in
text B (see Appendix) occurs immediately preceding a topicalized temporal
clause which was shown in (9) to be functioning as a boundary marker at
the end of that paragraph. In (17), the same type of preposed temporal
clause structure as in (9) occurs, this time, however, immediately preceding
a focus construction.

(17) **ekúlú eéye mbá** *wá mɛ laána iŋgimi cɛ bɔkɔ así ŋeé mi*
      time DEM then 3s me tell   root of thing REL PR me

      yeébi
      bother
      At that time then he should tell me the cause of what is bothering me.
      (Focus construction which follows: Here he is going to prescribe to me
      the type of medicine that I need to take.)

No reason has yet been found for this reverse order. One hypothesis is
that procedural discourse considerations may be involved since both

examples seem to be within embedded procedural texts. Another possibility is that the combination of the focus construction and the topicalized temporal clause plus *mbá,* regardless of which precedes the other, constitutes a pronounced paragraph end boundary.

2 Cohesion

2.1 Cohesion within the overall discourse

As previously noted, discontinuities are often marked in Nɔmaandɛ expository discourse with a topicalized element. While topicalization marks a break in the text, it is also anaphoric, thereby making a thematic link with the preceding unit (Givón 1990:846–47). In this way, coherence is maintained, even across paragraph boundaries.

The linking function of topicalized elements was shown in (11) where a rare expository text usage of tail-head linkage is involved. In (18), a topicalized temporal clause illustrates the dual functions of cohesion and discontinuity.

(18)　*ekúlú eéye o ŋoó túme ɔkála　　asana*
　　　time DEM 2s PR start toˆjudge case
　　　At that time you start to judge the case.

The temporal clause (in bold) refers back to the time of the preceding paragraph. At the same time, it is the 'point of departure' for what follows. In this way, the topicalized clause helps to advance the theme line.

Demonstrative adjectives also function bidirectionally in Nɔmaandɛ expository texts, sometimes within the paragraph (see §2.2) and sometimes (more rarely) at paragraph boundaries as shown in (19).

(19)　*buátá kána buɔsé á　　kaáháma*
　　　DEM same day (having) arrive
　　　That same day having arrived . . .

The topicalized element marks a major temporal gap in the text (see discussion with (10), which is repeated here); at the same time, the demonstrative component refers back to a day (previously mentioned in the text) that would be selected for hearing a certain court case in the village. Thus, a topicalized element can again be seen to aid in maintaining coherence across paragraph boundaries, while also marking discontinuity (in this case, an action discontinuity).

In text A, examples of coherence across paragraph boundaries may be seen in the usage of the connective word *tɔ́na* 'also' in Nɔmaandɛ as shown in (20).

(20)   *oónju   ti   ŋé lene tɔ́na ɔnyiɔ   buóli háyɛ ɔtáma*
       woman NEG PR like also toˆwork work like toˆclear
       A woman also does not like to work a job like clearing.

The restated noun phrase 'woman' is thematic in text A (see Appendix). The preceding paragraph states an activity that women do not like to do. The use of 'also' to introduce the second activity women do not like to do thereby serves as a cohesive device which gives continuity to the theme line.

2.2 Cohesion within paragraphs

Discontinuities of reference, situation, and action have not been found to occur within paragraphs in Nɔmaandɛ expository texts.[6] Cohesion within paragraphs, however, is maintained in one or more of the following ways: (a) through the use of demonstrative adjectives, (b) through the type of encoding of participant reference, and (c) through the use of subordinate clauses.

Demonstrative adjectives function bidirectionally (as discussed in §2.1). They are used as cohesive devices within paragraphs in three of the four expository texts studied and are illustrated in (21).

(21)   *u   ŋa cɔ́bana yɔ́ sɔ́ména   né otéŋí u bunɔŋɔ*
       3s PR take   3s complain to chief of village
       He takes (it) and complains to the village chief.

       bɛsɔ́ména eébi ŋe bíhembule anyía ɔ ŋɔ́ cɔbana ɛkɔké
       complaint DEM PR mean   that 2s PR take   chicken
       This complaint means that you take a chicken.

---

[6]Topicalization can occur within paragraphs. Although this device functions as a marker of paragraph boundaries in the overall discourse, it has a different function within paragraphs. Within paragraphs, topicalization functions as a highlighting device for what follows in the discourse. In addition, it should be noted that left-dislocation is not involved, but rather simple fronting only. This fact confirms the assertion made in §1.1 that left-dislocation is used to mark pronounced discontinuities in the text (namely, paragraph boundaries).

The demonstrative adjective in (21) provides cohesion with the previous sentence while also serving as a 'point of departure' for giving new information.

The type of encoding used to refer to participants is a major means of maintaining thematic continuity within paragraphs in Nɔmaandɛ. Givón (1983:17–18) lists the most common grammatical devices used to denote "topic accessibility": zero anaphora, unstressed/bound pronouns or grammatical agreement, and stressed/independent pronouns. The device most frequently employed to encode participant reference within paragraphs in Nɔmaandɛ is of the 'unstressed pronoun' variety. This is illustrated in the paraphrased paragraph in (22) taken from text A.

(22)	Some	they like to work	corn,
	because corn, with it,	**she** can eat	fufu.
	When	**she** has crushed	the corn,
		she will prepare,	
		she will eat	with her family.
		She takes	that which
		it is remaining,	
		she will sell	(it).
	There	**she** is going to have	money,
	or	**she** can buy	oil.

This paragraph begins by referring anaphorically to the women mentioned in the preceding paragraph as 'some'. At the same time, this topicalized subject serves as a point of departure for talking about a different work activity. The pronoun 'she' replaces the plural subject 'some' in this case, although it still refers to women in general. The repetition of the unstressed pronoun 'she' within this paragraph denotes that topic accessibility is sufficiently great and cohesion is maintained. The clause following this subunit repeats the complete noun phrase 'women', which marks the beginning of another paragraph about a different work activity.

Subordinate clauses also play a major role in maintaining cohesion within paragraphs. This is due, at least in part, to the type of conjunctions used in expository texts such as *anyía* 'because, so that', *ananyía* 'because', *ta anyía* 'or', *ekúlú ayé* 'when', *ɔkɔɔ́háma ahá* 'until when', and *ɔ́kɔ* 'if'. It is also due to verbs like *nyɛmána* 'need to'.

Text D, which discusses the major political parties in Cameroon, demonstrates the importance of subordinate clauses in providing cohesion within paragraphs. For example, the paragraph in (23), given in English translation, provides the Nɔmaandɛ conjunctions which precede subordinate clauses.

(23)   The first chief his party   was   the UNC.
                      They   chose   the motto: peace,
                                                    work, country.
                      They   chose   this motto
            anyía   peace   **may** exist,   not war with blood,
                      the country   **may** prosper
                      people   **may** work   well,
                      they   **may** remove   poverty from the
                                                    country,
                      people   **may** become   rich once again,
                      they   **may** live   well,
                      they   **may** do   great things,
        ɔkɔɔ́háma ahá life of people it changes,
                      cleanness   **may** again
                                     enter,
                      people   **may** build   good houses,
                      they   **may** eat   well,
                      life   *may* become   again 'tender'.

The verb forms translated 'may...' lack tense/aspect markers. These markers are obligatory in independent clauses. The first cluster of subordinate clauses are all dependent on the clause 'they chose this motto so that...' These subordinate clauses are introduced by the conjunction *anyía* which means 'so that' rather than 'because' when it occurs before a reduced verb form. The second group of subordinate clauses are dependent (in a different way) on the clause 'until when life of the people it changes'. The subordinate clauses that follow represent events which are viewed as occurring simultaneously with the main clause, because the first clause after the conjunction 'until when' is independent (i.e., the tense/aspect marker is present). Simultaneous actions are marked in Nɔmaandɛ by dropping the tense/aspect marker after the first action has been stated with the tense/aspect marker present.

3 Summary

This paper examines the devices used in Nɔmaandɛ to mark cohesion and discontinuities within expository discourse. Topicalization is a frequently used device within the overall discourse to mark both cohesion and discontinuities due to its bidirectional function. Left-dislocation of the subject or direct object marks referential discontinuities. Topicalization of a temporal or locative phrase marks situational discontinuities, while a preposed subordinate temporal clause or a positive-negative switch marks action discontinuities on the discourse level. Another marker of action discontinuities is focus constructions, which tend to mark the end boundary of paragraphs. They also function as summary statements about the paragraph.

Within paragraphs, left-dislocation of the direct object does not occur, and topicalization of a subject, direct object, or temporal clause functions as a means of highlighting what follows. Cohesion within paragraphs is maintained primarily through the use of pronouns versus full noun phrases when referring to participants, and through the use of subordinate clauses.

Appendix

(24)   Text A Likes and dislikes of women's fieldwork

a.		Women	like to work	cucumbers
	anyía(because)	they	know	
	anyía(that)	owner	having worked	her cucumbers
		she	them	will sell.
b.		She	may see	help there concerning money
	that(REL)	she	is going to have	
	when	she	may sell.	
c.	Some	they	like to work	corn
	ananyía(because)			
	corn it(EMP)	she	eats	fufu.
d.	When	she	has crushed	corn,
		she	will prepare	
		she	may eat	with her family.
e.		She	takes	
	that which(REL)	it	is remaining,	
		she	may sell.	
f.	*aáha*(there)	she	is going to have	money,
	or	she	may buy	oil.
g.		Women	do not like to work	in plantation
	ananyía(because)	they	see	
	how *ananyía*(that)	it	is not	work
	that(REL)	them	not concerns	
		it	is.	
h.	And	it	is not	
	ananyía(because)			
	them them(EMP)	they	it	sell.

i.		Woman		also does not like to work	job like clearing savanna
	ananyía(because)	owner		sees	
	anyía(that)clearing	it		may	
			her	ruin	body.
j.	*ɛ́ɛhɛ́*(that's why)	they		do not like to work	job like clearing savanna
	anyía(because)	it		is	hard.
k.		Women		like to work them alone	job like rework yams
	anyía(because)			having taken	others,
		they		will harm	yams
	if	they		are growing.	
l.	Or some	they		are jealous;	
		they		start to pull out	(the yams).
m.		Women		also like to work	job they alone job like rework taros
	anyía aáha (because there)	she		wants	
	anyía(that)	she		may rework	her taros well she alone.
n.	Sometimes	women		like to cut grass	with others
	ananyía(because)				
	work of cutting	it	is		very hard
	anyía(because) every time				
	that(REL)	you		enter	into work society,
		others		are going to work	a lot for you.
o.	Work also like weeding	woman		likes	
	ananyía(that) then	she		works	with others
	anyía(because) work like cutting, these				
	like hoeing	jobs		are	very hard
	that(REL)	person			
		alone	it	is not able to work.	

(25)   Text B Where court cases are judged

a.	Cases that(REL)	one		judges are	in the village the kind
	like that if	a man		has robbed	another man,
		he(DS)		brings	his complaint to the chief
b.		This complaint		means	
	anyía(that)	you(SG)		bring	a chicken,
	ɛ́cɛ ananyía (it is that)	money or a chicken with feathers.			
c.	At that time	the chief		will look for	a day
	that(REL)	you(PL)		should come	to judge the case.
d.		He		will tell	his judges
	that(REL)	we		call	'assesseurs'.
e.		That same day the accused		having arrived, will bring also	a chicken:
	thus	we		call	'lift up chicken'.
f.	At that time	you(SG)		start to state	your case
	that(REL)	you(PL)		are	in disagreement
	or thing that	he		did	to you
	or theft that	he	you	robbed.	
g.	*aáha*(there)	one		will hear	your case,
		the accused		may still defend	his case.
h.	At that time				
	mbá(then)	judges		having exited	outside,
		they		may look for	decision.
i.	Case that	one		does not judge	in the village
		it		is	a case
	that(REL)	one		may kill	a man: blood affair.
j.	That kind	one		does not judge	in the village
	or	you(SG)		can complain	to the chief
	mbá(but)	chief		having reflected	
	then	he	you	tells	
	ananyía(that)	this		not made	for his level.
k.		He		is going to send	you(PL) to those
	who(REL)	they	him	may be greater.	
l.	Like here	he	you	will send	to Bokito,
	aáha(there) these others who(REL)	they		have	uniforms
	that(REL)	one		calls	police;
	those(EMP)	they		may suffice	for that sort of case.
m.	A case like theft	one	it	judges	in the village.

n.	When	you(PL)		having stated	(your cases),
	you who(REL)	you(SG)		complain	and the accused,
		the judges		are going to study	
		they	you	may give	decision.
o.	aáha(here) man				
	who	he		complains	
	if	he		likes	decision,
	that(REL)	one		has decided,	
		he		can accept;	
p.	but if	he		does not like	
	then	he		says that	
		they	him	should give	letter
	that(REL)	he		should take	his case to the government.

References

Andrews, Avery. 1985. The major functions of the noun phrase. In Timothy Shopen (ed.), Language typology and syntactic description, 1:62–154. Cambridge: Cambridge University Press.

Brown, Gordon and Gillian Yule. 1983. Discourse analysis. Cambridge: Cambridge University Press.

Dooley, Robert A. 1990. The positioning of non-pronominal clitics and particles in lowland South American languages. In Doris L. Payne (ed.), Amazonian linguistics: Studies in lowland South American languages, 457–83. Austin: University of Texas Press.

Forster, Keith. 1976. The narrative folklore discourse in Border Cuna. In Robert E. Longacre and Frances Woods (eds.), Discourse grammar: Studies in indigenous languages of Colombia, Panama and Ecuador, 2:1–23. Dallas: Summer Institute of Linguistics.

Givón, Talmy, ed. 1983. Topic continuity in discourse. Philadelphia: Benjamins.

———— 1990. Syntax: A functional-typological introduction 2. Philadelphia: Benjamins.

Levinsohn, Stephen H. 1992a. Discourse features of New Testament Greek. Dallas: Summer Institute of Linguistics.

———— 1992b. Preposed and postposed adverbials in English. Workpapers of the Summer Institute of Linguistics, University of North Dakota XXXVI:19–30. Grand Forks.

Taylor, Carolyn. 1985. Relations entre les propositions en nɔmaantɛ. ms.

Wilkendorf, Patricia. 1985. Paragraph markers in Nɔmaantɛ narrative discourse. ms.

Preposed Constituents and Discontinuities in Makaa Discourse

Daniel P. Heath and Teresa A. Heath

Abstract

This paper describes how preposed constituents in Makaa discourse mark discontinuities, and looks specifically at the devices of topicalization and focus. Both complex noun phrases and simple noun phrases, as well as prepositional phrases and verbal phrases, are frequently preposed for topicalization. A complex noun phrase, consisting of a head noun modified by a relative clause, may express the time, manner, or reference of the following propositions. The study of topicalized phrases shows how each preposed constituent marks discontinuity of action, situation, or reference. Focus in Makaa involves preposing the focused constituent. However, it marks a different kind of discontinuity, an interruption of the argument, in order to highlight a main assertion.

Résumé

Le présent article décrit comment les constituants placés au début d'une phrase servent à marquer les discontinuités au sein du texte en mekaa. On examine plus particulièrement la topicalisation et la focalisation. Les syntagmes nominaux complexes et simples, tout comme les syntagmes prépositionnels et verbaux, sont souvent placés au début de la phrase à des

33

fins de topicalisation. Un syntagme nominal complexe, qui se compose d'un nom modifié par une proposition relative, peut exprimer le temps, la manière ou la référence de la proposition ou des propositions qui suivent. L'étude des syntagmes topicalisés montre comment chaque constituant placé au début d'une phrase permet de marquer des discontinuités d'action, de situation ou de référence. En mekaa, la focalisation se fait également en plaçant le constituant focalisé au début de la phrase. Toutefois, ce même constituant marque aussi une autre sorte de discontinuité, à savoir, une interruption de l'argument en cours, permettant ainsi à l'argument principal de se dégager.

1 Preposed constituents in Makaa

Coherent discourses contain discontinuities of action, situation, and reference which are marked by various devices to maintain coherence. This paper[1] looks at preposed constituents in Makaa[2] and shows that such devices signal discontinuities in discourse, thus supporting Levinsohn's claim to this effect in the introductory article of this section.

The term PREPOSED in this paper refers to any constituent of the sentence that occurs before the nuclear constituents of the main clause. A number of constituents can occur in this position, including vocatives, conjunctions, subordinate clauses, noun phrases, and other phrases. Preposed vocatives are illustrated in (1).[3]

(1)   *okóól bâm*
       sisters my
       My sisters!

---

[1]This paper was written during a course on discourse studies held in Yaoundé, Cameroon, from January through March 1993 under the auspices of the Société Internationale de Linguistique. The authors wish to express their grateful thanks to Dr. Stephen Levinsohn, who directed the course, and to Dr. James Roberts, for their stimulating insights and their valuable direction in the writing of the paper. Thanks also go to Mr. Zok Ntah Rigobert and Mr. Kouamb Alexis for their cooperation in providing and transcribing the texts used in this paper.

[2]The Makaa language is spoken in southeast Cameroon, West Africa. It is a Bantu language classified by Guthrie (1971:33) as A.83. The dialect used in this paper is the Mbwaanz dialect spoken along the Ndjoung Nkol road, approximately 50 km. from Abong Mbang. Though the name of the language is Məkaá, the English spelling of this language will be used throughout this paper.

[3]The following abbreviations are used in this paper: AM associative marker, EMP emphasis, F1 near future, F2 remote future, F-P focus-presupposition construction, FOC focus marker, HORT hortative mood, IMPER imperative mood, INF infinitive, ITER iterative/habitual, LOC locative, NEG negative, P1 recent past, P2 remote past, PERF perfect, PL plural, PR present, PROG progressive aspect, REL relative article.

osóŋgú óshé bwó á byá   shé
fathers our   they P2 beget us
Our fathers begot us.

Vocatives, as in (1), differ from other preposed noun phrases in that they are used by the speaker to address the audience and are not usually part of the rest of the clause syntactically.

The following examples illustrate a conjunction in (2) and a subordinate clause in (3), occurring before the main clause.

(2)   nji mə ji nə   mpimbə nə bwán   wâ budûm
      but I am with anger   with children AM male
      But, I am angry with the sons.

(3)   ijkí ijîm í   dɨ   dɨ́g mə e bá ɛ   kə shílə mpwə́lá a
      if   spirits they ITER see I F1 F2 him go ask debt   AM

      cínoŋg
      place
      If the spirits are watching, I will ask him for that debt (hold him accountable for his actions).

Of the several types of preposed constituents that exist, vocatives, conjunctions, and subordinate clauses are excluded from further consideration here. This paper is limited to the discussion of phrases and how they function in discourse, since phrases are the most common constituents occurring before the main clause in the texts studied.

Preposed phrases occur in two different constructions: topicalization, as described in §2, and the focus-presupposition construction, as described in §3. The study of these preposed phrases, as they occur in these two constructions, shows how preposed phrases mark discontinuities in Makaa discourse.[4]

2 Topicalization

Topicalization as used in this paper involves a phrasal constituent that is preposed before the main clause of the sentence and has a bidirectional function. Givón (1990:846–47) claims that the topicalized element plays a

---

[4]The texts used in this paper are oral texts given by Mr. Zok Ntah Rigobert from the village of Beul.

bidirectional role: it serves both as a point of departure for what follows, and also as the primary basis for linking what follows to its preceding context. The primary basis may link what follows to the preceding context in two ways—by repeating information from a previous clause, or by switching from a constituent in a previous clause to show a new or contrasting element, such as time or place (Levinsohn 1992:16). In this way the topicalized constituent provides linkage, contributing to the coherence of a discourse.

At the same time topicalized constituents also indicate discontinuities. Three types of discontinuities have been distinguished by Givón (1990:896–97): change of action, change of situation, and change of reference. Change of situation can be further subdivided into change of time and location. Change of reference can also be further subdivided into change of participants and topic. In discussing preposed constituents, each is described in terms of what kind of discontinuity is being marked.

Topicalized constituents are marked in Makaa only by their position at the beginning of the sentence, as illustrated in (4). There is no marker associated with topicalization.

(4) *sá   joŋgú   sógá   mimbií myêsh nó*
     thing this^aforementioned look^IMPER ways   every that

     bi   bág   byá bwân
     you^PL F2^HORT bear children
     For this reason, search out all ways that you will bear children.

The phrase *sá joŋgú* 'for this reason' is topicalized, occurring before the main clause. This preposed phrase is not marked in any way except by its initial position. In oral speech, the intonation shows that it is associated with the following clause, in that the topicalized constituent ends with suspended intonation (a high tone) rather than phrase-final intonation (a falling tone).

Example (5) shows that more that one constituent may be topicalized.

(5) a. *nji sá   ŋgúdú*
       but thing one

    b. *ja   shémó zó   béégya yí*
       time we   come separate REL

    c. *mó ji nó   mpimbó nó bwân   wâ budûm*
       I be with anger with children AM male
       But one thing, as we are about to separate, I am angry with my sons.

In this example, there are two topicalized constituents at the beginning of the sentence: a simple noun phrase, *sá ŋgúdú* 'one thing' in (5a), and a complex noun phrase 'time we are about to separate' in (5b). Both are fronted before the main clause in (5c).

This section discusses four types of phrases that may be topicalized: complex noun phrases, simple noun phrases, prepositional phrases, and a verbal phrase *kə jé kúl*. Complex noun phrases consist of a head noun modified by a relative clause and are the type of noun phrase most frequently topicalized. Simple noun phrases consist of a noun or pronoun that may be modified by an adjective.

2.1 Complex noun phrases

Complex noun phrases that are topicalized in Makaa consist of a head noun modified by a following relative clause (described in Heath and Heath 1984). In example (6b), there is a complex noun phrase headed by *ja* 'time'.

(6) a. *mudá   nyə ji mudá*
      woman she is woman

   b. *ja   bímɔ́   kɔ́ məbá   dí   yí*
      time you^PL go marriages LOC REL
      A woman is a woman when she gets married.

Verbal complements and sentence modifiers are normally found after the verb, because Makaa is an SVO language. In its position after the main clause, the *ja* phrase functions purely as a temporal adverbial, adding information to the main clause. The temporal phrase in (6b) specifies the time when the main clause will be true, when a woman is really a woman.

However, when such phrases occur before the main clause, they do more than situate the time of the main clause. They are topicalized, contributing to the coherence of the discourse, while indicating a discontinuity of action, reference, or situation, as stated in §2. In other words, they have added functions above the sentence level. These added discourse functions may be referred to as added implicatures, following Sperber and Wilson (1986) and Blass (1990:67ff). This is parallel to the way English 'when'-clauses function, according to Ramsey (1987:385). An example of such a topicalized phrase is found in (7).

(7) a. *ja   bwó mɔ́   byêl yí*
     when they PERF born REL

  b. *cúúmbá kɔ́ dʉ   ndêny mɔ́láámb*
     elder   go ITER set   traps
    When they were born, the elder (brother) set traps.

The sentence previous to (7) introduces the two brothers who are the
major participants of this folk tale. The topicalized phrase of (7a) not only
situates the main clause (7b) in time, but also marks the beginning of a
new section, giving a further description of the two brothers.

Further examples of such topicalized phrases are given in the following
sections. For purposes of discussion, these complex noun phrases have
been divided into three groups, according to their function: temporal,
manner, and reference.

Temporal noun phrases. The noun *ja* 'time,' as exemplified in (6) and
(7), is the most frequently used head noun in topicalized complex noun
phrases with a temporal function. Consider also (8).

(8) a. *ja   bwó mɔ́   ka   tééd nɔ́   bwó zɔ́   dɔ kúwo   yí*
     time they PERF then start that they come eat chicken REL

  b. *kumkoonz a   mú   dʉ́g múdá   tɔ́dʉ́gá   yé wêsh dʉ̌   bul*
     Ant   she then see woman thoughts her all   ITER lot

    kɔ mpyɔ́ dí
    go Dog LOC
    When they started eating the chicken, Ant then saw that all of the
    woman's thoughts were going to Dog.

The phrase in (8a) occurs at a major change of action. This sentence is
found in a narrative concerning Ant and Dog, who together go to ask for
the hand of marriage of a woman in another village. Immediately prior to
this sentence, Ant and Dog have been received by the woman and invited
to eat. With this temporal phrase, the action switches from the
preliminaries to the actual events which trigger the woman choosing to
marry one of them. *ja* phrases are frequently used in Makaa narratives to
signal such a major change in action, as discussed in Heath and Heath
(1990).

Other nouns that function as the head of temporal complex noun
phrases are *jwów* 'day' and *té* 'time', as in (9).

(9) a. *té   njówbúud íshé í mɔ́   cugə yí*
     time family   our it PERF live REL

  b. *ŋgwólɨ́ga múud nyə afwɛ́   bə nə   məga mə kɔ́ kyab*
     certain   person he not^yet be with luck   he go pass

    mɔ́vəgɨlɛ
    exams
Since the time our family has existed, no person has yet had the luck
to pass the exams.

This sentence is taken from a text where a father counsels his son, who is
about to join the military. Preceding this sentence, the father has described
what it means for a family in a village to have a relative in such a position.
Example (9) summarizes or applies the preceding thought, by saying that
their own family has never had anyone succeed in obtaining such a post.
The topicalized noun phrase (9a) marks discontinuity, indicating the end
of a section. In the following sentence in the text, the father changes the
topic, to describe the difficulties that the son will encounter in the military.
Thus, the topicalized noun phrase helps mark the change of topic.

    The marking of this discontinuity in (9) is unusual, since topicalization
usually follows a discontinuity, as in (8). In (9), the topicalized phrase
comes in the summary at the end of a section. It also signals the discontinuity that follows, i.e., the beginning of a new section, describing the
difficulties that the son will encounter.

    In addition to a temporal function, some temporal complex noun phrases
are used pragmatically to imply reason, even though they have a time head
noun. Observe (10), taken from a text recounting the farewell speech of a
dying father to his family.

(10) a. *kag*   *sámb* *mə* *mbwool* *kwaand*
        go^IMPER cut   me trunk   plantain

    b. *mə* *zɔ́g*   *lúgə* *bí*   *nə*   *ocúncésh*
       I   come^HORT leave you^PL with blessing

    c. *Nji* *sá*   *ŋgúdú*
       but thing one

    d. *ja*   *shémɔ́* *zɔ́*   *béégya*   *yí*
       time we   come separate REL

    e. *mə* *ji* *nə*   *mpimbə* *nə*   *bwān*   *wâ* *budûm* *kóómb* *zhíí*
       I   be with anger   with children AM male   side   path

       á   *byâ*
       AM birth

Go cut me a plantain trunk, so that I can give you a blessing. But one thing, as we are about to separate, I am angry with my sons about giving birth.

In (10a-b), the father is preparing to give the blessing. Then, with (10d), he switches topics, from talking about the blessing, to talking about a matter that he needs to deal with before he can give the blessing (thus, a change from blessing to reproach). The topicalized phrase of (10d) occurs before the main clause (10e).

The topicalized clause of (10d), with the head noun *ja,* has more of a reason meaning, 'as/since we are about to separate', than a temporal meaning, even though it literally means 'the time we are about to separate'. This use of a temporal head noun in a reason phrase is frequent in non-narrative discourse. This may be described again as an added implicature that a topicalized phrase has in certain contexts.

In addition, the *ja* phrase in (10d) indicates a major discontinuity, more than phrases with other time head nouns. It signals a major change of topic in this non-narrative discourse, just as it signalled a major change of action in a narrative in (8). The fact that (10) marks a major discontinuity is strengthened by the presence of a second topicalized constituent, the simple noun phrase of (10c).

Manner noun phrases. In addition to temporal noun phrases, manner noun phrases may also be topicalized. These are complex noun phrases with head nouns such as *mbií* 'way', or *nda* 'manner', as in (11).

(11) a. *nda ósóŋgú bâm bwó á lúgə mə nə mətə́lɛ nə́*
　　　 as　fathers my　they P2 leave me with blessing REL

b. *mɛ　mə́　ka　nə́mə́ nyiŋgə lúgə bí　　nə mətə́lɛ*
　 IʿEMP PERF then also　again　leave youʿPL with blessing
As my fathers left me with a blessing, I then also again leave you with blessing.

The phrase in (11b) indicates a point of discontinuity, signalling a change of action. Taken from the text of the dying father, the preceding sentences described the actual giving of the blessing, which included both the actions and the exact words. With (11a), a new section starts and the father now proceeds to explain what he has done. Thus, the topicalized manner phrase indicates a switch from the act of blessing to the explanation of the blessing.

Reference noun phrases. Other complex nouns are designated as reference noun phrases, because their function is to make reference to certain participants of the discourse. When preposed, these noun phrases are topicalized, usually indicating a change of participants, as in (12a).

(12) a. *baŋg bêsh bwó á shígé bə jwôw doŋgú dí　wá*
　　　 those all　they P2 NEG be day　that　LOC REL

b. *shílə　　yé nyə ó　bág　　ŋgə kə wá　　bwə mətə́lɛ*
　 daughter his she FOC F2ʿHORT PROG go putʿon them blessing
As for all those who were not present that day, his daughter, she would be giving them the blessing.

This topicalized noun phrase in (12a) is taken from the text of the father's farewell. The previous sentences in the text dealt with the blessing that was given to all those present the day the father spoke. With (12a), the narrator switches to talk about those who were not present, and how they would receive the blessing. It is logical, then, that he topicalize the noun phrase referring to the new participants in order to highlight a change of participants.

2.2 Simple noun phrases

As stated earlier, simple noun phrases consist of a noun or pronoun that may be modified by elements other than relative clauses. When these noun phrases are topicalized in Makaa, they usually function adverbially, as do most of the complex noun phrases. These noun phrases would be expected to occur after the main verb of the clause. Like the complex noun phrases, simple noun phrases also indicate points of discontinuity.

A common example of a topicalized noun phrase is a phrase with a temporal head noun, qualified by an adjective, as in (13).

(13) a. *mimbú myêsh*
      years   all

    b. *cúúmbá nyə ó   mɔ́ kɔ́ ndêny mɔ́láámb*
       elder   he FOC he go set   traps
    Every year, the elder (brother) went and set traps.

The noun phrase in (13a) functions as a temporal adverb, to indicate a change of time. The preceding clauses have introduced two brothers in a general way, saying that the elder was a hunter, while the younger had not even bothered to learn how to hunt. The phrase 'each year' situates the following discussion in a more specific time frame.

Noun phrases which are semantically associated with the main clause in some way can also be topicalized, as in (14a).

(14) a. *nji bí bwán   wâ búdúm*
      but you children AM male

    b. *mə adúgé   ónta   mɔ́ mɔ́ lúgə wá*
       I   NEG^PR^see grandchildren I   PERF leave REL
    But, of you male children, I do not see grandchildren that I have left behind.

The noun phrase *bí bwán wâ búdúm*, though it has no direct syntactic relationship with the following clause, is semantically associated with *ónta* 'grandchildren'. The sentence as a whole thus has the meaning 'I do not see grandchildren of (coming from) you sons, that I have left behind'. For this reason, this phrase is still viewed as topicalized, though it is not clear that it has actually been fronted from some position within the main clause.

This topicalized noun phrase also indicates discontinuity of topic. The father has just said that he himself has begotten more than thirty children. Now, with example (14), he switches to his sons ('you sons') and talks about their failure to bear children, the discussion of which continues for several more sentences.

2.3 Prepositional phrases

Although prepositional phrases normally occur after the verb in the main clause, just like adverbial noun phrases, these phrases may also be preposed. When preposed, the topicalized phrase often indicates a discontinuity of time or location. The category of prepositional phrases here includes phrases with postpositions as well as prepositions. The locative, for example, may be marked by a tonal preposition or by a postposition marker, as in (15).

(15) *wa jǫ́ bɛɛnd dí   mə mɔ́   lǘgə cúd*
      here my family LOC I   PERF left empty
      Here in my family, I have been left empty.

This sentence occurs in the dying father's farewell speech. In the preceding sentence, he has stated that the married daughters, who live in their husbands' villages, had borne children. In this sentence, with the topicalized locative phrase, he switches to talk about his own village, where his sons live, and where there are no grandchildren because his sons have not produced children. Thus, this topicalized phrase marks a change of location.

2.4 Verbal phrase *kə jé kǘl*

The phrase *kə jé kǘl* has the form of a verb phrase, since the morphemes literally mean 'go arrive place'. It most often appears thus, as a fixed phrase, but in some cases it is used without the *kǘl* 'place', and in a few others, the *kǘl* is replaced with *té* 'time'.

In its post-main clause position, the phrase *kə jé kǘl*, here translated as 'until', functions as a conjunction, as seen in (16).

(16) a. *bɨmɔ́   jəlá nə ji   baagʉlə mʉ́n*
       you^PL must with exist conserve your^PL

   b. *mɔ́bá   kə jé   kǘl jínɔ́ dâm í bá bə kú jímb*
      marriages go arrive place name my   it F2 be NEG disappear
      You (daughters) must conserve your marriages, so that (until) my name will not disappear.

The phrase here introduces a kind of temporal or causal clause, adding information to the main clause. In this post-main clause position, it does not mark any discontinuity.

However, when this same phrase is preposed, it definitely marks a point of discontinuity, usually a change in participants. It often occurs in a text with reported speech, in order to signal a change in the addressee, as shown in (17).

(17) a. *kǝ jé kúl nyɔ́ á nyiŋgǝ zǝ líína ókóól búsú dí*
go arrive place he P2 again come turn^to sisters our LOC

yí
REL

b. *nyǝ nǝ ókóól búsú nɔ́*
he with sisters our that...
Until he again crossed over to our sisters, he said to our sisters...

In (17a), *kǝ jé kúl* occurs in the text of a father's farewell at the point where the father has finished speaking to the sons and now addresses the women, including the daughters, sisters, and wives. Thus he switches to address a different group.

In the topicalized position, the phrase not only indicates discontinuity, but also contributes to the coherence of the action. The literal meaning of the morphemes of this phrase ('go arrive place') shows that this phrase links the previous clauses or actions to the subsequent clause. This explains why this phrase is sometimes translated as 'until', even though it might be translated equally well as 'and then'.

3 Focus-presupposition construction

Another construction in Makaa involving a preposed constituent is the focus-presuppositon construction (henceforth F-P).[5] This section shows how it is used to interrrupt the flow of an argument in order to give prominence to the assertion with which it is associated. Such interruptions constitute discontinuities of action, according to Givón.

The F-P is made up of a focused constituent followed by a presupposed statement. The focused constituent contains highlighted information, and the presupposition contains nonhighlighted or background information. In this construction, the highlighted information appears at the beginning of

---

[5]This paper uses the term focus-presupposition in the same way as Andrews (1985:77), who distinguishes three principal articulations of the sentence: topic-comment, focus-presupposition, and presentational.

the clause; less important (nonhighlighted and usually old) information is found toward the end of the clause.

After showing briefly how the focused constituent is marked, this section describes how it interrupts the flow of an argument.

3.1 Marking

The focused constituent is marked by the morpheme *ó* which immediately follows it, thus separating the focused constituent from the rest of the clause. A noun phrase may be focused, as in (18), or an entire clause may be focused, as in (19).

(18) *shílə   yé nyə ó   bág   ŋgə kə wá   bwə mətálɛ*
      daughter his she FOC F2^HORT PROG go put^on them blessing
      His daughter she's the one who would be giving them the blessing.

(19) *mə ŋgə́lə   wóós ó   ga*
      I   PROG^INF arrive FOC here
      It's my arrival here.

In these two examples, the item in focus is the subject of the main clause. In such cases, the particle *ó* that follows is the only marker of the focused constituent. Other constituents of the clause may be put into focus too, however, as seen in (20).

(20) *ja   jongú   ó   cʉg bá   jé í é bá kǎ bǒ*
      time this^aforementioned FOC life marriage his it F1 F2 go be

      mpwogé yí
      in^peace REL
      It's at that time his married life will go well.

The phrase *ja jongú* in (20) functions as an adverbial of time and normally occurs in nonfocus sentences in postverbal position. Here, in a F-P, the constituent in focus is fronted to the beginning of the clause, unless that constituent already occurs clause initially. In either case, the focused constituent is considered to be preposed with respect to the (rest of the) main clause.

3.2 Interrupting the flow of an argument

Focus is used in connection with the main assertion of the argument in order to give it prominence. In so doing, it not only highlights the main assertion, but also stops the progression of the argument, and thus causes some sort of discontinuity in the expected flow of the discourse.

This is similar to the use of repetition in tail-head linkage as "a rhetorical device that slows the story down prior to a significant development" (Levinsohn 1992:169) in order to highlight that event. Jarvis (1991:222–23), for example, shows how backgrounded information repeated in tail-head linkage is actually placed in the focus position of the Podoko sentence. Using repetition to slow down is similar to using simultaneous actions in a narrative discourse to stop the flow of action, thereby creating a discontinuity.

Using an example from daily life, this phenomenon may be compared to a tour of a museum. The tour guide gives an explanation of the displays. When he comes to a more important item, he is apt to slow down the tour, underlining its importance by using different words, or by pointing out how it is different from other items, or simply by enunciating it more emphatically or more clearly.

The F-P construction can do three things with the main assertion. It can (a) reiterate the main assertion, (b) state the contrastive item compared with the main assertion, or (c) identify a participant or topic in the main assertion.

Thus, in some cases, the F-P restates or reiterates the main assertion of the section in the text, in order to refocus on given information, as in (21).

(21)   *mə́ ó   mə́ ámə byá bí*
       I   FOC I   P1   bear you^PL
       I'm the one who fathered you.

This sentence is part of the dying father's speech, where he is advising his sons how to live after his death. The main assertion of the speech is that he wants them to live worthy of being his offspring. In the sentence quoted here, the focus is the father himself. The clause highlights the fact that the father is the one who begot those he is addressing. This is restating a known fact, since the audience knows that the father is speaking to his own children and is thus refocusing on given information. In emphasizing the importance of this assertion, this clause interrupts the flow of the argument.

Secondly, a constituent may be focused in order to highlight a contrasting argument, when it states the opposite of the main assertion (a negative antonym) in order to underline the main assertion of the argument. This is illustrated in (22).

(22) *bwán   wâ bwábudá bwɔ́ ó   bwó mɔ́   byá bwân*
      children AM girls   they FOC they PERF bear children
      The daughters, they bore children.

This sentence occurs in a section where the father is rebuking the sons for not having produced any offspring. The focus is on 'daughters', the subject of the clause. It is temporarily highlighting the fact that the daughters did bear children. However, this sentence serves to contrast the stated assertion (i.e., about the daughters) with the main assertion of the section, the fact that the sons have not produced any children. Thus, this focused clause underlines the main assertion by making a contrast.

Thirdly, the F-P in Makaa may also be used to identify a participant in the main assertion. In this case, it also stops the flow of the argument in order to draw attention to what is important, as illustrated in (23d).

(23) a. I must leave you with a blessing because it is very bad if I leave you without a blessing.

   b. And then he said to his wife that that banana trunk [used to give the blessing] must be kept.

   c. *baŋg bêsh bwó ɔ̀   shígé bɔ jwów doŋgú*
      those all   they P2 NEG be day   that^aforementioned

      dí   wá
      LOC REL
      As for all those who were not there that day,

   d. *shílɔ   yé nyɔ ó   bág   ŋgɔ kɔ wá   bwɔ mɔtɔ́lɛ*
      daughter his she FOC F2^HORT PROG go put^on them blessing
      his daughter, she will be giving them the blessing.

These sentences, from the same text as (22), occurs after the father has given his blessing to the children present on that day, ending with (23a). These sentences in (23) are part of a section which explains the giving of the blessing to those who were absent, beginning with (23b). The narrator identifies who will give the blessing to those who were absent, referred to as *bwɔ* 'them' in (23d). The daughter, designated to carry on the blessing, is a new participant, not mentioned before in the text. So, rather than restating a main assertion, according to the first function illustrated of focus, this F-P highlights a new participant who is relevant to the main assertion, the carrying on of the blessing. By adding the focus marker to the clause, it draws special attention to and interrupts the flow of the text.

In (24), a F-P is again used in the same text to identify an important point the father wants to make. The focused item of this example has the same general function as the one in (23), but this time it identifies a topic (rather than a participant) having to do with the main assertion.

(24) *ntúni ó   cʉg jísɔ́ yé*
      this FOC life is REL
      It is like this that life is.

This clause occurs at the very beginning of the dying father's speech. The focus is on the cataphoric *ntúni* 'this', and identifies that what is coming is an important point in the speech.

Similarly, the focus on an anaphoric noun phrase identifies that what was previously said was an important point, as in (25).

(25) *ja   joŋgú   ó   cʉg bá   jé í é bá kɔ̌*
      time that^aforementioned FOC life marriage his it F1 F2 go

      bɔ̌ mpwogé yí
      be in^peace REL
      It's at that time that his married life will go well.

This example, occurring in a text describing a marriage, comes after the family members have given their blessings to the daughter who is about to be married. The focused sentence summarizes or points out the importance of the previous blessings given.

Because the F-P construction reiterates, contrasts, or identifies the main assertion, it interrupts the flow of the argument, and thus constitutes a discontinuity. It is a more subtle kind of discontinuity than the discontinuity of change indicated by topicalization.

4 Conclusion

The study of preposed phrases, both simple and complex, has shown how discontinuities are indicated in Makaa discourse. Topicalized phrases mark discontinuities by indicating a change, whether of action, situation, or reference. This paper is limited to certain types of phrases, but its discussion suggests that other preposed constituents, such as vocatives, conjunctions, and conditional or other subordinate clauses, may be used to signal discontinuities in a manner similar to the pattern described in this paper.

Focused phrases signal discontinuity by interrupting the flow of the argument in order to highlight a main assertion. This type of discontinuity has not been discussed often in studies of discourse, which has dealt mostly with narrative discourse. This present study has made much use of non-narrative discourse, where the focus-presupposition construction and the discontinuity of interrupting the argument are more frequent than in narrative discourse.

References

Andrews, Avery. 1985. The major functions of the noun phrase. In Timothy Shopen (ed.), Language typology and syntactic description, 1:62–154. Cambridge: Cambridge University Press.

Blass, Regina. 1990. Relevance relations in discourse: A study with special reference to Sissala. Cambridge: Cambridge University Press.

Givón, Talmy. 1990. Syntax: A functional-typological introduction 2. Philadelphia: Benjamins.

Guthrie, Malcolm. 1971. Comparative Bantu 2. Farnborough: Gregg International Publishers.

Heath, Daniel and Teresa Heath. 1984. Relative clauses in Məkaá. Journal of West African Languages 14(2):43–60.

―――. 1990. Preliminary observations on a Makaa conflict narrative discourse. Yaoundé: Société Internationale de Linguistique.

Jarvis, Elizabeth. 1991. Tense and aspect in Podoko narrative and procedural discourse. In Stephen Anderson and Bernard Comrie (eds.), Tense and aspect in eight languages of Cameroon, 213–37. Dallas: Summer Institute of Linguistics and the University of Texas at Arlington.

Levinsohn, Stephen H. 1992. Discourse features of New Testament Greek. Dallas: Summer Institute of Linguistics.

Ramsey, Violeta. 1987. The functional distribution of preposed and postposed 'if' and 'when' clauses in written discourse. In Russell S. Tomlin (ed.), Coherence and grounding in discourse, 387–408. Philadelphia: Benjamins.

Sperber, Dan and Deirdre Wilson. 1986. Relevance: Communication and cognition. Oxford: Blackwell.

Section Two

Participant Reference Encoding

Demonstrative Adjectives in Mofu-Gudur Folktales

James N. Pohlig and Stephen H. Levinsohn

Abstract

Two sets of demonstrative adjectives qualify nouns in Mofu-Gudur. One set indicates the current center of attention and allows the speaker to convey physical or psychological distance between two or more participants when they are featured at the same time in the story. A second set, often occurring with the first, marks the relative salience of known referents. The interaction of these demonstratives and unqualified nouns permits the Mofu-Gudur storyteller to be very specific as to the orientation of the story and the relative status of each of the participants in it.

Résumé

Deux séries de démonstratifs servent à qualifier les nominaux en mofu-gudur. La première série renvoie à l'objet actuel d'attention et permet au sujet parlant de créer une distance physique ou psychologique entre deux participants ou plus lorsque ces derniers apparaissent au même moment de l'histoire. Une deuxième série de démonstratifs, que accompagne souvent la première série, indique l'importance relative accordée aux référants connus. L'interaction des démonstratifs en question et des nominaux non qualifiés permet au conteur mofu-gudur de préciser à la fois l'orientation générale de l'histoire et le statut relatif accordé à chacun des participants qui y sont présentés.

This study seeks to identify and explain the discourse functions of the demonstrative adjectives in traditional Mofu-Gudur[1] folk tales. The functions in question (a) help to indicate the degree and kind of salience of a participant,[2] (b) indicate identity or close association with a previously-introduced referent, and (c) indicate the nature of the 'stage' at any point in the narrative, whether all the participants are acting on a single stage, or whether the stage is divided and attention is directed to one side, rather than to the other.

Participants tend to be locally salient, central only for a time, following which attention is shifted to a different salient participant. Other participants may be marked as nonsalient.

In addition, this study notes secondary and specialized uses of the demonstratives.

1 Barreteau's inventory of demonstrative adjectives

An inventory of the demonstrative adjectives which are treated in this paper is given in (1), as they appear in Daniel Barreteau's (1988) lexicon.

---

[1]Mofu-Gudur (Mofu, South) is a Chadic language spoken by about 25,000 people in the Mayo Tsanaga Division, Far North Province, Cameroon. James Pohlig has worked for two years in the language, principally in the community of Mokong. Thanks go to Mr. Jean-Baptiste Almara, who has worked closely with him, and to others in the community for their help. This study has used a corpus of thirteen texts that were collected and transcribed by Mr. Kenneth Hollingsworth, most of which appear in Hollingsworth and Hollingsworth (1982, 1985). Acknowledgements go to the following storytellers: Mr. David Səkwar Way, Mr. Alioum Bayo Mana, Mr. Laban Zamakai, Mr. Moussa Sadjo, Mr. Jean-Claude Fandar, Mr. Hawa, Mr. Salomon Ndawa, and Mr. Goleved Galla. Sincere thanks go also to the Ministry of Scientific and Technical Research of the Republic of Cameroon, with whose permission this research was made possible.

The underlying segments in Mofu-Gudur are reflected in the following list utilized in this paper: *b, ɓ, c, d, ɗ, f, g, gw, h, hw, j, k, kw, l, m, mb, n, nd, ŋg, ŋgw, nj, p, r, s, ɬ, t, v, w, y, z, ɮ, ʔ, a, aa, e, ee, ə.* The underlying sequences *əy* and *əw* are represented by *i* and *u* respectively. Mofu-Gudur has two discrete tones, high and low; in this paper, high is marked (´), while low tone is left unmarked.

[2]The term 'participant' is employed, in this paper, to include both animate and inanimate referents. The terms 'animate participant' and 'prop' are employed when it is necessary to distinguish between these two categories.

(1)   á³   1. (déf.) - le, la (... en question)
                        2. (Adj. poss. 3 sg.) - son, sa
                        3. (anaphorique) - (ici) même, (ce ...) -ci

       héyey   (an.) - en question

       káa   1. (dém.) - ce, cet, cette
       (var. de kedé)   2. (loc.) - là
                        3. (temp.) - maintenant, aujourd'hui

       kedé, káa   (dém.) - ce, cet, cette; ceci, celui-ci

Another demonstrative, represented in Barreteau as *há*, is described in (2).

(2)   *há* (déf.) - (ce ...) -ci, le ... en question

This putative *há* is always found following the demonstrative *á*, and appears as *áha* or *ahá*, depending on the tonal shape of the preceding noun. This paper treats *áha* and its allomorph *ahá* as a unitary demonstrative adjective, given that Barreteau's definitions of *á* and *há* are very similar.

Barreteau cites other demonstratives, including *katáy* and *kaatáy* ('là, ce ... là' and 'au loin, ce ... là-bas' respectively), but these do not figure in the discussion which follows. They occur infrequently and their usage is accounted for by Barreteau's definitions.

2 A sketch of participant reference in Mofu-Gudur

This section first gives an overview of the semantic values of the demonstrative adjectives which are discussed in detail in the body of this paper. It then places these adjectives, together with the nouns they qualify, in the larger context of a hierarchy of topic identification based on Givón's (1983) iconicity principle.

---

[3]*á* has eight allomorphs: *á, a, é, e, há, ha, hé, he*. All are represented in this paper by *á*.

2.1 An outline of the semantic values of the demonstratives

The demonstratives considered in this paper may be organized according to two parameters: status and orientation. Examples (3) and (4) display these parameters; the contextual effects of using them are discussed respectively in §§3 and 4.

(3)   Status Parameter

$$\begin{bmatrix} h\acute{e}yey \\ +\ \text{salient} \\ +\ \text{anaphoric} \end{bmatrix}$$

$$\begin{bmatrix} \acute{a} \\ +\ \text{phoric} \end{bmatrix}$$

$$\begin{bmatrix} \acute{a}ha \\ +\ \text{anaphoric} \\ +\ \text{sameness} \end{bmatrix}$$

Absence of demonstrative

(4)   Orientation Parameter

$$\begin{bmatrix} ked\acute{e} \\ +\ \text{center} \end{bmatrix}$$

$$\begin{bmatrix} k\acute{a}a \\ -\ \text{center} \end{bmatrix}$$

Absence of demonstrative

The status on the stage of a given participant is defined in (3). Treating the demonstratives in descending order: *héyey* refers anaphorically to a previously introduced participant, and invests it with salience at that point in the text; *á* is marked solely as phoric; *áha* is marked as anaphoric and also as underlining the identity of the participant with an earlier reference ([+ sameness]).

The default value for the status parameter is carried by a noun which is not qualified by any of the demonstratives listed in (3). An unqualified noun is thus unmarked for the features concerned.

The parameter of (4), that of orientation, concerns whether attention is being directed to a particular participant or to all the participants that are on stage. If the storyteller orients his audience to a particular participant, he then has the choice of pointing to the center of attention (*kedé* marked [+ center]) or away to some 'other' (*káa* marked [- center]).

Again, when neither demonstrative listed in (4) qualifies a noun, the noun is unmarked for the feature concerned.

The two sets of demonstratives, in relation to each other and to the noun they qualify, occur in the order: noun–orientation–status.

However, the discussion of the two sets of demonstratives in §§3 and 4 treats them in the reversal order, namely, status first, then orientation. The sections concerned consider both the semantic values of the demonstratives, as indicated in (3) and (4), and the effects arising from their use in particular contexts.

2.2 The Mofu-Gudur ICONICITY HIERARCHY of topic identification

In accordance with his well-known iconicity principle, Givón (1983:18) offers the continuum in (5) "in the grammar of topic identification."

(5)   more continuous/accessible topics
        ↑   zero anaphora
        | unstressed/bound pronouns (agreement)
        | stressed/independent pronouns
        ↓   full NPS
        more discontinuous/inaccessible topics

Givón adds, "The iconicity principle underlying this scale must be simple: the more disruptive, surprising, discontinuous or hard to process a topic is, the more coding material must be assigned to it."

Before discussing how Givón's iconicity hierarchy applies to Mofu-Gudur, part of Barreteau's terminology concerning pronouns needs to be clarified. Barreteau (1988) establishes two series of personal pronouns, exemplified by the opposition between (a) *yá* (var. de *ya*, pr. pers. suj. 1 sg. devant une base verbale à ton haut antéposée) - je, and (b) *ya, yah* (pr. pers. subst. 1 sg.) - moi.

This paper considers (a), and the series of which it is a part, to be unstressed pronouns, in Givón's terms, i.e., phonological prefixes, bound to the verb stem or modifier that follows. The series of pronouns represented by (b) is that of Givón's stressed pronouns.

An unstressed pronoun is normally employed with a verb stem as in (6).[4]

(6)   *ya slǝkďawa*
      1   arise
      I arise.

A stressed pronoun is used when a pronominal referent is topicalized, as in (7), and a stressed pronoun is used also when a pronominal referent accompanies an ideophone, as in (8).[5]

(7)   *yah ná   ya slǝkďawa*
      1s   TOP 1   arise
      As for me, I arise.

(8)   *yah tál!*
      1s   arise
      I arise.

In applying Givón's iconicity principle to Mofu-Gudur, one finds that discontinuities in folkstories, as well as narrative peaks and highlighted turning points, are regularly reflected in the presence of full noun phrases, most often of the form noun +/− orientation + status.
A version of Givón's iconicity hierarchy specific to Mofu-Gudur is shown in (9).

(9)   Mofu-Gudup Topic Identification Iconicity Hierarchy

      more continuous/accessible topics
        ↑   zero anaphora
        │   unstressed pronouns
        │   stressed pronouns
        ↓   unqualified nouns and nouns + demonstratives
      more discontinuous/inaccessible topics

---

[4]Mofu-Gudur has first-, second-, and third-person unstressed pronouns. Plurality and plural inclusiveness (in the case of the first-person pronoun) are marked by verbal suffixes. The abbreviations used in this paper are DEMADJ demonstrative adjective, s singular, TOP topicalizing particle, UNQN unqualified noun, VIR virtual, Ø absence of a bound pronoun, 1, 3 first, third person.

[5]For ease of identification, an exclamation point (!) in this paper follows all and only ideophones.

Zero anaphora has been observed only preceding an ideophone, as illustrated in (10).

(10)   *a da njéy ná jǝ́kwám! a   ray   bégáney héyey*
      3 VIR sit   TOP sit   on head elephant DEMADJ
      He sat down, he sat on the head of that elephant.

In all other contexts, an unstressed pronoun is attached to a following verb or prefix, whether or not a stressed pronoun or full noun phrase also refers to the subject.

Mofu-Gudur may generally be said to follow, as far as sentence topics are concerned, a sequential strategy of participant reference. In other words, an unstressed pronoun, bound phonologically to a verb stem or modifier, looks back to the first eligible word functioning as a sentence topic for its referent. Such a word must be eligible in that (see Grimes 1978:viii) (a) the proposed referent word agrees with the verb and its unstressed pronoun in person and number, (b) the proposed referent word agrees with the verb in its degree of animacy, and (c) the proposed referent word is reasonable in fulfilling the expectations arising from the verb in question.

Some sort of analogous strategy is probably employed for participants in sentence rhemes, although this has not been thoroughly examined.

Unqualified nouns and noun + demonstrative combinations that are sentence topics typically occur following a discontinuity, at a peak, or in connection with an important turning point in the story.

3 Status on stage

This section considers the semantic values and contextual effects of the presence of *héyey, á,* or *áha,* together with the absence of any of these demonstrative adjectives with a noun.

3.1 Noun + *héyey*

Comrie (1989:199) describes salience as "relating to the way in which certain actants present in a situation are seized on by humans as foci of attention." Grimes (1975:337–38) points out that pronominal reference may reasonably indicate degree of salience.

This section argues that *héyey* is marked [+ salient]. *héyey* is also marked [+ anaphoric], since it always refers to a previously introduced or implied participant. The following discussion treats the various contexts in which *héyey* functions and the effects which are found in them. The effects are (a) to establish or, more generally, to reestablish a participant as salient, (b) to switch attention to a different action initiator or sentence topic when (s)he is salient, and (c) to help mark a narrative peak or turning point.

(Re)establishment of participants as salient. In connecting the main events of a story, *héyey* is used most frequently to reestablish a participant as salient and simultaneously to reintroduce it on stage. This is illustrated in (11). The donkey is reintroduced to the story (albeit negatively) and reestablished as salient by the use of *héyey*. The story from which (11) is taken is about a child thief. He steals a traveller's donkey, cuts off the donkey's ears, and plants them in a marsh. The episode in (11) relates the reaction of the traveller.[6]

(11)   a.   He-comes,
                       he-does not see   his donkey *héyey*.

       b.   He-seeks-it,
                       he-seeks-it,
                       he-seeks-it.

       c.   He-looks TOP,
               ears   planted   in water.

       d.   He-says, "Ah, my donkey
                       has fallen in water."

       e.   Take off! He-takes off   his clothes all from body.

---

[6]In this example and all others in which it is judged useful to denote elements of the sentence structure, a display of three columns is adopted. The first column contains all preverbal elements of any given clause, with the exception of the English word 'then' (standing for the Mofu-Gudur developmental marker *tá?*) when it occurs immediately prior to the verb. The third column contains only post-verbal elements which may be qualified by demonstratives, e.g., object nouns. The second column contains everything else, including the verb.

The Mofu-Gudur demonstratives are given in the language in their exact positions relative to the noun they qualify. No other material is given in the language. The unstressed pronoun is represented by a pronoun in English which is attached by a hyphen to the verb, e.g., 'he-comes.' The stressed pronoun is represented by an English pronoun placed in the first column, as in (11f).

     f. He   plunge! He-plunges   into water *káa héyey.*

He came, but did not see his donkey. He looked and looked for it. As he looked, he saw its ears which had been planted in the water. He said to himself, "Aha, my donkey has fallen in the water." He took off all his clothes and plunged into the water.

However, the reestablishment of a salient participant with *heyey* sometimes occurs independently of, and after, its (re)introduction onto the stage. Stative verbs or verbs of perception may (re)introduce an item without ascribing salience to it.

This is illustrated in sentence (11f). The water is referred to in (11c), in connection with a verb of perception, but it is only when the event line actually involves the water again, that it becomes qualified with *héyey.*

Much later in the same narrative, the child thief has fallen into the hands of the local chief, who tries to find a pretext to put him to death. He tells the boy to shave his head. The child agrees, but only if the chief at the same time will take off the kernels from the ear of corn which the boy has brought. The boy is thus the initiator of the actions, and it is in this context that the chief is reestablished as salient in (12c), with the boy not merely seeing him (compare (11c)), but actively watching him. The reason for marking the chief as salient (12c) is because he will pick a quarrel with the boy (see (12g)).

(12) a. Chief   he-begins to dekernel   corn.

      b.   He [boy]-begins to shave   head [of chief].

      c.   He-is shaving
                 he-is watching eye   on chief *káa héyey.*

      d.   He-shaves-him,
                 he-shaves-him,
                 he-shaves-him.

      e.   He-sees [that]
         corn   almost it-finish TOP,
                 he-rests   body,
                 he-rests   body.

      f.   Corn   finishes all,
                 he he-finishes-it   head also.

g. Chief
   káa   he-says-to him,
              "You must put that hair
              back on my head.
              Who told you to shave me?"

(In response,) the chief began to remove the kernels from the ear of corn. The boy began to shave the chief's head. While shaving, he kept an eye on the chief. He shaved and shaved. When he saw that the chief had almost finished the corn, he stopped shaving. When the corn was completely finished, the boy finished shaving, too. The chief said to him, "You must put that hair back on my head. Who told you to shave me?"

The next passage illustrates the need for an item to be introduced before *héyey* can mark it as salient. In this passage (see appendix (44v–w) for the context), the meat (13c) is introduced as a goat (13a), which the owner of the compound slaughters in honor of his guest. The meat turns out to be a salient prop because it is what the stranger refuses to eat.

(13) a.   They-go   to their house TOP
         man *káa héyey*   he-slaughters   goat.

      b.   He-says, "A stranger
                                has come to me."

      c. Then woman *káa*   she-prepares-it-
                                for them   food with meat *kedé*
                                                     héyey.

They [stranger and boy] went to their [the boy's] house. The man [of the house] slaughtered a goat. He said, "A guest has come to me." Then his wife prepared a meal with that meat.

In some cases, a participant is (re)introduced as salient by being placed in association with a previously introduced noun qualified by *héyey*. In (14), the fiancé is so reintroduced as a salient participant.

(14) a. Then   they-weed, they-weed.

     b.   They-weed,
       husband of girl
       káa héyey   he-says
                            "I am going to
                            relieve myself."

> They weeded and weeded. Then that girl's fiancé said, "I am going to relieve myself."

Here the fiancé, defined in terms of his fiancée, is reintroduced onto the main event line as salient. His simple intention to relieve himself turns out to important, for it leads to his fiancée seeing him in an embarrassing situation, which in turn leads him to end his life. Incidentally, if a different demonstrative had been used, his reintroduction in relation to his fiancée would have had the effect of downgrading his salience (see §3.2).

The establishment of participants as salient by means of association with *héyey*-qualified nouns occurs most commonly in patient-oriented episodes. Thus, in the story of the child thief, in which the student thief is following his mentor and stealing his clothing as he climbs a tree, it is not the man that is established as salient by the use of *heyey*, but rather his clothing, piece by piece.

(15) a. Man *káa héyey*   he-begins to climb.

     b. Child *káa*   he-puts   foot on their tree TOP,
                   he-pulls off   trousers from legs of
                                   man *káa héyey*.

     c.   They-reach   to top of tree TOP,
                   he-pulls off   underpants from
                                     buttocks of man *káa*
                                     héyey.

> The man began to climb. The child placed his foot on the tree and in one motion pulled off the trousers from the man. They got to the top of the tree, and he pulled the underpants off the man.

In another story, Squirrel and Elephant in turn persuade an old woman to spin his cotton instead of the other's. Each prop is reintroduced by association with a *héyey*-qualified noun.

(16) a. Elephant   he-complains,
                          "What? Is Squirrel
                          greater than I?"

      b.   "No, great chief."

      c. Old woman   take! she-takes   cotton of Elephant
                                               kedé héyey
                                                           . . .
      d. Old woman
          héyey   leave! she-leaves-it of Elephant.

      e. Then   she-spins-it   of Squirrel *héyey*.

Elephant complained, "Is Squirrel greater than I?" "No, great
chief." The old woman took the cotton of Elephant... The old
woman stopped spinning Elephant's cotton. Then she spun that of
Squirrel.

Switching from one salient sentence topic to another. When applied
to a participant that is already on stage and active in the scene, *héyey* has
the effect of switching the sentence topic to that participant and of
marking him or her as salient. Most commonly, the participant is the new
action initiator. For example, in the story of Elephant and Squirrel, Squirrel discovers that he is sitting on Elephant's head, and cries out to the old
woman for help. Then Elephant becomes the action initiator.

(17) Elephant *héyey*   seize! he-seizes-him,
                          enter! he-makes enter-him   into ear.

Elephant seized him [Squirrel] and put him into his ear.

See appendix (44dd) for another example in which a switch from one
salient action initiator to another is indicated with a *héyey*-qualified noun.
A participant may also be marked as salient in connection with a
background comment. In the story of the bird and the chief, for instance,
a marvelous singing bird performs. In (18a), the daughter is established as
salient in connection with a main event. This salience is reiterated in (18b),
in the background comment, probably because a climactic act (her acciden-
tally killing the bird) is about to follow.

(18)   a.   Daughter *káa*
            héyey TOP, she   climb! climb!
                                  she-climbs, she-goes,
                                  take! she-takes-it TOP,
                                  then it-begins   song,
                                  "Thank you ... "

       b.   Daughter *keɗé*
            héyey TOP,   it-pleases-her TOP,
            since   it-sang   song for her.

The daughter climbed up and took the bird. Then it began this
song, "Thank you ... " As for the daughter, she was pleased because the bird sang for her.

Heavy participant encoding using *héyey* at narrative peaks. Heavy participant encoding at climactic points in a story is probably a linguistic
universal. (Givón's iconicity priniciple hints at this when he refers to
"surprising" information being a motive for using more coding material.)
In Mofu-Gudur, *héyey* is commonly used in such contexts.
   In the story of the bird and the chief, for instance, the chief's wife and
daughter have been killed by monkeys. Their heads, scooped out and
covered over, are made into drums. The story continues in (19).

(19)   a.   They   they-cover over   drums TOP,
                      they-come TOP with singing   songs,
                      "*kwára, kwára ... *"

       b.   Others   they-do-it,
                      they-say,
                      "Thanks to the chief, where
                      did our drums come from?"
                      Boom! boom! boom!

       c.   They-beat-it   drums of heads
                                                héyey.

After they [the monkeys] had stretched covers over these drums,
they came and made music: *kwára, kwára ... * [ideophone for singing
of nonsense]. Others sang like this, "Thanks to the chief, where did
the drums come from?" Boom! boom! boom! They beat the drums
made of those heads.

The phrase 'the drums of heads *héyey*' in (19c) cannot be considered to reestablish the drums as salient, since they have been salient for the last several sentences. Rather, the shift from 'these drums' or 'the drums' to the possessive noun phrase qualified by *héyey* is typical of heavy participant encoding at peak.

3.2 Noun + *á*

The demonstrative *á* is marked as [+ phoric]. It most commonly references participants which have already been introduced (anaphoric), but may be used cataphorically or exophorically. Three contextual effects which may be conveyed by *á* are (a) to signal nonsalience, (b) to indicate a close association with something previously introduced, and (c) to function cataphorically or exophorically when no anaphoric referent is available.

***á* signals nonsalience.** In referencing previously introduced participants, *á* indicates nonsalience in the following contexts: (a) when qualifying references to a participant in an exchange of reported speeches; (b) when qualifying a reference to a major participant in connection with a background comment; and (c) when qualifying references to nonsalient props. These three contexts are now treated in turn.

In an exchange of reported speeches, *á* signals that a lack of dominance attaches to the participant which it qualifies. Thus, the speaker who is not qualified with *á* exercises an "authority role" (see Johnstone 1987). Typically, the participant who lacks dominance is first marked by *á* when he or she is the addressee of the speech concerned.

The example in (20) is drawn from the appendix, examples (44e–l) and (44s–t).

(20) a.   He-goes TOP,
                   he-perceives   children seated
                                                       under tree.

      b.   He-says-to them,
                  "Children, what are
                  you doing?"

      c.   "We are sitting here
                  guarding."

      d. Children   they-answer-him like this.

e.   "What are you guarding?"

f.   "We are guarding sheep
                and goats."

g.   They-answer-him   stranger á,
                "Are you a thief?"

h.   "Ah, am I a man who would
                steal from children?"

The stranger went and saw some children seated under a tree. He said
to them, "Children, what are you doing?" "We are sitting here guarding." The children answered him like this. "What are you guarding?"
"We are guarding sheep and goats." They in turn asked the stranger,
"Are you a thief?" "Ah, am I a man who would steal from children?"

[The stranger then addresses three children in turn; the participants
are unmarked for dominance. The story continues:]

o. Stranger   he-says   to child á,
                "Let's go to your home."

p. Then   they-go   to house with
                child á.

The stranger said to this child, "Let's go to your home." Then he
went to [the child's] house with the child.

In (20a–f), no participant is qualified with á; the children and the stranger
are presented on an equal basis. In (20g), the children seize the initiative
with a question that puts the stranger on the defensive, and reference to
him is qualified with á as the participant not in the authority role. The
stranger seizes the initiative over one of the children in (20o), and reference to the child is qualified with á. (See appendix (44z–cc) for another
example in which one participant exercises an authority role over another.)
    The fact that á continues to be used in connection with a further
reference to the same child in (20p) suggests that the authority role of a
participant extends beyond conversation to action(s) resulting from it.
    á is sometimes used in the context of a background comment to qualify
a reference to a major participant. The presence of á presumably reflects
the fact that the information of the comment is less important than the

foreground events that surround it. For example, a certain story presents a chief who is called upon to settle a dispute which has arisen because two deaf people have each misunderstood what the other has said.

(21) a. Chief   he-says-to them,
                            "Why are you quarreling?"

      b. Chief á TOP   is   deafmute also.

      c. Woman   she-says ...

      d. Man also   he-says ...

      e. Chief á   he-understands not even   one word.

      f.   He-says ...

The chief said to them, "Why are you quarreling?" Now the chief was deaf, too. The woman said ... Then the man said ... But the chief understood not even one word. He said ...

Examples (21a), (21c), and (21d) are on the event line, and the participants are unqualified (see especially (21a)). In contrast, (21b) and (21e) are comments in which the chief is qualified with *á:* the information is of a backgrounded nature.

This use of *á* may be contrasted with that of *héyey,* in connection with a background comment about a participant previously marked as salient by *héyey,* immediately preceding peak (see (18b), discussed in §4.1).

Anaphoric references to nonsalient props are qualified with *á*. In the following excerpt from appendix (45x–z), two props are thus qualified. The example begins after the tortoises have run under dry leaves in order to escape from the squirrel; the story concerns the squirrel and a particular tortoise, not the props.

(22) a. Fire   fall! it-falls   from mouth of pipe
                                                           TOP,
          fire á TOP   to light   with flint and steel.

      b. Then   it-spreads slowly   on dry leaves á.

      c. Tortoises   they-come out   from dry leaves á TOP,
                           they-do innumerable!

Fire fell from the pipe's bowl, fire lit with flint and steel. Then it slowly spread on the dry leaves. The tortoises came out from those leaves—they were innumerable!

Both the fire and the dry leaves are qualified with *á* as further references to props.

***á* indicates a close association with something previously introduced.** Barreteau (1988) points out that *á* is used with some lexical items to indicate possession. Many, but not all, kinship terms use *á* in that way, as well as certain other common nouns. A sampling of such nouns is given in (23).

(23)   *zel á*   'her husband'   (see appendix (44aa))
       slam á   'his place'   (see (24))
       way á   'his house'   (see appendix (45ee))

This kind of reference has the effect of conferring minimal salience upon a participant, probably because such referents are thus defined in terms of another participant.

Example (24) illustrates this effect in connection with a prop. In the story of the singing bird, the chief acquires the habit of removing the bird from its home in the granary.

(24)   a.   Whenever chief   wants TOP,
                               he-takes-it,
                               it-begins-for him to sing   song.

       b.   Later   he-put-it   into place *á*.

Whenever the chief wanted, he would take the bird out of the granary, and it would begin to sing for him. Later, he would put it back in its place.

Here the bird's home has no interest for the audience. It has been mentioned before, and there is no more to be said about it.

Similarly, minimal salience is conferred on animate participants who are eligible for this kind of qualification with *á*. Defined in terms of another character, such a participant is usually depicted as lacking in salience. In one story, a girl makes a black fruit drink for her fiancé.

(25) a.   It-boiled,
           then   she-goes
                        she-calls   fiancé *á* and
                                                         his comrade.

      b.   She-tells-them,
                        "Come and drink this."

      c.   They-come,
           fiancé *á*   he-says,
                        "I won't drink this drink of
                        yours, for at my home there
                        is sorghum everywhere."

[The black fruit drink] boiled; then she went and called her fiancé
and his comrade. She told them, "Come and drink this." They
came, but the fiancé said, "I won't drink this drink of yours, for at
my home there is sorghum everywhere [for the making of beer]."

Here, the girl occupies an authority role (§3.2) and the fiancé has little
salience. This fact is manifested in that he is on the receiving end of the
interaction. He receives the invitation to drink, and he reacts instead of
taking the initiative.

A similar evaluation can be made wherever an animate participant is
qualified with *á*. See, for example, lines (44z, aa, cc) of the appendix, which
were referred to in §3.2.

**_á_ functions cataphorically or exophorically when no anaphoric
referent is available.** When no anaphoric reference is possible, *á* may
function cataphorically in a speech margin, as in (26).

(26)   He-sings differently   with cry *á:*
                                                         kwédédédé.
        He sang differently with this cry: *kwédédédé.*

In an expression capable of indicating a gesture on the speaker's part, *á*
functions exophorically, with an external referent, as in (27).

(27)   Big monkeys
        kedé   they-do-to him   fingernails
                                                         thus *á* . . .
        The big monkeys scratched him like this . . .

3.3 Noun + *áha*

The features [+ anaphoric] and [+ sameness] are assigned to *áha*. The feature [+ sameness] denotes that the anaphoric reference is underlined, that attention is directed to the identity of the qualified noun with its previous referent.

The association of [+ sameness] with *áha* is consistent with the fact that the noun + *áha* combination so often occurs soon after its referent, in the same small unit of discourse, e.g., within the same sentence or within one or two sentences. For example, in the story of the two deaf people in (28), the man misunderstands the woman's words.

(28)   a.   He-says-to her,
                   "Woman *kedé*, did not
                   my sheep come by here?"

       b.   It-seems   to woman *káa* TOP,
                   "Where is the boundary of
                   the field you are farming?"

       c.   Woman *áha*   she-says TOP,
                   "The boundary of my field
                   is over there, over there."

       d.   She-points out-it-to him.

       e.   It-seems   to man again as if
                                                  she-says-to him TOP,

                  his sheep have gone to
                  place *áha* which woman
                  áha has pointed out to
                  him thus.

He said to her, "Woman, did not my sheep come by here?" It seemed to the woman that he said, "Where is the boundary of the field you are farming?" The woman said, "The boundary of my field is over there, over there." She pointed it out to him. In turn, it seemed to the man as if she said to him that his sheep had gone where she pointed to.

Three contextual effects of *áha*, associated with a low degree of salience
are (a) to assign a low degree of salience to a participant which is
reintroduced on stage, (b) to assign to the qualified noun a low degree of
salience in the context of a background comment, and (c) to assign
anaphoric reference to a qualified noun for which *á* denotes close
association.

áha **assigns a low degree of salience to a participant which is
reintroduced on stage.** Although *áha* is seen as unmarked for salience,
when it is used in connection with the reintroduction of a participant, it
contrasts with *héyey* in that the noun so qualified is not invested with much
salience. This is illustrated in the introduction to the story about the black
fruit drink.

(29) a. Man   there-is
          they with
          his friend,   they-go   to work party of
                                            his fiancée.

      b. Then   they-weed.

      c. Girl *áha*   then she-goes,
                        she-draws   water.

There was a man who went with his friend to work on his fiancée's
farm. They weeded. Then the girl went and drew water.

The existence of a fiancée is indicated in (29a). When she is actually
introduced to the scene in (29c), reference to her is with *áha*. If *héyey* had
been used instead of *áha*, this would have established the fiancée as a
salient participant. In fact, the story is about the fiancé, who is ultimately
solitary in his shame and his fate.

áha **assigns to the qualified noun a low degree of salience in the
context of a background comment.** Such an effect is possible because
áha is unmarked for salience. In a story of a lizard and a goat, Goat buries
the soup prepared for him by the wife of his friend Lizard. After he has
left for home, Lizard's wife finds the soup and calls her husband to witness
this culturally outrageous deed.

(30)   Then ...   he-runs ...
                    he-sees TOP,
        thing *áha*   like thus.

Then he ran and saw that the situation was just like [his wife had said].

The soup is a crucial prop in the story, in the sense that its rejection becomes the cause of war between all four-footed animals and all crawling animals. However, the soup itself figures no more in the events after this point. Had the soup remained salient in the following events, *héyey* would have been used instead of *áha*.

áha assigns anaphoric reference to a qualified noun for which *á* denotes close association. The nouns described in §3.2 take *á*, rather than a personal possessive pronoun, to denote possession or close association. Consequently, *á* cannot fulfill for these nouns its regular function of denoting anaphoric reference. For such nouns, *áha* is observed to take the place of *á* in denoting anaphoric reference.

This is illustrated in the story of the child thief, which closes with the words in (31).

(31)   Then   he-became   chief in place *áha*.

Then he became chief in that (same) place.

Contrast (31) with the line from the story of the bird and the chief in (32).

(32)   Afterwards   he-put-it   in place *á*.

Afterwards he [the chief] would put it back in its place.

3.4 The unqualified noun

The unqualified noun is seen as carrying the default value for the features discussed above. It is not [– anaphoric], [– salient], [– phoric], or [– sameness]. Rather, it is unmarked for these features.

Because an unqualified noun is unmarked for anaphoric reference, it is the appropriate means of introducing a participant for the first time. The exception to this generality occurs when a participant is introduced by association with a different and *héyey*-qualified participant (see §3.1). On the other hand, an unqualified noun may reintroduce a participant if there is no reason to suppose that the unqualified noun would refer to any other participant.

Because an unqualified noun is unmarked for the feature [salient], it implies nothing in and of itself about the degree of salience of its referent. Rather, its relative salience is to be deduced from the context. Thus, interacting participants may be deduced to be of equal salience when reference to them both is with an unqualified noun. This is illustrated in the story of the squirrel and the tortoise (see appendix (45a–f) for the context).

(33) a. Squirrel   he-is going   to feast.

      b.   He-had-put on   robe on body,
                     he-is going with
                     small movements!   with to play guitar.

      c.   He-goes TOP,
             Tortoise seated   at edge water.

      d.   He-says-to him . . .

      e. Squirrel   he-says-to him . . .

Squirrel was going to a feast. He had put on a robe, and was walking with small movements, playing a guitar. As he went, [he saw] Tortoise seated at the edge of a a stream. Tortoise said to him . . . Squirrel said to him . . .

Alternatively, a participant referred to with an unqualified noun may be deduced from the context to be ascendant over another one, as in the story of the squirrel and tortoise (see appendix (44w–z) for the context).

(34) a. Squirrel   he-goes,
                     he-smokes   pipe . . .

      b. Tortoises they-come out . . .

Squirrel went smoking a pipe . . . Tortoises came out . . .

Typically, when the references to all the participants are with an un-qualified noun, animate participants are assumed to be locally salient and props to be nonsalient. In the context of (33a–c), for instance, the props 'feast', 'robe', 'body', 'guitar', and 'water' will all be perceived as nonsalient. As the narrative progresses, the guitar and the water become very salient, but the other three props do not. However, when all five are first intro-duced, one has no way of knowing which, if any, will become salient.

4 Orientation on stage

The orientation parameter was presented in (4) and characterizes the demonstratives *kedé* and *káa*. The feature [+ center] is assigned to *kedé*, while [– center] is assigned to *káa*. These two demonstratives are now treated in turn.

4.1 Noun + *kedé*

kedé is marked as [+ center]. A participant qualified with *kedé* holds center stage; the attention of the audience is directed toward it. This is illustrated in the opening of a story about a fly and a flea, who meet their end together as a result of gorging themselves on meat.

(35) a. Flea and fly   they-fatten   steer.

      b.   Fatten! fatten!
                          they-fatten-it   steer *kedé*.

      c. Big,   it-grew up.

A fly and a flea were fattening up a steer. They fattened this steer, and it grew very big.

The steer is the story's only prop and, once introduced (35a), is marked in (35b) as the center of attention in the first paragraph of the story, while it grows, is caught, and is then slaughtered.

For other examples of a noun qualified with *kedé* to establish a prop as the center of attention, see appendix (44w) and (45s).

Highlighting one participant over against others. When one participant out of a group on stage is referred to with *kedé*, it has the effect of highlighting that participant, marking him or her as the center of attention.

This effect is illustrated in the following example, drawn from the story of the bird and the chief. The chief's daughter is highlighted rather than the chief and her mother. (For the use of *kedé* in (36a), see §4.2.)

(36) a. Day *kedé*,
          chief   departed   to field.

      b. His daughter at
          house of husband   she-heard   [that] mother *á*
                                                     had not gone to
                                                     field that day;
                                                     she was at home.

      c. Daughter *kedé*   she-comes   to mother *á* TOP
                                 she-says-to her,
                                 "Mother, they say
                                 that father has a
                                 singing bird.
                                 Where is it?"

      d. Mother *á*   she-says-to her,
                                 "It is in the gran-
                                 ary. Go fetch it."

      e. Daughter *káa*
          héyey TOP she   climb! climb!
                                 she-climbs,
                                 she-goes take!
                                 she-takes-it TOP,
          then   it-begins   song,
                                 "Thank you, wife of
                                 the chief... "

      f. Daughter *kedé*
          héyey TOP   it-pleases-her TOP,
                                 [that] it-had sung-
                                 it-for her   song.

      g. Daughter *kedé*   put! she-returns-it   to granary *héyey* TOP,
                                 she-drops-it TOP,   into calabash
                                 filled with oil.

h. Bird *kedé héyey*
    TOP, oil   it-killed-it.

One day, the chief was away in the fields. His daughter at her
husband's home heard that her mother had not gone to the fields
that day, that she was at home. The daughter came to her mother
and said, "Mother, they say that father has a singing bird. Where is
it?" Her mother said, "In the granary. Go fetch it." The daughter
climbed and climbed and took out the bird. It began to sing for her,
"Thank you, chief's wife..." The daughter was pleased because the
bird had sung for her. The daughter put it back into the granary; she
dropped it into a calabash filled with oil. So the oil killed the bird.

Different participants become the center of attention in this excerpt. The
daughter is highlighted with *kedé*, rather than the chief or her mother in
(36c). After the center of attention has ceased to be the daughter (see §4.3
on *káa*), she is again marked in (36f) and (36g) as the center of attention,
rather than the bird. She is highlighted with *kedé* first, in connection with
a background comment (see (18)), then, in connection with the next
foreground event. Finally, in (36h), the bird becomes the center of attention, as it is killed by the oil.

4.2 Other contexts in which *kedé* is used

The following are three particular contexts in which *kedé* indicates the
center of attention.
In direct address in reported speech, kedé *can be used to reinforce a
vocative and mark the addressee as the center of attention.* In the story
about two deaf people, for instance, the man addresses the woman,
"Woman *kedé*, did not my sheep come by here?" Even though the man
and the woman are alone, *kedé* is used.
In the story of the hungry stranger, the stranger addresses three boys
within a group, one by one. Each time he says (see also appendix (44m, o,
q)), *káa* child *kedé!* 'You there!'.[7] The presence of *kedé* serves to highlight
each boy in turn as the center of attention.
A series of two noun + kedé *combinations indicates that one participant
after another is selected as the center of attention.* This is illustrated in (37).
(In appendix (45bb–cc), *kedé* is used as a demonstrative pronoun.)

---

[7]A prenominal *káa* such as this is described by Barreteau (1988) as having a locative
sense, *'là'*, which seems to be an adequate description here.

(37) a. He   strike!   on *kedé* TOP
                     to kill.

      b. He   strike!   on *kedé* TOP
                     to kill.

He struck and killed this one. He struck and killed that one.

In connection with a series of noun + kedé *forms,* kedé *may be used with a time word to indicate one time after another.* The example in (38) is drawn from the story of the child thief.

(38)   With day *kedé*   he-sleeps   with wife other *kedé,*
                          he-sleeps   with wife other *kedé,*
                          he-sleeps   with wife other.

One evening he slept with one wife, the next with another, and the next with another.

4.3 Noun + *káa*

káa is marked as [– center]. This feature is not a default value, but rather one which implies a divided stage. Under most circumstances, it places the participant so qualified on the other side of the stage from that side to which the audience's attention is directed.

When producing a divided stage, participant(s) referred to with the noun + *káa* combination are often contrasted with participants referred to with an unqualified noun. This is illustrated in the second half of a story about an old woman who planted groundnuts. The old woman administers a test to determine whether the squirrel or the monitor is guilty of stealing her peanuts, and in this section she is regularly qualified with *káa*. As she fills the functions of judge and then executioner, she is thus placed on one side of the stage against both the squirrel and monitor, who remain unqualified. (The squirrel and monitor remain equal in salience, pitted against each other until the judgment is delivered.)

As indicated above, placing participants on different sides of a stage implies distance between them. This distance may be psychological, as in the above story, or physical. Physical distance is illustrated in examples below. For a further example of psychological distance between participants, see the use of *káa* to refer to the chief in (12), in connection with his interaction with the child thief.

Two contextual effects are observed to arise from the noun + *káa* combination. First, if two participants on stage are both referred to with *káa*, there is distance between them, and second, if two participants are referred to with *káa* and *á* respectively, the first dominates the second.

If two participants on stage are both referred to with *káa*, there is distance between them. Physical distance between participants is illustrated in the long excerpt from a story of a goat and a leopard in (39); the leopard is about to spring on the goat.

(39) a. As goat *káa héyey*   he-looks eye,
          leopard   almost near to him.

      b. Goat *káa*   he-does bare teeth!

      c. Leopard *káa*   he-says-to him,
                                  "What happened to your teeth?"

      d. Goat *káa*   he-says-to him,
                                  "Before, I ate only dried leopard meat,
                                  but today I have found fresh."

      e. Leopard   he-says-to him,
                                  "Where is it?"

      f.   "It's you."

      g.   "Me?"

      h.   "You."

      i. Leopard, fear   it-seizes-him,
                                  he-returns backward,
                                  he-flees, he-runs.

      j. Goat   he-inches forward,
                                  he-eats,
                                  he-inches forward,
                                  he-eats.

      k. Leopard *káa*   to back.

l.   Goat   he-says,
                             "Let's get this over with."

m.   They-go like there TOP,
     goat   he-does cry TOP,
     leopard *káa*   cry! cry!
     excrement   splat! splat!,
                             to run off.

n.   Finished.

As the goat looked up, the leopard was almost upon him. The goat
bared his teeth, and the leopard said to him, "Why, what has
happened to your teeth?" The goat said, "Before, I ate only dried
leopard meat, but today I have found fresh." The leopard said to
him, "Where is it?" "It's you!" "Me?" "You!" Fear gripped the
leopard; he turned around and went back, running. The goat inched
forward and grazed a bit, inched forward and grazed. The leopard
backed up. Finally the goat said, "Let's get this over with." They
were going like this, when the goat let out a big cry; the leopard
screamed, his bowels gave way with a splat, and he fled. The story
is finished.

In (39a–d), the physical distance between the goat and the leopard is
indicated by marking them both with *káa;* they occupy different parts of
the stage, but attention is not directed to either part. As they converse, the
division of the stage disappears (39e–j), until the leopard starts to move
offstage (39k) and flees (39m). By marking the leopard with *káa* but not
the goat (39k–m), attention is directed to the goat and how he triumphed
by forcing the leopard to flee from him.
   A more complicated use of *káa* occurs in (40). (See appendix (44t–w)
for the context.)

(40) a.   Then   they-go   to house with
                                                   child *á* next.

      b.   They-go   to their house TOP,
           man *káa héyey*   slaughter!
                               he-slaughters   goat.

c.   He-says,
                            "A stranger has
                            come to me."

d.   Then woman *káa*   she-prepares-it-
                            for them   food with meat
                                              kedé héyey.

Then they [the stranger and the child] went to [the child's] house.
When they had gone there, that man [the owner of the compound]
slaughtered a goat. He said, "A guest has come to me." Then that
woman prepared food with that meat.

Example (40a) presupposes the existence of the owner of the house, i.e.,
the child's father, who is then referred to in (40b) with the words 'man *káa*
héyey'. The presence of *káa* divides the stage between this man and the
stranger. In (40d), the man's wife, also qualified by *káa*, is put on the same
side of the stage as her husband. The two are separated physically from
the stranger; they are surely talking out of earshot.

The referents may be pictured in (41), with the husband and wife on the
other side of the divided stage from the stranger.

(41)   UNQN   distance   *(káa = káa)*

       stranger   husband   wife

**If two participants are referred to with respectively *káa* and *á*, the
first (the 'other') dominates the second.** The function of *á* in reported
conversations has been discussed in §3.2; it indicates that the other participant occupies an authority role. The use of *káa* in connection with the
dominant participant places both on the other side of the divided stage. This
is illustrated in (42) (appendix (44z–cc)), which is a continuation of (40).

(42)   a.   Woman *káa*   to husband *á*,
                            "Give him it, then,
                            maybe he has need
                            of it."

       b.   Husband *á*   he-says-to her,
                            "Never! I slaughter a goat
                            for him; how will I give
                            him only a foot *káa*?"

c.   Woman *káa* TOP,   she-says,
                        "Ah, I am going to the
                        river."

d.   Husband *á*   stand up! to go,
                        he-looks for   something for
                                                  stranger.

The woman said to her husband, "Give him the foot. Maybe he has need of it." Her husband said to her, "I slaughter a goat for him; how can I give him only the foot?" The woman said, "Ah, I am going to the river." The husband got up to go look for something for the stranger.

In (42), the man and his wife talk about how to handle the stranger's odd request to be given only a foot of the slaughtered goat to chew on. Reference to the wife is qualified by *káa*, while the use of *á* in connection with her husband indicates that she occupies an authority role over him in the exchange. Both of them are separated physically from the stranger (who is referred to by an unqualified noun); thus, they are on the other side of the divided stage from him.

A schema comparable to that given in (41) is presented in (43) to reflect the authority role that the wife has over her husband in the exchange.

(43)   UNQN   distance   *(káa > á)*

       stranger   wife   husband

Summary

Two sets of demonstratives qualify nouns in Mofu-Gudur. The set whose members immediately follow the noun indicates the current center of orientation and contains two members. *kedé* marks a referent as the center of orientation. *káa* indicates a divided stage which has physical or psychological distance between the referent, on the one hand, and one or more other participants, on the other. Frequently, some other participant is the center of attention.

The second set of demonstratives indicates the status of the referent in the context and contains three members. *héyey* marks a known referent as salient. When *á* is used anaphorically, its referent is nonsalient or nondominant. When used exophorically or cataphorically, however, no such implicature is conveyed. The principal function of *áha* is to mark a known referent as nonsalient when attention is directed to the identity of the referent who has been mentioned previously.

Both sets of demonstratives contrast with their absence. An unqualified noun is used to introduce participants and, in appropriate circumstances, to make further reference to them, when the referent is unmarked for orientation or status.

Appendix

The sentences in the following two stories are arranged as nearly as possible with each clause on one line. The three column array puts preverbal elements in the first column, postverbal elements which are capable of being qualified by demonstratives in the third column, and everything else in the second column. Unbound personal substantive pronouns, referred to in this paper as stressed pronouns, are glossed by English pronouns in column 1, while pronouns bound to verbs (unstressed pronouns) are glossed by English pronouns attached by hyphens to verbs in column 2. The absence of a bound pronoun is indicated by Ø. The English distinction between genders in the pronouns does not carry over into Mofu-Gudur and is indicated for convenience only. Similarly, the English singular/plural distinction does not carry over to the Mofu-Gudur unstressed pronouns; number is instead encoded by a verbal suffix.

The Mofu-Gudur developmental marker *tá?* is glossed as 'then'. The topicalizing particle *ná* is glossed as TOP. All the demonstratives which are treated in this paper are noted in Mofu-Gudur. All other material is given in English. The exclamation point (!) indicates ideophones.

(44)   Text 1 The Story of the Hungry Stranger

a.	Stranger	there is.	
b.	His wife	she-does not find	something,
	he	he-does not find	something.
c.	Next hunger	it-strikes-him.	
d.	Then	he-goes	
		he-journeys.	

e.   He-goes TOP,
                       he-perceives   children seated
                                                          under tree.

f.   He-says-to them,
                       "Children, what are
                       you doing?"

g.   "We are sitting here
                       guarding."

h.   Children   they-answer-him like this.

i.   "What are you guarding?"

j.   "We are guarding sheep
                       and goats."

k.   They-answer-him   stranger *á*,

                 "Are you a thief?"

l.   "Ah! Am I a man who would
                       steal from children?"

m.   "You, there! You're the big-
                       gest child here; in your
                       home, when food is prepared
                       and when you eat it, where
                       do you wipe your hands?"

n.   Child   he-says,
                       "When we eat food, I wipe
                       my hands like this."

o.   "Ah! You, there, is it like
                       that at your home, too?"

p.   Child   he-says,
                       "In our home, when we eat,
                       I wipe my hands like this,"
                       gesturing   like a deaf-mute.

q. Stranger   he-says,
                    "You there! In your home,
                    when you eat, where do you
                    wipe your hands?"

r.   "As for me, when we've
                    eaten, I wipe my hands like
                    this, and I wipe my face
                    like this. After that, father
                    gives me soap. He tells me,
                    now wash your hands. I
                    wash my hands, then we sit."

s. Stranger   he-says   to child *á*,
                    "Let's go to your home."

t. Then   they-go   to house with
                                                child *á* next.

u.   They-go   to house their TOP,
    man *káa héyey* Ø slaughter! he-slaughters goat.

v.   He-says,
                   "A stranger has come to me."

w. Then
    woman *káa*   she-prepares-it-for them   food with meat
                                                kedé héyey.

x. Then   they-eat-it.

y. Stranger   he-says,
                   "Please, as for me, give me
                   foot *á*. I will only
                   crunch meat, I will not eat
                   it, it would make me swell
                   up. For three days *káa*
                   I have not eaten meat."

z. Woman *káa*   to husband *á*,
                   "Give him it, then! Maybe
                   he has need of foot."

aa.	Husband *á*	he-says-to her, "Never! I slaughter a goat for him; how will I give him only a foot *káa?*"	
bb.	Woman *káa* TOP,	she-says, "Ah, I am going to the river."	
cc.	Husband *á*	Ø stand up! to go he-looks for	something for stranger.
dd.	Stranger *héyey,* TOP,	Ø go on tiptoes! Ø enter! he-steals	to kitchen, foot *héyey.*
ee.		He-steals he-crunches-it TOP,	foot,
	husband of woman *káa* *héyey*	Ø return!	
	woman *káa* *héyey*	Ø return!	from river.
ff.	Next, shame	it-fills-them rooted to the spot!	
gg.	Stranger	he-says-to them, "Just leave me foot *á.* Just don't make trouble."	
hh.	Story *á*	finished.	

(45)   Text 2 The Story of the Squirrel and the Tortoise

a.	Squirrel	he-is going	to feast.
b.		He-had put on he-is going with small movements!	robe on body, with to play guitar.

c.		[Song of the squirrel]	
d.	Tortoise	He-goes TOP, seated	at edge water.
e.		He-says-to him, "Please, Squirrel, give to me, that I may play, too."	
f.	Squirrel	he-says-to him, "You, tortoise, are very wily, you will take it into the water with you!"	
g.	Tortoise	he-says-to him, "Please, Squirrel, I won't take it in. I just want to play it a little."	
h.	Squirrel	he-says-to him, "All right, take it. Anyway, I'd also like a swim."	
i.	Tortoise	take! he-takes-it.	
j.	Then	he-plucks-it he-sings, "If I jump into the water, what will you do to me, Squirrel? If I jump into the water, what will you do to me, Squirrel?"	
k.	Squirrel	he-says-to him, "That is my guitar; you're going to take it into the water!"	
l.	Tortoise	he-says-to him, "No, Squirrel, I'm just practicing on it."	

m.		He-plucks-it again, "If I jump into the water, what will you do to me, Squirrel? If I jump into the water, what will you do to me, Squirrel?"	
n.	He	Ø plunge suddenly!	into water with guitar *héyey.*
o.	Squirrel *héyey* TOP,	he-looks	eye with tears.
p.		He-says, "Ah, Tortoise, is that how you play games with me? If I do not hurry back here to- morrow and scoop out this water, I am not Squirrel."	
q.		Going his	to feast.
r.		He-returns he-sleeps.	in evening later,
s.	In morning TOP	then he-invites to work they-scoop out	people; water *kedé héyey.*
t.	water all	Scoop! scoop! it-is emptied.	
u.	young tortoise one	They-look TOP,	in it small.
v.	The rest of tortoises TOP,	Ø scurry away suddenly!	under dry leaves.
w.	They	they-scurried suddenly	under dry leaves TOP,
	Squirrel	he-goes he-smokes	pipe TOP.

x.	Fire	fall! it-falls	from mouth of pipe TOP,
	fire *á* TOP,	to light	with flint and steel.
y.	Then	it-spreads slowly	on dry leaves *á*.
z.	Tortoises	they-come out	from dry leaves *á* TOP,
		they-do innumerable!	
aa.	He who with guitar his *héyey*	he-is coming out clasped!	in one hand.
bb.	He	Ø strike! to kill.	on *kedé* TOP,
cc.	He	Ø strike! to kill.	on *kedé* TOP,
dd.	Basket	Ø full.	
ee.		He-goes cook! cook! he-cooks-them.	to house *á*,
ff.	he	Mixed together! eat! eat! he-eats-them all.	
gg.	Story *á*	is finished.	

References

Barreteau, Daniel. 1988. Déscription du mofu-gudur: Langue de la famille tchadique parlée au Cameroun. Livre II: Léxique. Paris: Editions de l'ORSTOM. Collection TRAVAUX et DOCUMENTS no. 206.

Comrie, Bernard. 1989. Language universals and linguistic typology. Chicago: University of Chicago.

Givón, Talmy, ed. 1983. Topic continuity in discourse. Philadelphia: Benjamins.

Grimes, Joseph E. 1975. The thread of discourse. The Hague: Mouton.

———, ed. 1978. Papers on discourse. Summer Institute of Linguistics Publications in Linguistics 51. Dallas.

Hollingsworth, Kenneth and Judith Hollingsworth, eds. 1982. Mamba hay ta méy ngá ngwa 1: Contes en langue mofu-gudur 1. Yaoundé: Société Internationale de Linguistique.

——— and ———, eds. 1985. Mamba hay ta méy ŋga ŋgwa 2: Contes en langue mofu-gudur 2. Yaoundé: Société Internationale de Linguistique.

——— and Charles Peck. 1992. Topics in Mofu-Gudur. In Shin Ja J. Hwang and William R. Merrifield (eds.), Language in context: Essays for Robert E. Longacre, 109–23. Dallas: Summer Institute of Linguistics and the University of Texas at Arlington.

Johnstone, Barbara. 1987. 'He says ... so I said': Verb tense alternation and narrative depictions of authority in American English. Linguistics 25:33–52.

Participant Reference in Nɔmaandɛ Narrative Discourse

Carolyn P. Taylor

Abstract

Study of narrative texts in Nɔmaandɛ shows that there are five participant categories: primary, secondary, tertiary, impersonal, and prop. This article describes how participants in each category are introduced in a text by nouns, pronouns, or zero anaphora. The maintaining of reference to each participant is influenced by the presence of a discontinuity, by the buildup to a climax, and by the backgrounding of an event or participant. Finally, reference to each participant is also affected by direct speech and speech margins within the text.

Résumé

L'étude des textes narratifs en nɔmaandɛ révèle qu'il existe cinq catégories de participants, soit primaire, secondaire, tertiaire, impersonnel, et accessoire. Cet article décrit la manière dont les participants associés à chaque catégorie sont présentés dans un texte, soit par un nom, soit par un pronom, ou bien encore par un zéro anaphore. Le maintien de la référence à chaque participant est influencé par la présence d'une discontinuité, par la montée de la tension jusqu'à un point culminant et par la mise en arrière-plan des événements ou des participants dans le texte. Enfin, la référence aux participants est aussi influencée par la présence d'un discours direct et ses marges dans le texte.

Nɔmaandɛ is a Narrow Bantu language, classified by Guthrie (1967:31) as A.46, and spoken in the Center Province of Cameroon. The present work was done on the basis of a corpus of 13 recorded folktales and two short historical narratives, and it accounts for participant reference in the subject position of the clause. With two exceptions, the data are written phonologically; the exceptions are the following orthographic conventions: (a) for the two contrastive tones, low is unmarked and high is marked with [´]; (b) although there is no contrast between voiced and voiceless consonants, voiced allophones that occur next to nasals are written voiced [t/d, c/j, and k/g].

1 Participant categories and introduction of participants

In Nɔmaandɛ narrative discourse, participants belong to one of the following categories: primary, secondary, tertiary, or impersonal. There are also props.

1.1 Primary participant

The primary participant[1] of a story is characterized by being one of the first participants to be introduced, and also by the higher frequency of his appearances and the importance of his role in the narrative.

He is introduced in a presentative or setting clause; these are illustrated in (1)–(3). He is again referred to by a noun when he first begins in action. The presentative clause usually includes the 'be' verb and the name and/or title of a person, as in (1).[2]

(1)   bɔ́tɔ́okɔ ŋaá bá   e ekúlú eeye oténí
        Bɔ́tɔ́okɔ T/A was at time DEM chief
        Bɔtɔɔkɔ was chief at that time.

In this presentative clause, Bɔtɔɔkɔ is presented by his title, chief. A presentative clause may also simply present an attribute of the primary participant, as in (2).

---

[1]Levinsohn (1992:100) calls the primary participant the "central character"; Dooley (1992:76) refers to him as the "global VIP." Both Levinsohn and Dooley refer to secondary and tertiary participants as "major" and "minor" participants, respectively.

[2]The abbreviations used in this paper are: C5, C14 noun classes (5, 14), DEM demonstrative, EXCL exclamation, NEG negative marker, CN connective-noun class, as in (2); invariable, as in (4b), QM question marker, T/A tense/aspect, 1s, 2s, 3s first-, second-, third-person singular, 1p, 3p first-, third-person plural.

(2) *ofule u kíléke ŋaá bámɔ́kɔ́nɛ́na yaáta*
     Spoon CN Taboo T/A be   ugly
     Taboo Spoon was ugly.

Here, Taboo Spoon is not introduced by his name, but by his most salient attribute, his ugliness!

When the primary participant is presented in a setting clause, it is a description not of the character, but of what the story will be about, as well as introducing him. This is illustrated in (3).

(3) *ɔɔcɔ u buáyá   u ŋaá tánáka   úyé obúme*
     person of long^ago 3s T/A arranged his hunt
     A long time ago a man organized his hunt.

The hunt organizer is introduced in a way that shows that the story will be about his hunt.

The primary participant may be mentioned before he is formally introduced but, even if he is included as part of a group, he will later be reintroduced individually in a presentative or setting clause, as in (4).

(4) a. *ɔɔcɔ ŋeé bíéne   bááyɛ baáná béfendí*
        man T/A gave^birth^to his   two   children
        A man had two children.

    b. *ooci a wɔ́mɔté wuúci mubúmébúme*
        DEM CN certain himself hunter
        One of them was a hunter.

In this story of two brothers, the father is mentioned only to establish the relationship between the two sons. One son is then formally introduced as the hunter.

The primary participant often is referred to by different nouns according to the story's development. In one story, the primary participant is referred to by his name (hunter), a family relationship (brother), and a name that refers to a major event in the story (animal killer). If the conclusion of the story has a moral, the primary participant will be referred to with his character generalized in a manner applicable to the human race. This is illustrated by example (5).

(5)   *basɔ́ biinyí   te   óo bíene ɔ́nɔ́ u yaáta a tɛ   sɛ wuúci*
       we   mothers even 2s beget child CN ugly   2s NEG   him

       sɔmɔ́   ɔ   ɔwɔ́ ɔmbana u baáná
       take^out of your number of children
       We mothers, even if you give birth to an ugly child, don't take him
       out of the total of your children (don't neglect him).

In this example, the primary participant, Taboo Spoon, is referred to in the
concluding moral of the narrative as 'an ugly child'.

1.2 Secondary participants

Like primary participants, secondary participants are also introduced in
a setting or presentative clause, then are referred to again by a noun in
connection with an action. Since they are referred to in ways similar to the
primary participant, special treatment is often needed to distinguish them.
In the case of the hunter's brother cited in (4), the hunter is the primary
participant, and his brother is later introduced in a way that reinforces the
primary participant status of the hunter, as shown in (6).

(6)   a. *sɔ́ɔkɔ ooci awɔ́ ŋaá bamɔ́kɔ́nɛ́na mubúmébúme*
          other DEM who T/A was   hunter

       b. *úyé onyíinyí mbá ú me síke a cɔba e bukendinyi*
          his brother then 3s T/A later 3s go   to friendship
       This person who was a hunter, his brother later started a friendship.

The setting clause that introduces the hunter's brother (6b) is preceded by
a fronted relative clause that shows the superior status of the hunter.

1.3 Tertiary participants

While primary and secondary participants are on stage for the bulk of
the action in a narrative, tertiary participants represent most of the 'extras'
on stage. They are usually introduced in the object position, as in this
introduction of the wife in (7).

(7)   *onyíinyí ŋaá cɔba e bukendinyi ne   oónyí u otéŋí*
       brother T/A went to friendship with wife   of chief
       The brother began an affair with the chief's wife.

After the wife is mentioned in this way, she is not mentioned again until she is involved in a conversation with her husband later in the story.

(8)   *mbá ú ma láana oónyí ɔ-sɛ   yó súéte ɔkanda*
      then 3s T/A told wife 2s-say 3s go trip
      Then he (husband) told his wife he was going on a trip.

Tertiary participants may appear on stage without having been previously mentioned, as in the case of the wife of Ɔmbɔnɔ in (9).

(9)   *ahé ú ŋa ka hámánana ehétú o ooki   oónyí ŋɔ tɔléá ehétú*
      when 3s T/A arrive^with   plum at house wife T/A soak plum
      When he got home with the plum, his wife soaked it (in water).

Tertiary participants can also simply appear on stage after they are mentioned in some context such as the noun phrase in (10).

(10) *bá maá ka kuana buliómólíómo bú ɛbála*
      3p T/A go find   fruit   of leopard
      They found Leopard's fruit.

Here Leopard is mentioned only in describing the fruit, but he is neither the actor nor the goal of an action. He does not appear until much later in the story and, when he does, he simply appears on stage.

(11) *ɛbála   ŋa kaá háma e buliómólíómo bú ɛbála*
      leopard T/A arrive   at fruit   of leopard
      Leopard came to his fruit-tree.

Tertiary participants are infrequently introduced in a presentative clause, such as (12).

(12) *ɔɔ́nɔ́ u buúse ŋa bámɔ́kɔ́néna ne   nyiínyi anyía bílíke*
      child CN first T/A be   with name that Bilike
      The first child's name was Bilike.

      u ɔlata bikóŋó u ɔlata maána
      of follow Bikoŋo of follow Maána
      The next was Bikoŋo, the next was Maána . . .

Although the above participant, Bilike, is introduced in a presentative clause, he is not assigned primary participant status by this kind of

introduction because he is not given unique treatment. The clause introducing him is followed by a list of the names of five children (of which one
is the primary participant). This participant is merely one of a crowd.

When tertiary participants first enter the event line, they are introduced
by a noun, which tends to be in the object position. When they are in
subject position, what they do is often just a reaction to the act of another
participant, rather than an independent action. This is often found in
speech, as with the character of the wife in one story, whose only actions
are speech in (13).

(13) *eéye ekúlú mbá ú ma laana yéye ekendinyi*
      DEM time then 3s T/A told her friend
      Well, then she told her friend.

Tertiary participants are referred to differently if they are grouped with
a higher-status participant. An example of this involves four brothers of
Taboo Spoon, the primary participant of one story. Whenever the five
brothers are referred to as a group, they appear in the subject position but,
if the four tertiary participants are set off against the major participant,
they appear in the object position.

Other tertiary participants are introduced in groups, then individually
speak or act in some way and afterwards disappear from the stage. In one
story, birds are called upon to take action (carry news). Although they are
first referred to as a group, a series of individuals is then involved in a
series of events. The first is called, told what to say, and is sent. When it
returns, not having accomplished its mission, it is sent away and does not
come back. The same series of actions occurs for the second bird. Only the
third is able to tell the message, and is sent to do so, but also disappears
after the message is received.

1.4 Impersonal participants

Impersonal participants form a special category, which uses a pronoun
for backgrounded, unidentified subjects (see §2.1). A third-person plural
pronoun *bá/bé* occurs which has no referent among the participants already introduced. This pronoun is used to refer to some unspecified wider
group, such as a community. In one story, for example, a woman dies and
there is a need to tell the news of her death to her children. In a scene
where all participants previously introduced are either off the scene or
deceased, the clause in (14) appears.

(14)   *mbá báyɛ   bá aambáka tunonyí*
        then 3p^say 3p look^for birds
        Then they said they should look for birds (to tell the news).

In other stories a group may be mentioned, but they are not formally
secondary participants, as evidenced by the fact that the first time they act
they are not referred to by a noun. This may be seen in one text about an
Nɔmaandɛ chief where the Nɔmaandɛ community is referred to in an
impersonal way. The community is introduced in the object position
('Bɔtɔɔkɔ was the chief of all Nɔmaandɛ; he brought the first Protestant
teacher to his village. When he brought the teacher . . .'):

(15)   *yaalɛ   bá   ŋaá falɛfa na   bɛcala*
        shelter they T/A build with palms
        They built a palm shelter.

The fact that the pronoun *bá* is unspecified in the context means that its
referent is impersonal, rather than tertiary.

1.5 Props

Props are objects or personalities which are important to the story,
reappearing several times. However, they neither appear in the subject
position as a noun phrase nor are they formally introduced. Although they
are sometimes referred to by pronouns in the subject position, they never
take an active role. In one story, the hair of the primary participant plays
an important part. It is referred to first by a noun and then by a pronoun.

(16) a. *ofule   u   kílíke nyɛ-lɔbɔ eényi   aatɔ́ fákálákéna*
        Spoon CN Taboo C5-staying DEM^C5 head messy

   b. *yɛ́ ŋá faáya   ɛmaŋa ícіéci*
        it T/A became hairdo unhealthy
        Taboo Spoon stayed with his head all messy; it became a head of
        unhealthy hair.

A prop which appears in an important event of a story may represent
that entire event when it is referred to later in the story. An example is a
cut finger in one story. The finger was cut off by a chief who later paid
dearly for this deed. Because he was unable to find enough money, he was
forced to begin taxing his subjects. This situation exposed the major theme
of the story, shown in (17).

(17) *ɛɛhɛ́ yaáŋa anyía bitéési abɛ́ tɔbaka   túásɔ́ ɔ́ndɔ́kɔ ɛ́ɛhɛ́ yá*
      so   it^is   that   taxes   that 1p^often 1p   pay   thus it

      báka anyía   hɛnɔ́nɔ́ hi onyíinyí u muɔ́nɔ ɛnyama híe
      often because finger   of brother of killer animal to

      hiíhi tɔbaka túásɔ́ ɔ́ndɔ́kɔ
      it   often we   pay
      So it is that the taxes we often pay are because of the finger of the
      animal killer; that's what we're paying for.

The importance of the role played by the finger, its frequent reappearance
in the narrative, and its centrality to the plot is evidence for establishing a
prop category distinct from other objects. In addition, the pronominal
references to certain objects and their frequent appearances show that
there is indeed a prop category of participants.

2 Maintenance of identification

As one clause follows another in the narrative, reference to participants
can be by noun, pronoun, or zero anaphora. The means of reference is
partly influenced by whether the following clause has the same or different
subject as the preceding clause. Reference follows different rules if the
subject of the second clause is the addressee of the speech or action of the
first clause.

2.1 Same subject

When the subject of one clause is the same as in the preceding one, the
default or normal way of referring to the subject of the second clause is a
pronoun, as in (18).

(18) a. *iinyí   ŋaá bá weé lénéke baáná   eebe benyise*
        mother T/A be 3s love   children these four

   b. *u ti   léne ofule   u   kíléke*
      3s NEG love Spoon CN Taboo
      The mother loved the other four children; she didn't love Taboo
      Spoon.

Here mother is the subject of both clauses, so a pronoun is used to refer to her in the second clause.

Marked reference to the same subject as in the preceding clause is either by a noun or by zero anaphora together with a certain verb form.

Identification by a noun. At points of discontinuity in the text, whether of situation or of action,[3] the identification of participants is done by nouns instead of pronouns. The example in (19) illustrates such a discontinuity of situation. Although the referent of clause (19b) has the same subject as (19a) and the identification would normally be made with a pronoun, the noun 'brother' is repeated in the second clause.

(19) a. *mbá onyíinyí ɔ-sɛ   nyiána míɔ cɔba ɔ yɔ́ɔ hɔɔ*
       then brother 3s-say leave 1s   going to you save
       Then his brother said, "Forget it, I'm going to take care of you."

    b. *mbá onyíinyí ú ma cɔba ne otéŋí*
       then brother 3s T/A go   to chief
       Then the brother went to the chief.

The reason that a noun is used in (19b) is that there is a major change of scene at this point in the story. The first scene takes place with two brothers and the second includes one of the brothers and their antagonist, the chief.

Zero anaphora. Zero anaphora occur with GERUNDS in the verb position of the clause. These gerunds consist of a noun class prefix and a verb root. The prefix is either class 5 *(nyi/nyɛ)* or class 14 *(bu)* 'the act of' (doing something). These constructions occur during the buildup to and at the climaxes of stories. When the gerund is class 5, it occurs with a demonstrative of the same class, while class 14 gerunds do not. In contrast to normal verb phrases, the gerunds do not contain any pronominal reference, so the only identification can be by a noun preceding them.

In example (20) illustrating gerunds, there is nominal reference to a participant (husband) in clause (20a) and zero anaphora in clauses (20b) and (20c).

---

[3]See Levinsohn's introductory article in this volume for definition of these terms.

(20) a. *ɔnɔ́mɛ   bu-hiite yandá yé ɛngíásɛ́na*
      husband C14-take big   of scissors

  b. *yɛ-bébaábɛ́na eényi   o   okoki*
     C5-stick   DEM^C5 to door

  c. *bu-sɔ́mbɔ hɛnɔ́nɔ́*
     C14-cut   finger
     The husband took big scissors . . . He lay against the door . . . he cut
     the finger!

In (20a), the actor is identified by a noun which is followed by a clause
with a different subject. In the following clauses, since the husband is still
the subject, normal reference should be by a pronoun. Since the gerunds
are used to build up to a climax, however, there is zero reference to the
actor.[4]

Backgrounding by pronoun. The third-person plural pronoun, *bá* or
bé, also functions as a generic pronoun, very similar in use to the French
'on'. This impersonal use of the pronoun, which is in a sense a 'refusal to
identify' the actor (Grévisse 1986:1113), allows the referent of the pronoun
to remain unspecified, as in (21).

(21) *memé bá   nyíána aána e*
      mom   they leave   thus QM
      Mom, shall we leave it like that? (i.e., shall we stop?)

In narratives, this pronoun is given a marked usage when its antecedant
is a previously introduced (singular) participant. The use of the pronoun
has the effect of backgrounding the character in order to highlight the
action. Sometimes its referent is identified by a noun in a following clause,
as in (22).

---

[4]The class 5 gerunds can also occur with a possessive pronoun of the same class,
which has a backgrounding rather than an identifying function (see §2.3).

(22) a. *hiáha a hiɔŋɔ ɛnyama ŋaá bámɔ́kɔ́nɛ́na a buábɔ́ bunɔŋɔ*
      every - year animal T/A was   in their village

    b. *mbá bá aáfɛna ɔɔcɔ*
       well 3p give   person

    c. *otéŋí mbá ú hiite ɔɔcɔ*
       chief well 3s took person
       Every year an animal was in their village. They would give a person
       to it; (that is,) the chief would take a person . . .

In (22), a specific person, the chief, is the one referred to in the preceding
clause by the third-person plural pronoun. For the speaker, it was the
action that was important and not the person who did it.

2.2 Different subject

When the subject of a clause is different from the preceding one, the
normal or default way of referring to the subject of the second clause is a
noun. This noun may appear in the object position that precedes the
clause where this different participant is the actor. In (23), the chief (23b)
is a different subject from that in (23a), so he is referred to by a noun.

(23) a. *ɛ́ɛhɛ́ ɛ ma kaá mɛ tɔ́ma umi onyíinyí*
      so   1s T/A go 1s send my brother

    b. *anyía wáa kaá laána otéŋí*
       to   3s go tell   chief

    c. *bu-kasɔ́mba hɛnɔɔ́nɔ́*
       C14-cut   finger
       So I sent my brother to tell the chief, (but he) cut (his) finger!

In the buildup to a climax, however, a pronoun is sometimes used
instead of a noun, as in (24), where *buliómóliómo* 'fruit' is represented by
the noun class pronoun *bú*.

(24) *bá nyíáka bú sóomoko bá nyíáka bú sóomoko*
    3p eat   C14 wasˆsweet 3p eat   C14 wasˆsweet
    They ate, it was sweet! They ate, it was sweet!

One pronoun follows another as the tension builds up in the story.

2.3 Backgrounding of an event

The class 5 gerund occasionally occurs with a possessive pronoun. The gerund and pronoun occur after a climax, and have the effect of backgrounding a clause which has less important information than other clauses preceding it. This is because the exciting events tend to have less pronominal information than backgrounded ones. In (25), there is a string of class 5 gerunds which build up the tension in the story. In clauses (25a)–(25d), a series of actions occur which are extremely important in the story. All are expressed by gerunds. Then (25e), which contains a gerund plus a possessive pronoun, is backgrounded.

(25) a. *nyifununeke eényi*
    digging   DEM^C5

   b. *nyiketúluleke ciabɔ́ iinyí   eényi*
    dragging   their mother DEM^C5

   c. *nyɛháya eényi   aáha*
    putting DEM^C5 over^there

   d. *nyihúéke eényi*
    covering DEM^C5

   e. *nyiabɔ́ nyieélue eényi   ɔ ɔkɔ́bɛtabɔna nyionyí*
    their   returning DEM^C5 to get^ready   market
   They dug, dragged their mother, put (her in) there, and covered (her). So they returned to get ready for market.

The important events here are the children's actions towards their mother, not their going home to get ready for market, so the latter event is backgrounded.

 When the gerund with a possessive pronoun has a different subject from that of the preceding clause, it appears to act like a pronoun to indicate the change in actor. The fact that the event is unimportant is the reason for the possessive, as shown in (26).

(26) *ofule u kíléke ŋe hiite bɛtámá u ŋá béháya a ɛmaŋa cí*
Spoon CN Taboo T/A take fruits   3s T/A put   in dirty   -

   tuhúnyi eéci nyiabɔ́ nyieélueke eényi
   hair   DEM their   returning DEM^C5
   Taboo Spoon took some fruits and put them in that dirty head of
   hair. So they returned.

It was Taboo Spoon's actions that were crucial to the ongoing of the story,
so the event of the group's return was backgrounded.

2.4 Addressee of a preceding speech

In cases where the subject of a clause is different from the preceding
one, but is the addressee of a preceding speech (or, occasionally, the
recipient of a preceding action) by another participant, the normal identification of this previously addressed participant is a pronoun. In one
story, one brother asks another the question.

(27) a. *mbá aáté yɔ́ yɔ́ sɔmbá hɛnɔ́nɔ́ e*
    but what it 2s cut   finger QM
    So how did you cut your finger?

   b. *u me bíketikinyi onyíinyí*
      he T/A told   brother
      He told his brother (everything).

The second brother, being the previous addressee, is referred to by a
pronoun.

The exception to the use of a pronoun for the previous addressee is
when the new subject makes a new initiative, rather than going along with
the intention of the previous speech. He is then referred to by a noun
which indicates the change of initiative and sometimes includes a change
in the status of the participant.

In one story, for example, the chief is one of the secondary participants,
while his wife is a tertiary participant. In a dramatic scene between the two
of them, he is suddenly referred to by the noun 'husband', instead of by
the normal pronoun, shown in (28).

(28) a. *oónju ɔ-sɛ   u ti   lene okuune*
      wife 3s-say 3s NEG want open

   b. *mbá ɔnɔmɛ   ɔ-sɛ   ké ké kuúne*
      but husband 3s-say go - open

   c. *oónju ɔ-sɛ   ɔ tɛ   áa kɛla wɔ cɔba okuune*
      woman 3s-say 3s NEG 3s do 3s go   open
   The wife said she didn't want to open (the door). Then the husband
   said, "Come and open up!" The wife said she could not go and open
   (it).

At this point in the story, there is a change in the role of the chief,
reflected by the repetition of the noun referents to husband and wife.
Normally, the chief would be referred to by a pronoun but, in this scene,
the chief is now the jealous husband instead of the chief and he is referred
to by a noun.

3 Identification in speech

In speech, two considerations for participant reference are the speech
itself and the margin.

Reference to the participant who is the agent of a speech act is carried
by a dummy verb, *ɔsɛ* '(he) says' or *báyɛ* '(they) say'. (It is a dummy verb
because it is marked for person and number, as verbs are, and refers to a
real action, a speech act. However, it is not marked for tense or aspect,
nor does it have other morphological properties of a verb.) The dummy
verb appears at the beginning of each speech and again when there is a
change of addressee. While the dummy verb is most commonly in third
person, there exist forms for second and third persons, which are rarely
used in narrative discourse except in conclusions.

Marked speech margins have a verb of speech or communication in
addition to the dummy verb. This indicates that the speech act is an
important part of the event line. The verbs used in these margins include
'send a message', 'write', and 'announce'.

(29) a. *bá báka bá láakɛna otéŋí*
 3p often 3p tell chief

 b. *bá-yɛ ɔɔcɔ ɔ́ báka u síke fáakɔna aaha*
 3p-say person 3s often 3s later come here
 They often told the chief, "Someone often comes here later."

The event of someone telling this news to the chief is one of the turning points in the story, leading to drastic action on his part. The speech is made to stand out by the use of the speech verb 'tell', in addition to the dummy verb.

3.1 Identification in direct and indirect speech

In direct speech, the agent of the dummy verb (and another verb of speech, if there is one) is referenced in the speech by a first-person pronoun, while, in indirect speech, it is referred to by a third-person pronoun.

Direct speech is the normal usage in discourse. Indirect speech is used rhetorically, to mark the 'trigger' of a major development in the story. In one story, for example, Leopard, angered by the absence of fruit on his tree, asks who has eaten all his fruit. Mother, the eater, is hidden from him, but eventually answers his furious questions. When she thus reveals herself, Leopard's response (in indirect speech) indicates his intention to kill her.

(30) a. *oónju ɔ-sɛ*
 woman 3s-say

 b. *bé ŋe mi iínjíe*
 3p T/A me gave

 c. *mbá ɛ́ ɔ́kéténa buliómólíómo buɔ́wɔ́ oo*
 then 1s taste fruit your EXCL

 d. *ɔ-sɛ u ŋée téŋíti onyike ocinyíé*
 3s-say he T/A greet meat DEM
 The woman said, "They gave it to me, then I tasted your fruit oh!"
 He said he greets that meat over there.

It is common for a trigger to comprise an action plus an indirect speech as response. The response is often negative, as in (31). This negative response also initiates a major development in the story.

(31) a. *u ŋáa náakɛna tukóló tɔ mɔɔnyɛ́*
         3s T/A fill   boxes of money

     b. *u ŋe iínjíékíne na muɔɔnɔ ɛnyama*
         3s T/A give   to killer   animals

     c. *muɔɔnɔ ɛnyama ɔ-sɛ u tɛ   ŋa léca tabɔkɔ*
         killer   animals 3s-say 3s NEG T/A see   nothing
         He filled boxes with money and gave them to the animal killer. The
         animal killer said he couldn't see anything (it wasn't enough).

Indirect speech can also be followed by an action, as shown by the speech in (32) about what the woman says who has tasted Leopard's fruit.

(32) *mbá ɔ-sɛ   bé wuúci cɔbana híe   e eciké bé wuúci tóŋínyi*
      then 3s-say 3p her   take   there to forest 3p her   show

      bɔɔté eebu mbá baáná   nyɛkahámanana iinyí eényi
      tree   DEM then children arriving^with   mother DEM^C5

      e buliómólíómo bú ɛbála
      to fruit   of Leopard
      Then the mother said to take her to this tree. Then the children
      arrived with the mother at the fruit tree of Leopard.

This example of the combination of a speech and an action as a trigger represents a turning point in the story which leads to the downfall of the woman. She craves the fruit and gorges herself on it so much that she becomes incontinent. Her children abandon her, which leads to her being devoured by Leopard.

3.2 Embedded speech

As was stated in §2.2, in direct speech in Nɔmaandɛ, the agent of the speech verb is referred to by first person. Embedding adds a second agent of a speech within this first speech. This is rare in Nɔmaandɛ, but there are instances of direct speech with indirect embedding. In the examples available, these are all in clauses where the direct speech verb is in the imperative mood. An example is cited in (33).

(33) a. *ciínu   ŋá laána oónyi ɔ-sɛ*
      Tortoise T/A told   wife 3s-say

   b. *mbɔ́kɔ yémi ekendinyi é síke á faaya*
      if   my   friend   3s later 3s comes

   c. *wuúci laána a-sɛ́*
      him   say   2s-say

   d. *é maá mɛ cɔba ɔ ɔkanda*
      1s T/A 1s go to walk
      Tortoise told his wife, "If my friend comes later, tell him I've gone for a walk."

In (33), the agent of 'tell' in (33a) is the tortoise and, in (33b), he is referred to by a first-person pronoun. His addressee, the wife, is referred to by a second-person pronoun in (33c), and another participant, friend, is referred to by third-person pronouns in (33b). The second speech verb is in the imperative mood, so the agent of the verb is the wife, the second-person pronoun in (33c). The verb in the embedded speech (33d) is in the first person, however, so the speech is from the tortoise's subjective viewpoint and not the wife's.

4 Summary

The rules determining participant reference in Nɔmaandɛ discourse include various devices for the introduction of five different categories of participants. These are primary, secondary, tertiary, impersonal, and prop. Maintenance of reference to them, whether by noun, pronoun, or zero anaphora, depends on the context. This may be in a clause whose subject is the same as or different from the preceding one. Alternatively, the subject may have been the addressee of a preceding speech or action. Participant reference is influenced by the presence of a discontinuity, by the building up to a climax, and by the backgrounding of events or characters. Direct speech is the norm in narrative. Indirect speech is used to mark the 'trigger' of a major development in the stories.

References

Dooley, Robert H. 1992. Analyzing discourse: Basic concepts. Grand Forks: Summer Institute of Linguistics and the University of North Dakota.

Ennulat, Jürgen. 1978. Participant reference in Fali stories. In Joseph E. Grimes (ed.), Papers on discourse, 143–48. Dallas: Summer Institute of Linguistics.

Grévisse, Maurice. 1986. Le bon usage. Paris-Gembloux: Editions Duculot.

Grimes, Joseph E. 1975. The thread of discourse. The Hague: Mouton.

Guthrie, Malcolm. 1967. The classification of the Bantu languages. London: Dawson.

Hedinger, Robert. 1984. Reported speech in Akɔɔsɛ. Journal of West African Languages 14(1):82–102.

Levinsohn, Stephen H. 1992. Discourse features of New Testament Greek. Dallas: Summer Institute of Linguistics.

Perrin, Mona. 1978. Who's who in Mambila folk stories. Yaoundé: Société Internationale de Linguistique. ms.

Robinson, Clinton R. 1978. Participant reference in Gunu narrative discourse. Yaoundé: Société Internationale de Linguistique. ms.

Wilt, Timothy. 1987. Discourse distances and the Swahili demonstratives. Studies in African Linguistics 18(1):81–89.

Zander, Lynn. 1988. Tracking participants when they are not named. In Evelyn G. Pike and Rachel Saint (eds.), Workpapers concerning Waorani discourse features, 93–98. Dallas: Summer Institute of Linguistics.

Field Procedures for the Analysis of Participant Reference in a Monologue Discourse

Stephen H. Levinsohn

Abstract

A methodology is offered for identifying the different factors which affect the amount of encoding that is used when a speaker refers to participants throughout a discourse. The methodology involves eight steps: (1) drawing up an inventory of the different ways that references to participants are encoded in the language; (2) preparing a chart of how participants are referred to in a text in the language; (3) tracking all references to individual participants in the text; (4) proposing default amounts of encoding for various contexts; (5) identifying the context in which each reference to a participant occurs; (6) inspecting the text for instances in which the amount of encoding is less than or more than predicted; (7) incorporating any modifications to the proposals of step 4; and (8) determining the motivations for the remaining deviances from default encoding.

Résumé

L'auteur propose une méthodologie permettant d'identifier les facteurs qui régissent le degré d'encodage auquel le sujet parlant a recours lorsqu'il fait

109

référence aux différents participants introduits dans un texte donné. Huit
étapes sont proposées, comme suit : (1) faire l'inventaire des différentes
façons dont les références aux participants sont encodées dans la langue
étudiée ; (2) dresser un tableau montrant la façon dont la référence aux
participants se fait dans un texte de la langue concernée ; (3) suivre, d'un
bout à l'autre du texte en question, l'évolution des références qui sont faites
pour chaque participant mentionné ; (4) proposer un degré d'encodage
"normal" selon le contexte ; (5) identifier le contexte dans lequel chaque
référence à un participant donné se fait ; (6) examiner le texte afin d'en
dégager les cas où le degré d'encodage est, soit inférieur, soit supérieur au
degré d'encodage jugé "normal" ; (7) apporter aux valeurs proposées à
l'étape no 4 les modifications qui se dégagent à l'étape no 6 ; et, enfin, (8)
étudier les autres "exceptions à la règle" afin de déterminer les raisons pour
lesquelles le degré d'encodage utilisé s'écarte de la norme.

The present work outlines some analytic procedures for determining the
amount of coding material a speaker employs in different contexts to refer
to a previously introduced PARTICIPANT.[1]

Givón's ICONICITY PRINCIPLE (1983:18) states, "The more disruptive,
surprising, discontinuous or hard to process a topic is, the more *coding
material* must be assigned to it." Encoding of references to participants is
typically on the scale (beginning with the least amount of coding material
and ending with the greatest amount): zero–unstressed pronoun–stressed
pronoun–full noun phrase. In this scale, ZERO is the absence of any coding
material whatever, while an UNSTRESSED PRONOUN is often a bound
pronoun or concord affix that is associated with the verb.

Givón and his coresearchers used statistical counts to establish the
general validity of the above iconicity principle. To determine precisely
which form of encoding is to be used in a specific context, however, the
individual factors which come into play must be isolated.

Two sets of factors which affect participant encoding are recognized in
this paper: (a) those related primarily to the iconicity principle itself
(variations due to the presence of referents which are "disruptive, surprising, discontinuous or hard to process" (p. 18); and (b) those related
primarily to indicating the status of a participant and the position of a
participant in relation to a spatial point of reference.

Although these two sets of factors do interact, the first set tends to affect
the amount of encoding material used, whereas the second tends to affect
the selection of determiners within noun phrases. It is not unusual, however,
for the use of a stressed pronoun to be associated with the status of a
particular referent in a story (see Levinsohn 1978).

---

[1]'Participant' is used in this paper as a cover term for animate and inanimate
referents, both concrete and abstract. Givón (1983) uses 'topic' in a similar sense.

Among the factors which relate primarily to the amount of encoding material used are: (a) the number of participants featuring in the discourse at the point in question; (b) whether or not the referent occupies a role in the previous sentence; (c) if so, whether or not the referent occupies the same role in the current sentence; (d) the presence or absence of a discontinuity;[2] and (e) whether the sentence is unmarked for prominence, is backgrounded, or is highlighted.

Among the factors which tend to affect the selection of one determiner rather than another within a noun phrase are: (a) whether or not one participant occupies an "authority role" (Johnstone 1987; Pohlig and Levinsohn this volume); (b) whether or not the referent is spotlighted (Mfonyam this volume) or is salient (Levinsohn 1992:100); (c) the position of a participant in relation to a spatial point of reference (Pohlig and Levinsohn this volume); or (d) "the association of the narrator with one participant, in contrast with others" (Levinsohn 1978:69); and (e) the status of the participant: whether the participant is globally or locally a "VIP" (Dooley 1992:76), a major or a minor participant.[3] This last factor also influences the amount of encoding material used.

The remainder of this paper presents a methodology for identifying how different factors affect the AMOUNT of encoding material used. It does not discuss how to identify the factors involved in the selection of one determiner over another.

The methodology for identifying the different factors that affect the amount of encoding material used is now described in eight steps.

---

[2]For a full discussion of discontinuities in coherent texts, see the author's paper of the same title, earlier in this volume. Discontinuities may be of REFERENCE (involving changes in the topic of the text and its participants), of SITUATION (involving changes in the time and location of the contents of the text), or of ACTION (most commonly, when any events described are not in chronological sequence). Crosslinguistically, the principal device associated with these discontinuities is topicalization.

[3]Typically, minor participants (including inanimate props) "just appear and disappear in a story, without any formal introduction ... Major participants, in contrast, are formally introduced in some way and typically are involved in a series of events" (Levinsohn 1992:113). Taylor (this volume) divides participants into five categories: primary (the global VIP), secondary, tertiary, impersonal, and prop. Of these categories, the first two would denote major participants; the remainder, minor ones.

1 Draw up an inventory of ways of
encoding references to participants

A list is made of the different ways in which reference to a participant
can be made in the language. Typically, these ways may be grouped into
four categories or amounts of encoding, specifically, those listed on the
scale of encoding associated with Givón's iconicity principle.

The Mofu-Gudur text in section 2 which is used to illustrate the points
of this paper, employs all of the four categories: zero (the absence of both
a noun phrase, represented by —, and a verb affix, represented by $\emptyset$-); an
unstressed pronoun, affixed to the verb; a stressed pronoun (represented
by PRONOUN); and a noun with or without qualifiers (so indicated).

When a stressed pronoun or noun (phrase) is employed in Mofu-Gudur,
an unstressed pronoun is affixed to the verb. The total absence of reference to a subject (zero) is found only in connection with ideophones or
when a reported speech lacks an opening or closing margin such as 'A
says.' See Hollingsworth (to appear) for the conditions under which an
unstressed pronoun that refers to the direct object or benefactor may be
accompanied by a noun (phrase) with the same referent.

2 Prepare a chart of participant encoding in a text

A chart is prepared with separate columns for displaying how references
to subjects and nonsubjects are encoded.

The chart is based on the first Mofu-Gudur text which appears in the
appendix to Pohlig and Levinsohn's paper in this volume. The information
is arranged in four columns. The first column records intersentential connec-
tives. The second column indicates how references to subjects are encoded
(see §1 for details). The third column provides a free translation (abbreviated, where appropriate) of the remainder of each clause or sentence.
This includes the contents of reported speeches, since these may be viewed
as being embedded in the overall structure of the narrative. Ideophones are
signalled in the third column by an exclamation mark after the gloss.[4] The
fourth column records how references to nonsubjects are encoded.

---

[4]The abbreviations used in this chart are: TOP topicalizing particle, $\emptyset$ zero anaphora
(absence of pronominal affix), 3p third-person plural pronominal affix, 3s third-person
singular pronominal affix.

		Subject		Non-Subject
(1)		stranger [1]	3s-be	
(2)	a	wife á [2]	3s-not find something	
	b	PRONOUN [1]	3s-not find something	
(3)	next	hunger	3s-strike	-3s [1]
(4)	a then	— [1]	3s-go	
	b	— [1]	3s-journey	
(5)	a	— [1]	3s-go TOP	
	b	— [1]	3s-perceive	children seated under tree [3]
(6)		— [1]	3s-say "... what are you doing?"	-to^3p [3],
(7)			"We are sitting guarding."	
(8)		children [3]	3p-answer like this	-3s [1]
(9)		— [1]	— "What are you guarding?"	— [3]
(10)		— [3]	— "... sheep and goats."	— [1]
(11)		— [3]	3p-answer "Are you a thief?"	stranger á [1],
(12)		— [1]	— "Would I steal from children?	— [3]
(13)			You there ... where do you wipe your hands?"	
(14)		child [3a]	3s-say, "... I wipe them like this."	
(15)		— [1]	— "You there, is it like that at your home, too?"	
(16)		child [3b]	3s-say, "... I wipe them like this,"	
		— [3b]	gesturing like a deaf-mute.	
(17)		stranger [1]	3s-say, "You there ... where do you wipe your hands?"	
(18)		— [3c]	— "My father gives me soap ... I wash my hands, then we sit."	
(19)		stranger [1]	3s-say "Let's go to your home."	to child á [3c]
(20)	then	— [1/3c]	3p-go	to house with child á [3c]
(21)	a	— [1/3c]	3p-go	to their house TOP,
	b	man káa héyey [4]	Ø-slaughter! 3s-slaughter	goat [5]

	Subject		Non-Subject
(22)	— [4]	3s-say, "Stranger has come to me."	
(23)	then woman *káa* [6]	3s-prepare	-3s-for^3p food with meat *kedé héyey* [5]
(24)	then — [?]	3p-eat	-3s (food) [5]
(25)	stranger [1]	3s-say, "... Give me the foot..."	
(26)	woman *káa* [6]	— "... Give it him, then!..."	to husband *á* [4],
(27)	husband *á* [4]	3s-say "... How will I give him only a foot?"	-to^3s [6],
(28)	woman *káa* [6]	TOP 3s-say, "... I'm going to river."	
(29) a	husband *á* [4]	Ø-stand up! to go	
b		3s-look for something	for stranger [1]
(30) a	stranger *héyey* [1]	TOP Ø-tiptoe! Ø-enter!	into kitchen
b		3s-steal	foot *héyey* [5]
(31) a	— [1]	3s-steal	foot [5]
b	— [1]	3s-crunch	-3s [5] TOP,
c	husband of woman *káa héyey* [4]	Ø-return!	
d	woman *káa héyey* [6]	Ø-return!	from river
(32)	next shame	3s-fill	-3p [4/6] ...
(33)	stranger [1]	3s-say "Just leave me foot...!"	-to^3p [4/6],
(34)	story *á*	3s-finished.	

3 Track the participants

Each participant which is referred to more than once in the text is allocated a number. References to participants (including zero) are labelled on the chart.

In the Mofu-Gudur text, the numbers used to refer to the participants are given in (35).

(35) [1]   the stranger
      [2]   his wife
      [3]   the children
      [3a], [3b], [3c]   individual children
      [4]   the children's father
      [5]   the food
      [6]   the children's mother

4 Propose default encoding values for various contexts

Based on either a statistical count or an inspection of the data, default values are proposed for participant encoding in certain contexts in the absence of a discontinuity. This section lists typical contexts for which default values for encoding subjects and nonsubjects are to be proposed.

Default values for encoding SUBJECTS in the absence of a discontinuity are proposed initially for the contexts in (36).

(36) S1   the subject is the same as in the previous sentence
      S2   the subject is the addressee of a speech reported in
           the previous sentence
      S3   the subject is involved in the previous sentence in a
           nonsubject role other than addressee
      S4   other changes of subject than those covered by S2 and S3

The four contexts are illustrated in (37), using English sentences based on the Mofu-Gudur text. The reference which fits the context concerned is given in small caps.

(37) S1   The stranger entered the kitchen. HE stole the foot.
      S2   The boys asked the stranger, "Are you a thief?" HE replied ...
      S3   Hunger afflicted the stranger. HE went to look for food.
      S4   While they were eating, THE STRANGER said ...

Typically, the value proposed for context S1 applies also to contexts in which the subject and nonsubject of the previous sentence combine to form a single, plural subject, as in (38).

(38) The stranger said to the boy, "Let's go to your house!" THEY went.

Default values for encoding NONSUBJECTS in the absence of a discontinuity are proposed initially for the contexts in (39).

(39)   N1   the referent occupies the same nonsubject role as in
             the previous sentence
       N2   the addressee of a reported speech is the subject
             (speaker) of a speech reported in the previous sentence
       N3   the referent is involved in the previous sentence in a
             different role than that covered by N2
       N4   other references to nonsubjects than those covered by N1–N3

The four contexts are illustrated in (40), using English sentences based
on the Mofu-Gudur text. The reference which fits the context concerned
is given in small caps.

(40)   N1   He stole the foot. When he stole THE FOOT . . .
       N2   He said to them . . . The children answered HIM . . .
       N3   Shame filled them. The stranger said to THEM . . .
       N4   The stranger said, "Give me the foot." The woman said to
             HER HUSBAND . . .

In the Mofu-Gudur text, provisional default values for encoding subjects
might be as in (41). (NP indicates a noun, with or without qualifiers,
together with the obligatory unstressed pronoun. See §2.)

(41)   S1   unstressed pronoun or zero, as appropriate (see §2)
       S2   NP
       S3   NP[5]
       S4   NP

Discussion of default values for nonsubjects in Mofu-Gudur is not
covered in this paper.

5 Identify the context in which each reference to a participant occurs

For each reference to a participant in the text, identify which of the
contexts of the last section is applicable. For subjects, each reference is
labelled as S1, S2, S3, or S4. For nonsubjects, each reference is labelled as
N1, N2, N3, or N4.

---

[5]The only example of this context in the text is sentence (4a) in the chart, the
encoding of which is an unstressed pronoun. However, if the default values for both
of the other contexts which involve changes of subject are a noun (phrase), the same
default value would be expected for this context.

For example, selected clauses and sentences of the Mofu-Gudur text would be labelled as in (42) for subject encoding contexts.

(42)   clause   (2b)   S4
        clause   (4a)   S3
        clause   (4b)   S1
        sentence   (8)   S2

6 Inspect the text for other than default encoding

Each reference to a participant in the text is then labelled as to whether the encoding material used is or is not the default amount for the context in which it is found. If the encoding is not the default amount, it is useful to distinguish whether the amount is less than or more than the default value.

For example, the clauses and sentences of the Mofu-Gudur text considered in the last section would be labelled as in (43) for the amount of subject encoding used.

(43)   clause   (2b)   S4: less than default
        clause   (4a)   S3: less than default
        clause   (4b)   S1: default
        sentence   (8)   S2: default

The amount of encoding in clause (2b) is less than default, because the default amount of encoding for context S4 is a noun (phrase), but only a pronoun is used. The same is true for clause (4a); the default amount of encoding for context S3 is a noun (phrase), but only an unstressed pronoun is used.

Reasons for the amount of encoding being less or more than predicted are now considered in turn.

6.1. When the encoding is less than predicted. When encoding is less than what is considered to be a default value, this is typically due to the referent being the VIP (globally or locally), only one major participant being on stage, or a cycle of events being repeated.

In the Mofu-Gudur text, less than the proposed default value for subjects occurs in the clauses or sentences given in (44).

(44)   context S4: (2b)   (stressed pronoun
                                                       instead of NP)
        context S3: (4a)   (unstressed pronoun
                                                       instead of NP)
        context S2: (9), (10), (12), (15), (18)   (unstressed pronoun
                                                       instead of NP)

Possible explanations for the use in (2b) of a stressed pronoun instead
of a noun (phrase) in context S4 (when the subject was not involved in the
previous sentence) are that the referent is the VIP, the referent is a major
participant, and the only other participant on stage is a minor participant
(the stranger's wife features no further in the story).

The referent in (4a) is the VIP and is the only participant on stage
(assuming that his wife has faded out of the story). It is common for a
reference to a VIP to be less than the default amount used for other
participants (see, for example, Levinsohn 1992:123).

Regarding the sentences for which encoding is less than that predicted
for context S2 (when the subject is the addressee of a speech reported in
the previous sentence), each one occurs within the repetition of a cycle of
reported speeches. Two types of cycles may be distinguished.

Sentences (6)–(13) concern a conversation between a stranger and a
group of children. The participants remain unchanged throughout the
conversation, and the new speakers are overtly identified only on the first
occasion that they speak ((8)). The fact that the unstressed pronouns of
Mofu-Gudur distinguish singular and plural, and the speakers in this
conversation are alternatively singular and plural, assists in identification.

The cycles of speeches reported in (14)–(18) involve the stranger and
different individual children in turn. Since all the speakers are individuals,
the unstressed pronouns of Mofu-Gudur do not assist in identification.
Overt reference to the speaker is omitted only in sentences (15) and (18).
Further examples of this type of repeated cycle would be needed in order
to determine why these particular references, rather than others, were
omitted.

6.2. When the encoding is more than predicted. A similar procedure
to that described in §6.1 is followed for instances in which encoding is
greater than what is considered to be the default value.

Increased encoding typically occurs immediately following points of discontinuity and in connection with the highlighting of information, whether
or not that information is "disruptive, surprising" (Givón 1983:18). Rather,
"sentences may be highlighted and a full noun phrase employed, [even]

when the information concerned is important but neither disruptive nor surprising" (Levinsohn 1992:116).

The following extract from a Mofu-Gudur text illustrates increased encoding material, in connection with context S1 (when the same subject occurs as in the previous sentence). The default value for context S1 in Mofu-Gudur is an unstressed pronoun only. The initial adverbial phrase 'one day' indicates that (46) occurs immediately following a discontinuity, hence the motivation for the increased encoding material.

(45)   After that,   —(chief)   3s-put   -3s (bird) in its place.

(46)   One day,   chief   3s-left   for field.

Pohlig and Levinsohn (this volume) show that the qualifier *héyey* is often used with a noun in Mofu-Gudur, both following a discontinuity and in connection with highlighted events of a narrative. This is exemplified in clauses (21b), (30a), and (31c) of the chart. Each is an instance of context S4, for which the default value for referring to the subject is probably an unqualified noun, rather than the general NP proposed in §4. The presence of *héyey* may therefore be interpreted as an example of increased participant encoding. All three sentences begin with a topicalized constituent, reflecting a discontinuity in the story. In addition, sentence (30) is probably of a climactic nature (*héyey* also modifies the nonsubject 'foot', in the same sentence).

7 Incorporate any modifications to the proposals of step 4

Once the factors which are involved when encoding is more or less than predicted have been determined, it may be appropriate to modify the list of contexts for which default encoding amounts are proposed when no discontinuity is present. As has already been suggested in §6.1, modifications might be proposed to reflect the presence of a VIP in the story, or the involvement in the story of only one major participant.

For example, if the amount of encoding for context S3 is frequently less than the default value proposed, the default encoding might be modified to give different values, according to the number of participants on stage. An example might be, "If a nonsubject in one clause becomes the subject of the next and a major participant is interacting with a minor participant or is alone ... " (Levinsohn 1992:117).

8 Generalize the motivations for deviances from default encoding

Having eliminated all references which may be interpreted as instances of default encoding, the remaining deviances are judged to be marked forms of encoding. The motivation for each instance of marked encoding is then determined, and generalizations drawn. As indicated in §6.2, common motivations for marked encoding include the presence of a discontinuity and the highlighting of information.

9 Summary

The present work offers a methodology for identifying the different factors which affect the amount of encoding that is involved when a speaker refers to participants throughout a discourse. Eight steps are described.

1. Draw up an inventory of the different ways that references to participants are encoded in the language.
2. Prepare a chart of how participants are referred to in a text in the language. Distinguish the encoding of subjects and nonsubjects.
3. Track the way references to each participant in the text are encoded.
4. Propose, for both subjects and nonsubjects, default encoding values for various defined contexts which do not involve a discontinuity.
5. Identify the context in which each reference to a participant occurs.
6. Inspect the text for instances in which encoding is other than the default amount predicted.
7. Incorporate any modifications to the proposals of step 4.
8. Generalize the motivations for deviances from default encoding.

References

Dooley, Robert A. 1992. Analyzing discourse: Basic concepts. Grand Forks: Summer Institute of Linguistics and University of North Dakota.

Givón, Talmy, ed. 1983. Topic continuity in discourse. Philadelphia: Benjamins.

Hollingsworth, Kenneth. To appear. Transitivity and the pragmatics of object suffixes on Mofu verbs. Journal of West African Languages.

Johnstone, Barbara. 1987. 'He says ... so I said': Verb tense alternation and narrative depictions of authority in American English. Linguistics 25:33–52.

Levinsohn, Stephen H. 1978. Participant reference in Inga narrative discourse. In J. Hinds (ed.), Anaphora in discourse, 69–135. Edmonton, Canada: Linguistic Research Inc.

————. 1992. Discourse features of New Testament Greek. Dallas: Summer Institute of Linguistics.

Section Three

Semantic Constraints on Relevance and Prominence Devices

Semantic Constraints on Relevance
in Lobala Discourse

David Morgan

Abstract

This paper takes a Relevance Theory approach to utterance interpretation, as expressed by Sperber and Wilson. It particularly employs Blass' insight into particle typology. The paper discusses three particles used in discourse in Lobala, a Bantu language of Northwest Zaïre. It first shows that, whenever *ná* occurs, the inherent function of indicating a relation of addition between two constituents is always present. In utterance interpretation, *ná* is said to constrain either a parallel relation or, if this is not possible, a backwards confirmation effect, similar to English *even*.

The paper then discusses *ka* and shows that this particle indicates a backwards countering relation between two utterances. *ka* also constrains the hearer to access two optimally relevant assumptions that counter each other.

Finally, the paper examines *nde,* which functions as an excluder. In its marked, preverbal position, it acts as a spacer between verb and subject. This causes the preceding topicalized constituent to be highlighted, creating appropriate contextual effects.

Lobala speakers use these three particles either to constrain a particular interpretation at a point of ambiguity or to create additional effects. What is implicated by their presence, though insufficiently relevant to be stated, nonetheless forms an integral part of the interpretation process.

Résumé

L'auteur aborde l'interprétation de la parole du point de vue de la théorie de la pertinence, théorie pragmatique proposée par Sperber et Wilson. Il emploie surtout la typologie des particules formulée par Blass. Dans cet article, il présente trois particules du lobala, langue bantoue de la Région de l'Equateur du Zaïre. La première, *ná,* indique partout une relation d'addition entre deux éléments similaires. En ce qui concerne l'interprétation de la parole, *ná* contraint une relation parallèle ou, dans le cas où ceci n'est pas possible, il se produit un effet de 'confirmation en arrière', qui ressemble à l'anglais *even.*

L'auteur présente ensuite la particule *ka* qui indique une relation 'd'opposition en arrière' entre deux expressions. Cette même particule, *ka,* oblige l'auditeur à adopter les deux postulats les plus pertinents pour les faire opposer l'un à l'autre.

Finalement, il présente la particule *nde* qui exclut tout élément sauf celui mentionné. Quand *nde* se trouve avant le verbe, ce qui dénote l'usage marqué, elle fait fonction de barre d'espacement entre le sujet et le verbe. Ceci fait ressortir l'élément topicalisé précédent, produisant ainsi un effet supplémentaire.

Les locuteurs du lobala utilisent ces trois particules soit pour éviter l'ambiguïté, soit pour créer des effets supplémentaires. Ce qui est impliqué par ces particules n'est pas suffisamment pertinent pour être exprimé par le locuteur. Néanmoins, c'est une partie intégrante du processus de l'interprétation de la parole.

This paper[1] illustrates the use of three particles from the Lobala language[2] and, within a RELEVANCE THEORY (henceforth RT) framework, discusses how they are used in discourse. A secondary aim is to show that not only is RT a comfortable framework within which to work, but that it

---

[1] I wish to acknowledge the help of many Lobala-speaking friends, especially Mr. Enyanga Ndanga, who provided a number of the oral texts used in this paper, and Mr. Botɔkɔ Mokpengbe who answered my many questions. I also thank Dr. Stephen H. Levinsohn for his willingness to spend time in entering into the details of Lobala discourse and for his prompting and guiding my thoughts. All deviations from accuracy and clarity are very much my own.

[2] Guthrie (1971 2:39) classifies Lobala as C.16. Bastin (1978:140) retains the C.16 listing but also lists Lobala as C.31j. By doing so, she places Lobala in the Bangi-Ntomba group with the languages that are geographically closest to it. Guthrie's comments on C.16 Lobala apply to Bastin's C.31j Lobala. There is no evidence for there being two languages in Northern Zaïre both called Lobala; see Morgan and Fultz (1985). The language is spoken in Zaïre by about 50,000 people who live in the forest and swamplands on the eastern bank of the Ubangi River in the Kungu and Bomongo Zones of the Equateur Region. No previous study has been made of the Lobala language. For an account of phonological aspects of the language, see Morgan (1993).

is actually a valuable tool with which to operate, prompting the researcher to look in profitable places for implied meaning.

The paper begins with a brief outline of RT and the developments of the theory as it concerns particle typology. It then considers the particle *ná* 'and', demonstrating that its inherent meaning of addition is found in every instance of its use. When it is used as a CONSTRAINT in UTTERANCE INTERPRETATION, it may either guide the hearer towards a parallel interpretation or it may have the effect of backwards confirmation. *ná* contrasts, in this respect, with *ka* 'but', which is shown to have a backwards countering role in utterance processing. Finally, the paper discusses the particle *nde* 'only', which functions as an excluder. It is the very act of excluding that highlights the unmentioned, excluded item. The particle is discussed in its default and marked positions. The paper shows how the three different particles act, in all cases, as a constraint on the hearer's interpretation process, enabling him to retrieve the intended contextual effect.

Relevance Theory

RT, as proposed by Sperber and Wilson (1986), is a theory of cognition which offers a model of how the mind works. According to RT, the human mind pays attention only to phenomena which it deems relevant. It processes those phenomena, not on the basis of some code or mutual knowledge context, but quite simply in the context that is most relevant. This cognitive theory throws considerable light on how language is both used and understood. That is to say, it serves as a theory of pragmatics.

Sperber and Wilson define relevance in terms of CONTEXTUAL EFFECTS and PROCESSING EFFORT. The human mind only focuses on information from the outside world that is deemed relevant on the basis of whether it will provide sufficient contextual effects to offset the processing effort. Contextual effects are categorized as being of three different types: (a) contextual implications, (b) strengthening, and (c) contradicting.

These three effects are exemplified with a nonlinguistic case: I have been waiting in an airport lounge for a long time for my flight. Finally, I see a plane arrive on the tarmac and I note that it belongs to the airline I am booked with. Based on past experience that, when the plane arrives outside the passenger lounge, it is not long before passengers embark and the plane leaves, I am able to draw the CONTEXTUAL IMPLICATION that it will not be long before I leave.

I then notice general activity around the plane. It is being fuelled and luggage is being taken on board. This is relevant because it STRENGTHENS my earlier assumption.

I now observe that the plane moves off to the runway and takes off. This observation is said to achieve relevance because it CONTRADICTS my earlier assumptions.

All of the three visual observations described above were relevant to me because they had effects on the context of my wanting to start my journey. It may have been that I would have had to walk upstairs and look over a wall in order to make these observations. In other words, I might have been prepared to make a considerable effort in order to arrive at these effects. It would have been worthwhile in order to settle my anxieties. Conversely, I would have paid little or no attention to the discussion of coffee prices held by two business men seated opposite me. It would not have been relevant. Effort and effect have to balance each other.

Constraints on relevance: The work of Blakemore and Blass

Grice (1975) suggested that such particles as *therefore* and *but* involved the truth-functional logical operator '&' plus an additional IMPLICATURE resulting from the content of the lexical item. Grice called this implicature a conventional implicature.

Blakemore (1987), rejecting Grice's suggestion and working within an RT framework, proposed that particles such as *so* and *also* have both nontruth conditional and semantic content. She proposed that these particles guide the hearer in processing the utterance. That is to say that such particles do not affect the truth conditions of the proposition, i.e., that they have no effect on the semantic content of the proposition. They do, nonetheless, constrain the hearer's processing of the utterance. Specifically, they help him to know which of the above three contextual effects the utterance might be intended to have.

Blakemore (1987:84–85) pointed out that, where a newly presented proposition, together with supplementary premises, entails the proposition expressed by a preceding utterance, it is naturally interpreted as providing a strengthening effect, i.e., confirmation of the preceding utterance. This is exemplified in (1).

(1)   Mary is a linguist; she speaks half a dozen languages.

Blakemore further claimed that the function of *also* is to indicate that two syntactically parallel clauses stand in a relation of addition to each other, as in (2).

(2)   Mary is a linguist; she **also** speaks half a dozen languages.

The use of *also* does not allow the hearer to assume that 'she speaks half a dozen languages' strengthens 'Mary is a linguist'. It constrains a PARALLEL interpretation. That is to say, the intended contextual effect is not to provide strengthening but to create a contextual implication, presumably on the lines of 'if she speaks half a dozen languages, she is a very able person.'

Blass (1990a:145ff) demonstrated that German *auch* and Sissala[3] *ma* were unlike English *also* in that they permitted what she called BACK-WARDS CONFIRMATION. She gave a number of examples illustrating the difference between English *also* and German *auch*, one of which (1990b:15) is reproduced here as (3).

(3)   *Karin ist Übersetzerin geworden;*
       *sie ist ja **auch** gut in Linguistik.*

       Karin has become a translator;
       after all she is good at linguistics.

Blass comments, with respect to *auch* and *ma* (1990a:146), that, "though there may be parallelism in form, the formally similar utterances are not processed in parallel ways." Precisely because of the danger of processing an utterance in the wrong way, German *auch* achieves relevance because it constrains the hearer to process the utterance as strengthening a previous utterance. Lobala *ná*, like Sissala *ma*, can constrain both parallel interpretation and confirmatory interpretation. Its precise limits are discussed in the next section.

1 Marker of addition *ná*

In its default usage in Lobala, *ná* conjoins semantically similar entities within the noun phrase, as illustrated in (4).[4]

---

[3]Sissala is spoken in Burkina Faso and Ghana. Like Lobala, it is also part of the Niger-Congo language family. It is a Gur (Voltaic) language, of the subgroup Gurunsi (Blass 1990a:2).

[4]Lexical high tone only is marked. The abbreviations used in this paper: APPL applicative, AUG augmentative, C1, C2, etc. marker of noun class 1, 2, etc. (out of 14), DEM demonstrative, DIM diminutive, FUT future, IMPF imperfective, LOC locative, NEG negative, O object, P plural, PF perfective, RT Relevance Theory, s singular, 1, 2, 3 first-, second-, third-person, Ø zero marker.

(4) a. *kóbá   ná   ŋgbábé*
     tortoise and monkey
     the tortoise and the monkey

     b. *baŋgá ná   wɛ*
     1p   and 2s
     you and I (literally, we and you)

     c. *ndéngyé ná   ndéngyé*
     manner   and manner
     all sorts of ways

When conjoining such semantically similar entities, *ná* is obligatory. Neither constituent is signalled as being more important than the other in this default usage. *ná* is used to indicate addition, which is taken to be its inherent meaning.

From Guthrie (1970 4:243) onwards, it has been noted that low tone *na,* which occurs in many languages including Lobala, covers a much broader semantic range in Bantu languages than English *and.* For instance, English *with,* both in its instrumental and accompaniment sense, falls within the scope of *na.* Likewise, *na* following the verb *ba* 'be' creates the sense of English *have.* The relationship between this low tone *na* and the high tone *ná* under discussion in this paper is not altogether clear. Research into the patterns of tone shift in Lobala is under way. This section, however, focuses on the constraints that *ná* brings to bear on how two juxtaposed utterances are to be interpreted.

In other words, this paper regards all those cases where *ná* stands complete within an utterance as the default usage of the particle. All other occurrences of the word are regarded as marked. It will be found that, in all these occurrences, *ná* necessarily implies or refers to a previous utterance. In this sense, *ná* constrains the hearer to interpret the relation between the two utterances in the way the speaker intended.

1.1 Cases where *ná* is not used. In order to better define the use and meaning of *ná,* two examples are presented to illustrate what *ná* does not do. First, coordination effects are not indicated by *ná.* Specifically, *ná* does not link sequential actions. Juxtaposition of events described with the perfective verb form is quite sufficient to indicate that one completed event happened after another in the order in which the speaker mentions them (compare, Hopper 1982:9–10). This is illustrated in (5).

(5)   *na-ut-í   o   moséngye na-síy-é*
1s-leave-PF LOC Mosengye 1s-go^downriver-PF
I left Mosengye and paddled downriver.

   Second, to indicate that events are parallel and sequential, a verbal
auxiliary, *-kul-* 'repeat', is used, as in (6).

(6)   Monkey and family ate their food at table until it was finished.

   bá-kul-í   ya   nywá maleku o   mésa
   3p-repeat-PF come drink wine   LOC table
   They then also drank wine at table.

According to Blass (1990a:137), who was at this point building on the work
of Wilson and Sperber (1979), (6) entails the proposition that 'someone
had earlier done something'. *-kul-* has the function of signalling to the
hearer that this is the background against which to interpret (6). In this
instance, he will retrieve 'monkey and family ate their food at table' as the
preceding parallel proposition. *-kul-* has a more restricted function, however, than English *also*. It constrains not only a parallel interpretation, but
also a sequential interpretation, because of the perfective form of the
auxiliary. As is demonstrated in §1.2, *ná* does not allow a sequential
interpretation.

1.2 *ná* and parallel addition. *ná* may be used to add a new constituent
into an established context, as in (7).

(7) a. *wakyendé ɔngó ná nyɔngó o   inzabi*
        went   father and mother LOC field

   b. *ná   we ko-kyend-é omó*
      and 2s 2s-go-IMPF there
   When your father and mother go to the field, you too should go.

Example (7b) cannot be interpreted as subsidiary, explanatory, or confirmatory of (7a). Instead, the constituent in the scope of *ná*, i.e., *we* 'you', is
to be added into a previously established context. The hearer is guided by
balancing effort and effects as to which context to select. He selects 'father
and mother' because these are the most recently mentioned, semantically
similar items—in other words, this represents minimum effort—and because it makes sense in context, i.e., there are offsetting contextual effects.
He can thus be sure this is the relevant context. This is only a slight

development from the examples of conjoined noun phrases presented in (4). This use of *ná* produces a 'you too' sense.

In (7), the new constituent was added to an exactly similar context. Example (8) illustrates that the context does not have to be exactly similar.

(8) a. *nwásí wa ngbábé   a-mbá   ya   lámba ntóma ntóma ndáa*
       wife of Monkey 3s-went came cook food   food good

   b. *a-mo-bom-es-í   masóó*
      3s-C1^O-kill-APPL-PF chickens

   c. *a-kyes-í   ná malɛku*
      3s-make-PF and wine

   d. *a-mo-tuaky-es-í   ná makɔ*
      3s-C1^O-pound-APPL-PF and plantains
      Monkey's wife had cooked some really good food. She killed some chickens for him. She also made some wine and she pounded plantains for him, too.

Inasmuch as (8b) entails (8a) and represents a specific example of the generic (8a), it can easily be interpreted as providing confirmatory evidence for (8a) (see Blakemore 1987:84–5). It does not need to be marked in any special way for the hearer to arrive at this interpretation. On the other hand, (8c, d) are marked with *ná,* which signals that the constituents 'wine' and 'plantains' are added to the context of the chickens in (8b). It overrides a sequential interpretation of the relationship of (8c, d) to (8b) and constrains a parallel interpretation.

1.3 *ná* and correlation—both . . . and, neither . . . nor. The *both . . . and* construction in English brings two constituents together without uniting them. An example requiring a *both . . . and* translation is given in (9).

(9) *bo wand-é   bé ná mandu ná nkoto   bábona*
      as beat-IMPF 3p and drums and tom-toms thus
      bá-bín-el-é   mosi   nya wɛ
      3p-dance-APPL-IMPF brother of 2s
      As they are beating both the drums and the tom-toms, they are dancing for your brother.

In (4b), the expression *bangá ná wɛ* 'you and I' is to be interpreted as a self-contained unit. By contrast, the expression in (9), *ná mandu ná nkoto* 'both drums and tom-toms', is not a self-contained unit in that the first *ná* has no preceding constituent to conjoin. The first *ná* is like a hook with nothing to latch onto. It cannot be that there are yet other types of drums implied but not mentioned: there are only two sorts. This marked use of *ná* must create additional contextual effects. In this case, it is that one might expect one kind of drum for a normal feast, but to beat both kinds runs counter to expectation. The expected *nkoto* has been added to by the unexpected *mandu*. In this way, *ná* achieves relevance.

A similar example in the negative is presented in (10), where an employer sends a workman out to work in the fields.

(10) *moto mɛ t-a-iká   mo-phέ ná baphalángá ná ntóma*
      man DEM NEG-3s-PAST Cl^O-give and money   and food
      The man gave him neither money nor food.

Again the constituents *ná baphalángá ná ntóma* 'neither money nor food' are individualized rather than united by *ná*. It would be expected that an employer give his employee either food or money as reward for his labor. Not to give one of the items may be expected; the additional fact that he didn't give either is contrary to expectation. This is the extra contextual effect of the marked use of *ná* in this case.

1.4 *ná* and backwards confirmation. In (7b) and (8c), the constituent in the scope of *ná* was added into a context previously made explicit by the speaker. In (11), there is no previously mentioned context to which the constituent in the scope of *ná* can be added.

(11) a. *a-mbá kyela nzelá   yɔnɔ́yɔ e-láa*
        3s-went make C9^road C9^one C9-good

    b. *nzelá   mɛ t-e-lí   ná na mabáku*
        C9^road DEM NEG-C9-be and with obstacles
        He made a very good road. It didn't even have any obstacles.

If *ná* were absent from (11b), (11b) would, by default, be interpreted as a specific instance of what a very good road means. The presence of *ná*, however, overrides such an interpretation. This provides a contrast with (8a, b), where the relation was generic-specific. In the case of (11b), *ná* creates an implicature that there are other features of the road that are unmentioned. They are not mentioned because they are not relevant. The fact that the road is devoid of obstacles is more relevant than other features because it represents an extreme that is contrary to expectation.

It can thus be translated by English *even*. Blass (1990a:156), following the work of Karttunen and Peters (1979), comments that *even* has a scalar implicature. The constituent within the scope of *even* is "low on the scale of likelihood." Indeed, a path through the forests of Zaïre is virtually never obstacle-free.

This marked use of *ná* creates an additional contextual effect. Blass shows how *even*, unlike *also*, is used in backwards confirmation. She shows how Sissala *ma* is also used in this way. It is likewise claimed in this paper that Lobala *ná* may function to prevent the hearer from assuming a generic-specific or other default relation with a previous utterance and to constrain a backwards confirmatory interpretation. This is what happens in (11).

ná is used sparingly. Blass (1990a:140) points out, with reference to the use of *also* functioning to override backwards contradiction, that it is typically used when there is a risk of misinterpretation. Indeed, *ná* is used to constrain utterance interpretation by indicating one particular relation over another. Just such a case of this is illustrated in (12).[5] If *ná* were absent, the hearer would have no difficulty in processing the utterance. Its presence, however, indicates a particular relation to the hearer and that there is some further contextual effect to be retrieved.

(12)   One day, the younger brother said, "Father, give me my share of your estate. Let me enjoy it while you're still alive."

   a. *ángó   t-a   ná kanga*
       father NEG-3s and refuse

   b. *a-es-í   ya   bá-káb-ela   mbóló*
       3s-come-PF come C2^O-divide-APPL C4^things
   Indeed the father did not refuse. He divided out his things for them.

Two processes are going on here. First, a knowledge of the world as it is would suggest that the son's request is an impertinence, in Lobala culture as much as any other. The hearer thus has access to the real world context in which someone who asks you for their share of your estate while you are still alive is being impertinent and should be refused. In this way, the hearer can easily arrive at the expectation expressed in (12i).

(12i)   The father refused this impertinent request.

---

[5]The example is extracted from a freely told version of the Biblical parable 'The Prodigal Son'.

That is the response to be expected of the father. However, the father didn't refuse. That is why the speaker uses the negative construction in (12a). He counters the hearer's expectation given as (12i). Indeed, it is (12a) that enables the hearer to assume (12i), on the grounds that it would not have been relevant to negate the refusing if it had not been expected.

Second, and more important than this consideration, the hearer will have access to what Longacre (1976:150) calls an EXPECTANCY CHAIN. That is to say, he will be able to supply the assumption given as (12ii).

(12ii) When someone asks for something, it is to be expected that he is given it.

The assumption in (12ii) is not as obvious to the hearer as (12i). Yet it is precisely because it is not obvious, that (12a) is marked with *ná* in order to constrain the hearer to access this expectation. Therefore, *ná* confirms the implication of (12ii). The effort expended is not inconsiderable. Native speakers report that it is a hard expression to process. The result, however, is a fascinating instance of the economy of language. Unstated but implied in those four words in (12a) are, on the one hand, the impertinence of the son and, on the other, brought to the fore by *ná*, the gracious acceptance of the request by the father.

Now consider (13), in which the speaker moves from collateral to real information, i.e., from that which was not done to that which was done. In such circumstances, the hearer will typically assume a generic-specific relationship between the two utterances.

(13) a. *ina   ibanza   phe*
        C4^DEM protecting NEG

    b. *a-kyé   mikyela **ná** maphɔɔ ma bunza-bunza*
        3s-go^PF making and things of disorder
        He didn't look after those things. He even went off doing bad things.

Such a generic-specific interpretation is overridden by *ná*. It indicates that there is a relation of addition between the two utterances. It is possible that (13b) directly adds on to (13a), giving the sense of 'Indeed he went off doing bad things'. As far as Lobala is concerned, however, the evidence is to the contrary. First, there is the consideration that *ná* always relates back to a syntactically parallel utterance, unlike (13a, b). This is perhaps because of its inherent function of adding a new constituent into an already established context. Second, when it is used to indicate backwards confirmation, *ná* always does this by means of an implicature. In the *even* use illustrated in (11), *ná* created an implicature that there were other features of the road.[6]

For these reasons, it is suggested that *ná* in (13b) implicates other activities that the man engaged in, amongst which 'doing bad things' is held to be a scalar extreme.

In a further example, the particle *ná* combines with the conditional marker *bo* to create a frozen form, *ná bo* 'even if'. The fact that it is a frozen form accounts for the unusual sentence-initial position of *ná*. Despite this fact, it still produces the same contextual effect as in the previous three examples. This is illustrated in (14). The context is that Leopard has built a very good road so he can collect his palm wine and come home drunk without falling over. This follows (11).

(14) a. *mokɔlɔ ná mokɔlɔ ka-kyɛ   bá   nde omɔ́*
       day   and day   3s-go^IMPF climb only there

    b. ***ná* *bo enzɔmbi   e-leky-í   ka-ye   nde boesi***
       and if C7^darkness C7-pass-PF 3s-come^IMPF only coming
       Every day he used to climb (palm trees) just there. Even if it got very dark, he would still just come along.

ná has the conditional clause in its scope, but constrains the hearer's interpretation of the entire utterance of (14b). If *ná* were not present, the topicalized conditional clause 'if it got very dark' would indicate a switch from 'every day' to a new setting. The hearer would interpret this as a new development in the story. *ná*, however, overrides this interpretation. It creates an implicature that there are other conditions under which Leopard comes along the road. It is relevant to mention only this particular one because it is the least expected condition under which one would walk along a road in the forest when drunk! Thus *ná* not only overrides a sequential interpretation, it has the additional effect of constraining the hearer to interpret (14b) as providing backwards confirmation for (14a).

1.5 Summary. In all of the various uses of *ná*, the inherent meaning of addition is present. In its marked usage, further effects can be retrieved pragmatically, guided by the principle of relevance. Whereas *ná* is always used to conjoin two semantically similar noun phrases, it is not used to conjoin two syntactically similar sentences. The presence of *ná* overrides a

---

[6]In this respect, *ná* diverges from Sissala *ma,* which confirms both implicatures and explicatures (Blass 1990a:146–51).

default interpretation, which might have been sequential or generic-specific. Instead, it constrains a parallel interpretation where there is a preceding parallel utterance. Where no such preceding utterance is present, a parallel interpretation is not possible. *ná* is then said to create an implicature, allowing an *even* interpretation. In these cases, particular attention has been given to the role of *ná* in constraining the hearer to interpret the utterance with which it is associated as strengthening or confirming a previous utterance.

The table in (15) demonstrates the breadth of the functions of *ná*. English has a stock of different words to cover the same functions of *ná*. All languages have ways of creating these effects, but the precise strategy of achieving them constitutes one of the major mismatches between languages.[7]

(15) Lobala English

ná	and	noun phrase coordination
ná	also	sentence coordination
Ø	and	parallel interpretation
ná	even	unexpected backwards confirmation
ná	indeed	clarifying backwards confirmation

2 Marker of counter evidence *ka*

The second particle under consideration, *ka,* achieves relevance by indicating to the hearer that the utterance with which it is associated counters a previous utterance. If such an utterance is not present, *ka* constrains the hearer to access relevant assumptions. To this extent, *ka* functions as a counterpart to *ná*.

In ordinary conversation, *ka* introduces an utterance and signals the speaker's intention to counter the previous speaker's words or expectations. Consider (16).

(16)   A: I have no plans to visit place X.

B: *ka* you and I are going there next week.

A can be said to have produced a proposition P (that A has no plans to visit X). B then produces a proposition Q which, as Longacre (1976:146) points out, carries the implication in (17).

---

[7]The mismatch between German *auch* and English *also* has already been addressed. Sissala *ma* shares the *also, even,* and *indeed* functions of *ná*, but is not used for noun phrase coordination. It does, however, have other uses not shared by *ná*.

(17)   Q → ~P

Given Q, the hearer can derive ~P. He is then left with the contradiction of P & ~P. According to Sperber and Wilson (1986), when the hearer discovers that he is entertaining two contradictory propositions, it is the weaker one that is abandoned. *ka* will always mark the stronger proposition. Q thus counters and cancels speaker A's proposition. *ka* constrains the hearer to search for two contradictory propositions and to abandon the weaker one.

2.1 Contrastive coordination. Syntactically, *ka* always occurs in sentence-initial position. It never occurs midsentence between two clauses. As a result, it never functions as a straight contrast marker. Contrast between clauses is normally expressed by simple juxtaposition, i.e., as a type of coordination. The interpretation of the juxtaposed clause structure, whether as sequential, contrastive, conjoining, etc., can be determined pragmatically. Sequential coordination has already been illustrated in (5); contrastive co-ordination is illustrated in (18).

(18) a. *na-mó-taa ba o   imese*
         1s-FUT-DIM be LOC Imese

    b. *iwɛ o-mb-é   kyɛndɛ o   mbombe*
        2s 2s-go-IMPF go   LOC Mbombe
    I'll remain a while in Imese, but you'll be going to Mbombe.

ka is used differently from English *but*, inasmuch as it is not a marker of contrast. *ka* would be inappropriate in (18) because (18b) does not counter (18a). These are merely two juxtaposed utterances and the hearer will, by default, interpret them as contrastive. Alternation or sequential interpretations would have insufficient contextual effects.

2.2 *ka* and countering implicatures. In narrative, *ka* commonly introduces narrator comment into the flow of action. Consequently, verb forms following *ka* will be distinct from those employed on the main event line, i.e., they will be future, imperfective, or stative, rather than perfective. This is illustrated in (19).[8]

(19) a. *ngbábé   a-kúnyos-í sɛ   a-kúnyos-í sɛ*
         Monkey 3s-wash-PF fingers 3s-wash-PF fingers

   b. ***ka** ko-éb-e   ma-bɔ́kɔ ma   kata   ma-índ-á*
       but 2s-know-IMPF C6-hands C6ˆof blackˆmonkey C6-darken-PAST
       Monkey washed and washed his hands. But, as you know, black monkeys have very dark hands.

Example (19b) represents an intrusion by the narrator into the course of events. He addresses his audience directly. Now, the hearer may assume that any ostensive communication is relevant (i.e., that there are contextual effects to be retrieved), but he will still need help to know exactly how it is relevant. After all, the hearer is asked to process two seemingly unrelated utterances.

(19) a'. Monkey went on washing his hands.

(19) b'. You know black monkeys have very dark hands.

ka helps the hearer to understand that (19b) is relevant to the context of (19a) in a particular way. It constrains the hearer to process (19b) as countering the preceding utterance or some expectation created by that utterance. It achieves relevance because it guides the hearer to access particular contextual effects, in this case, that of contradicting an expectation. If *ka* were absent, the hearer would be at a loss as to how to interpret the second utterance.

   Example (19b) cannot be said to directly counter (19a). The interpretation process is more complicated. Both (19a) and (19b) create their own contextual assumptions and it is these assumptions that counter each other. Using Longacre's (1976:150) concept of the expectancy chain—that if someone washes his hands, his hands become clean—the hearer can assume (19i) from (19a).

---

[8]Since the remaining examples of this section are extracted from the same oral text 'Monkey and Tortoise', it is worthwhile explaining the background to this story. The two characters concerned make a friendship pact. Tortoise visits Monkey and is received with honor but is invited to eat at table. This is designed to cause Tortoise maximum shame and so he returns home. He later takes his revenge when Monkey pays him a visit. He has him wash his hands and refuses to accept that Monkey's hands are clean on account of his black skin.

(19i)   Monkey's hands became clean.

On the other hand, based on the fact that the word used for 'dark' may also be used to indicate 'dirt', the hearer may assume (19ii) from (19b).

(19ii)   Monkey's hands will never become clean.

It is these two assumptions that contradict each other. The second one is derived from the utterance marked with *ka* and the hearer is assured that this is the stronger one. He can thus abandon (19i).

ka consistently functions in this way, as a marker of backwards countering of either an explicature or an implicature. But, just how does the speaker know what is being countered? Consider (20), which follows the same pattern as (19).

(20)   a. Monkey and his family now drink wine at table.
        b. *ka* Tortoise will never be able to climb up to the table.

ka constrains the hearer to interpret (20b) as countering something. It encourages him to look for the most relevant proposition to be countered. The most relevant one is found by balancing the least effort with the greatest effect. In the case of (20), the hearer has easy access to the normal cultural context of (20i).

(20i)   If a host drinks wine, he invites his guest to join him.

From this he can assume (20ii).

(20ii)   Tortoise will join Monkey and his family at table.

He can be sure that this is the most relevant assumption precisely because it is the one assumption that will be countered by (20b). In other words, (20ii) will be the assumption that produces the greatest contextual effects for the least effort. (20b) implies (20iii).

(20iii) Tortoise will be not be able to join them at table.

It is (20iii) that counters (20ii) and, since it is marked with *ka,* it also cancels (20ii). *ka* constrains the hearer to access these assumptions precisely in order to have the one counter the other. They are certainly not worth the effort of stating explicitly. The advantage of RT for the discourse

analyst is that it provides a tool with which to dig out such hidden assumptions.
Much the same process is to be observed in (21).

(21) a. *bá-es-í   ya   tanda ntóma o   sé*
        3p-come-PF come spread food   LOC ground

   b. *yo kye ka ngbábé   obokye o-taa   kuma ntóma ya izá*
       3s that but Monkey before 2s-DIM touch food   of eating

      ko-taa kúnyola nde sɛ
      2s-DIM wash   only fingers
      They then spread the food out on the ground. He said, "However,
      Monkey, before you touch the food, just go and wash your hands!"

In the culturally accessible context where, once the food is put out, all those invited to eat start to eat forthwith, it will be easy for the hearer to assume (21i) from (21a).

(21i)   Monkey will go to eat straight away.

However, in the context provided by (21b) 'if Monkey has to wash his hands first, he will not be going to eat straight away', the hearer may assume (21ii).

(21ii)   Monkey will not go to eat straight away.

In all these examples, the logical process is the same. There are two juxtaposed propositions, P and Q. In (21), proposition P is 'they spread food on the ground' and proposition Q is 'go wash your hands'. Each proposition implies another proposition, given as (21i) and (21ii). These are labelled R and ~R respectively. The logical process is formally represented below in (22).

(22)   i. P
       ii. P → R
      iii. Q
       iv. Q → ~R
        v. R
       vi. ~R
      vii. R & ~R

Lines (22v) and (22vi) are derived by the IMPLICATION ELIMINATION rule; line (22vii) by the CONJUNCTION INTRODUCTION rule. *ka* constrains the hearer to search for the contradiction of R & ~R, just as was the case with (17). *ka* is associated with Q and by implication with ~R. It marks the stronger assumption and the hearer can therefore abandon R.

Now, compare (23) with (24), discussed earlier as (12).

(23)   a. Tortoise said, "Scrape your hands with this knife!"
        b. *ka*, with the hunger he felt, Monkey was not able to refuse.

(24)   One day, the younger brother said, "Father, give me my share of your estate. Let me enjoy it while you're still alive."

        ángó t-a   ná kanga
        father NEG-3s and refuse
        Indeed the father did not refuse.

In both examples, an impertinent request is made. Equally, in both examples, the recipient of the request 'does not refuse'. Example (24), however, is marked with *ná*, producing the effects discussed earlier. In (23), the utterance is marked with *ka* to achieve quite different effects. Reference has already been made to Longacre's (1976:150) concept of the expectancy chain that, when A asks B to do something, it is to be expected that B does it. So, in (23), we have the unusual case of what might be said to be expected being marked as countering some expectation. *ka* constrains the hearer to search out an assumption or expectation to be countered. This must be along the lines of (23i).

(23i)   If someone asks you to scrape your hands with a knife, this is such an unreasonable request that it has to be refused.

In (24), it was the gracious agreement of the father that was highlighted by *ná*. As a result, the unreasonableness of the request was backstaged. In contrast, by implying an assumption along the lines of (23i), *ka* brings to the fore the unreasonable request in (23a). This is done because it is part of the speaker's purpose to portray Monkey as a helpless fool.

2.3 Summary. This section has shown that *ka* functions as a marker of counterevidence. It may counter both explicatures and implicatures. The principles of RT are sufficient to guide the hearer as to which implicatures or assumptions are to be countered. It constrains utterance interpretation, particularly at points of potential ambiguity, by encouraging the hearer to search out two contradicting assumptions or propositions and to abandon the weaker one. It may also have the effect of highlighting additional assumptions.

3 Marker of exclusion *nde*

The particle *nde* functions as an excluder. It can best be translated as 'only' and it retains this meaning in all situations. By excluding all constituents apart from one, the speaker regularly uses *nde* as a device to highlight just one of the excluded constituents. Its default position is postverbal. In addition, it has a marked position which is preverbal. In its marked position, *nde* has the extra effect of spotlighting the topicalized constituent that it immediately follows.

3.1 Default position of *nde*. In its default position, *nde* occurs postverbally. It either occurs directly after the verb, in which case its scope may be the constituent to its right or the whole of the utterance, or it may occur elsewhere postverbally, in which case its scope is only the constituent to its right. Consider first (25).

(25) *to-zé   nde o   ikoló sá mesa*
      1p-eat^IMPF only LOC top   of table
      We only eat at table.

nde excludes all possible alternative constituents in its scope. In (25), there is potential ambiguity. It could mean 'we do nothing else but eat at table'. In the context, however, the only relevant interpretation is to assume that the other places to eat are being excluded, 'only at table and nowhere else'.

'Nowhere else' is a conventional implicature, derived from the semantic content of *nde*. As a result of the extra effort of processing *nde*, however, and in view of the principle of relevance, the hearer can be sure that there is a further intended effect, for why else did the speaker employ *nde?* He can be assured that one thing in particular is excluded: 'only X and nothing else AND CERTAINLY NOT Y'. The speaker's real interest is Y.

In the case of (25), where the context is that of Monkey detailing house rules to Tortoise, the identity of Y cannot be worked out by the hearer. It is withheld by the speaker until the following sentence: 'we do not eat on the ground'. Thus is set up the trigger to the main dilemma of the story, the fact that Tortoise cannot climb up onto the chair.

It is consistently found that a constituent is marked with *nde* precisely in order to highlight another constituent—whether stated or implied—that is, the constituent that is actually excluded. In (26), a case is provided in which it is the principle of relevance, rather than the explicit words of the speaker, that guides the hearer to select the one thing that is really excluded.

(26) *a-mo-lámb-es-í*   *ntóma* **nde** *bo wakyeláka ngbábé*
      3s-C1^O-cook-APPL-PF food   only as done   Monkey
      He cooked food for him just like Monkey had done.

Here the narrator states the exclusive manner of Tortoise's reception of Monkey. The details of Monkey's warm, earlier reception of Tortoise have already been spelled out and so this use of the particle *nde* states that this second reception was the same way and no other way. In particular, it was not the expected snub of Monkey. A snub would have been expected in view of the disgraceful way in which Tortoise had been subsequently treated by Monkey.

In (27), the particle *nde* occurs immediately after the verb. Its scope, however, cannot be solely the constituent to the right.

(27) *kúnyola* **nde** *sɛ*
      wash   only fingers
      Just wash your hands!

In context, the utterance cannot mean 'wash just your hands' (and not your feet or face). It must mean 'just wash your hands', i.e., 'wash your hands before you do anything else'. What is excluded are other activities, specifically the expected 'come and eat with us'.

Now consider two more complex examples and the contextual implications that are created. The statement in (28) occurs in a narrative in which the speaker tells how a man ran away from a friend who was bitten by a snake. The moral and conclusion is that a true man has courage.

(28) *e-koky-í*   **nde** *obokye to-bé*   *na*   *ikpí*
      C7-be^right-PF only that   1p-be^IMPF with   courage
      What's right is just that we have courage.   ·

nde has everything to the right within its scope. What it excludes specifically is the action of running away from someone who has been bitten by a snake. Therefore, the contextual implication of using *nde* in (28) is the censuring of the man who ran away. Since all the preceding discourse has been about this man, it is reasonable to conclude that, as far as the speaker's purpose is concerned, this unstated implication is every bit as much a part of his conclusion as 'that a true man has courage'.

In (29), *ka* and *nde* function together. The context is that of a man coming upon Python and Leopard engaged in a fight to the death in Frog's house. The man had intended to collect money owed to him by Frog. The man shot both Leopard and Python.

(29) *ka na-wén-έ* **nde** *obokye eye e-m-pέ   nde nwâphóngó*
      but 1s-see-PF only that   DEM C7-C1^O-given only God
      But I just think that this is a gift to me from God alone.

The constituent in the scope of *nde* is 'this is a gift to me from God alone'. Being marked with *nde*, a conventional implicature is created as in (29i).

(29i) He does not think it is anything else other than a gift from God.

The hearer is guided to access a particular contextual implication from (29) by the presence of *ka*. From the preceding utterance 'the man shot both Leopard and Python', the hearer can readily assume (29ii).

(29ii) He is a very skilled hunter and the credit goes to him.

The hearer can then access the particular contextual implication from (29i) and know that it is the relevant one because it contradicts (29ii). It is given as (29iii).

(29iii) He does not think he shot both Leopard and Python because he is
         a very skilled hunter.

Being marked with *ka*, it will also cancel out (29ii).

From this discussion of the default position of *nde*, one can observe that exclusivity is the inherent meaning associated with *nde*; that its scope is usually the constituent to its right (exceptions may occur when *nde* is placed immediately after the verb and are handled pragmatically); and that *nde* constrains the hearer to access a particular contextual implication. The principle of relevance will guide the hearer as to which implication to choose.

3.2 Marked position of *nde*. Relevance theory claims that placing *nde* in a marked position creates additional contextual effects to compensate for the extra processing effort involved. This subsection shows that *nde*, in marked position, acts as a SPACER between the constituent that precedes it and the rest of the sentence. A spacer (Dooley 1990:477) is used to separate information of unequal importance. In this instance *nde* has the effect of highlighting the topicalized constituent concerned, which acts as a FOIL for what follows. The concept of a foil in discourse has been discussed by Levinsohn (1992:84). One constituent is highlighted temporarily in order to present a contrast with a following, corresponding constituent.[9]

This is illustrated in (30), where the context is of two characters complaining about a third who, against accepted social norms, has been going off on his own to drink palm wine in his field and coming back without sharing it with them.

(30)   *nwɛbí na bangá **nde** k-amb-é   langa   malɛku ndéngyé eye*
       friend of 1p   only 3s-go-IMPF be^drunk wine   manner what
       How come it's only our friend who is getting drunk?

What is excluded by *nde* in (30) is 'other people getting drunk'. In its preverbal position, the particle also functions as a spacer with the effect of highlighting the topicalized constituent 'our friend'. However, the speaker is not primarily interested in 'our friend'. 'Our friend' is but a foil to his real concern which is 'us'. His next utterance is 'he is not giving US any wine'. The implication of (30) is 'how come WE are not getting drunk as well?'.

The context of (31) is the same as (29). The man is considering whether to shoot Python or Leopard first.

(31) a.   *ka bo na-tat-í   iwanda ngúma*
          but if 1s-begin-PF hitting Python

     b.   *mbáká ngɔ   **nde** a-es-í   ya   lota*
          then   Leopard only 3s-come-PF come escape
          However, if I shoot Python first, then Leopard just escapes.

ka, in (31a), implies a presupposition 'it is best to shoot Python first'. The utterance beginning with *ka* offers counterevidence to this implied suggestion. *nde*, in (31b), excludes other possible outcomes. In particular, it excludes the desired consequence (shared by anyone living in rural Zaïre)

---

[9]Epée (1975) reported a very similar construction in the Duala (A.24) language of Cameroon, which he discussed from a syntactic point of view.

that he should shoot both Leopard and Python! This is why it is not best to shoot Python first. The unstated implication is that the man will actually shoot Leopard first.

The hearer is helped to retrieve this unstated implication by the marked position of *nde*. *nde* highlights 'Leopard' by acting as a spacer between the subject and the verb to topicalize the subject. Whereas Leopard and Python were previously two matched participants, neither more prominent than the other, *nde* now highlights Leopard as a foil in contrast to Python. It implies that Python is to be left alone for the moment; he will be shot afterwards.

Example (32) presents a counterfactual conditional sentence in which *nde* constrains a counterfactual interpretation. If it were absent, it would mean something along the lines of 'when it is day time, I will show you'. The utterance was made at night by a traditional healer who was describing a particular leaf he used in his work. He was communicating the fact that he was not going to show it, together with an apologetic reason for failing to do so.

(32)   *bo moo   mo-bákyí   nde   na-e-téy-é*
        if C3^sun C3-be^past only 1s-2s^O-show-PF
        If it were day time, I'd just show you.

For convenience, let us consider (32) as two separate propositions.

(32) a. It is day time.

    b. I will show you.

Example (32b) is marked with *nde* and this excludes other possibilities, most notably, 'I will not show you'. *nde*, in this marked position, again has the additional effect of highlighting the preceding constituent, namely, (32a). This highlighting of (32a) causes it to act as a foil to real world considerations, i.e., that it is the middle of the night.

That is to say, in a nighttime context, (32) creates insufficient contextual effects to be relevant. The hearer is guided by the marked position of *nde*, which highlights the foil, to assume that, in a context of NOT day time, 'I will NOT show you'. The hearer is justified in this assumption by the principle of relevance which assures him that there are contextual effects to be retrieved from ostensive communication. In fact, the speaker has communicated more than simply 'I will NOT show you'. He has employed a face saving device offering a reason why he is not going to show the hearer the leaves in question.

The following observations summarize the effects produced by *nde* in its marked position. The inherent meaning of *nde* is retained—it still functions as an excluder—indeed, all the contextual effects noted in connection with the default position are present. In occurring in a marked preverbal position, *nde* functions as a spacer with the effect of highlighting the preceding constituent. This constituent then acts as a foil to another constituent. It is in connection with this foil that the additional contextual effects of the marked position are to be retrieved.

4 Concluding remarks

This paper has sought to demonstrate the functioning of three particles in Lobala by appealing to the insights of Relevance Theory. *ná* consistently indicates a relation of addition. In its marked use in discourse, it assists the hearer in the interpretation process by overriding a default relation between two utterances and constraining either a parallel interpretation or a backwards confirmatory interpretation. Equally consistently, *ka* indicates a relation of countering. In utterance processing, it constrains the hearer to access optimally relevant assumptions in order to satisfy the countering requirement of *ka*. The particle *nde* was shown to have an inherent meaning of exclusion. Its use in a marked position causes the preceding constituent to be highlighted and this guides the hearer towards a further intended effect.

A consideration of these particles leads to the observation that much information lies hidden behind them. This is because speakers often do not use language explicitly. Subtleness, overtones, and implications are the hallmarks of good language use. Relevance Theory, a useful tool with which to dig out the hidden implications, helps to draw the attention of the researcher to the details of the interpretation process and offers an account as to why implications are left unstated in the actual text.

References

Bastin, Yvonne. 1978. Les langues bantoues. In Daniel Barreteau (ed.), Inventaire des études linguistiques sur les pays d'Afrique noire d'expression française et sur Madagascar, 123–85. Paris: Conseil International de la Langue Français.

Blakemore, Diane. 1987. Semantic constraints on relevance. Oxford: Basil Blackwell.

Blass, Regina. 1990a. Relevance relations in discourse: A study with special reference to Sissala. Cambridge: Cambridge University Press.

————. 1990b. Constraints on relevance, a key to particle typology. Notes on Linguistics 48:8–20.

Dooley, Robert A. 1990. The positioning of non-pronominal clitics and particles in lowland South American languages. In David L. Payne (ed.), Amazonian linguistics: Studies in lowland South American languages, 457–83. Austin: University of Texas Press.

Epée, Roger. 1975. The case for a focus position in Duala. In R. K. Herbert (ed.), Proceedings of the 6th conference on African languages, 210–26. Ithaca: Cornell University.

Grice, H. Paul. 1975. Logic and conversation. In P. Cole and J. L. Morgan (eds.), Syntax and semantics. Vol. III Speech acts, 41–58. New York: Academic Press.

Guthrie, Malcolm. 1967–71. Comparative Bantu, vols. 1–4. Farnborough: Gregg International Publishers.

Hopper, Paul J. 1982. Aspect between discourse and grammar. In Paul J. Hopper (ed.), Tense-aspect: Between semantics and pragmatics, 3–18. Philadelphia: Benjamins.

Karttunen, Lauri and Stanley Peters. 1979. Conventional implicature. In C. K. Oh and D. A. Dinneen (eds.), Syntax and semantics. Vol. XI Presuppositions, 1–56. New York: Academic Press.

Levinsohn, Stephen H. 1992. Discourse features of New Testament Greek. Dallas: Summer Institute of Linguistics.

Longacre, Robert E. 1976. Anatomy of speech notions. Lisse: Peter de Ridder Press.

Morgan, David J. 1993. Vowel harmony, syllable structure and the causative extension in Lobala: A government phonology account. Journal of West African Languages 23(1):41–63.

———— and James W. Fultz. 1985. Enquête dialectale de l'Ubangi-Mongala: Première partie–Zone de Kungu. ms.

Sperber, Dan and Deirdre Wilson. 1986. Relevance: Communication and cognition. Oxford: Basil Blackwell.

Wilson, Deirdre and Dan Sperber. 1979. Ordered entailments: An alternative to presuppositional theories. In C. K. Oh and D. A. Dinneen (eds.), Syntax and semantics. Vol. XI Presuppositions, 229–324. New York: Academic Press.

Thematic Development and Prominence in Tyap Discourse

Carl M. Follingstad

Abstract

The concepts of thematic development and prominence are used to explain the distribution of two sets of preverbal particles in Tyap narratives. The first set has two members: *kan* and *kin*. *kan* indicates that the proposition concerned is viewed as representing a new development in the thematic flow of events; the information is "relevant in its own right" (Blass 1990:256–57). The additive particle *kin* closely associates the proposition concerned with previous utterances, rather than representing a new development. It typically strengthens the previous utterances (or assumptions behind them) and is pragmatically motivated in other ways as well. The second set of particles has three members: *si, sii,* and *sisi*. *si* correlates with propositions which present foreground events. The lengthened vowel of *sii* reflects a lapse of time between foreground events. *sii* is also used to indicate focus prominence on a particular event. The reduplicated form of *sisi* indicates emphatic prominence on a particular event, typically because it is pivotal in some way.

Résumé

L'auteur invoque les notions de développement thématique et de proéminence pour expliquer la distribution de deux séries de particules

151

pré-verbales dans les narratifs tyap. La premiere de ces séries comporte deux membres, *kan* et *kin,* dont le premier *kan* indique que la proposition qui la contient est considérée comme représentant un nouveau développement dans le déroulement thématique des événements ; cette information est pertinente "en soi" (Blass 1990:256–57). La particule additive *kin* représente une as-sociation étroite de la proposition en question avec le (les) énoncé(s) précédant(s), plutôt que de représenter un nouveau développement. Normale-ment, il renforce ce même énoncé précédant (ou les suppositions qui le sous-tendent) ; il trouve également d'autres motivations pragmatiques. La deuxieme série de particules comporte trois membres : *si, sii* et *sisi.* La particule *si* est utilisée dans des propositions qui présentent les événements de premier plan. Quant a *sii,* sa voyelle rallongée reflete le passage d'un laps de temps entre les événements de premier plan ; il indique également qu'un certain événement est focalisé, donc proéminent. La forme redoublée *sisi* indique une proéminence accentuée qui est accordée a un certain événement, souvent a cause de son rôle de charniere.

This paper[1] represents an investigation of certain hitherto problematic preverbal particles in the Tyap language.[2]

---

[1]This paper is based on data collected primarily in Mabukhwu, a village area about 5 kilometers south of the main town of Zango Kataf, although data were collected also from the Gora, Әbweap, and Jankassa village areas.

A large portion of the data was provided by Mr. Ishaku Ayok (Mabukhwu). Mr. Michael Bamayi (Gora) also contributed data. Other data were gathered and transcribed by Mr. Dimos Haruna and Mrs. Rahab Bityong from the Әbweap and Jankassa village areas. Without their kind assistance, this paper would not have been possible. Thanks must also be given to the District Head of Zangon Kataf, Mallam Bala Ade Dauke, and Major General (rtd.) Zamani Lekhwot for their guidance and support.

My studies of the Tyap language are carried out under the auspices of the Nigeria Bible Translation Trust (NBTT) which specializes in Bible translation, literacy, and linguistic work among the minority languages of Nigeria. Thanks must be given to the Director of NBTT, Dr. John R. Adive, Don Lindholm, and my wife Joy who helped make it possible for me to attend the workshop during which the data for this paper were analyzed. I thank Dr. Stephen Levinsohn and my wife Joy for making helpful suggestions on this paper. The paper would not have been possible without the insightful guidance of Dr. Levinsohn. All errors remain my responsibility.

It should be noted that this is an initial attempt at an analysis of Tyap discourse features. Further investigation will no doubt confirm or modify the conclusions presented here.

[2]The Tyap language is spoken by approximately 100,000 people in the Zangon Kataf Local Government of southern Kaduna State in the Middle-Belt of the Federal Republic of Nigeria. In addition, more than 20,000 people speak the language in various cities outside of the heartland. The language *Tyap* and people *Әtyap* are sometimes referred to as 'Kataf' in the northern Nigerian language of wider communication (Hausa). The Tyap language is classified by Gerhardt (1989:364–65) as a member of the (Niger-Congo, Benue-Congo), Platoid, Plateau, Central group, South-Central Sub-group, Katab cluster.

One set of preverbal particles with two members is explained in terms of the concepts found in Levinsohn (1987) and Blass (1990) to describe particles which facilitate the interpretation of utterances by providing "semantic constraints on relevance" (Blakemore 1987). *kan* is classified as a "development marker" (Levinsohn 1992:32–37), which indicates that the information concerned is "relevant in its own right" (Blass 1990:256–57) because it represents a significant development in the thematic flow of events as far as the author's purpose is concerned. *kin* is classified as an additive marker, which indicates that the information concerned is closely associated with, rather than developing from, previous utterances. It typically functions to strengthen previous utterances.

The differences among the three members of a second set of preverbal particles are partially explained in terms of Callow's (1974) three kinds of prominence. Thematic prominence is "what I am talking about"; focus prominence involves highlighting items of particular significance; emphasis prominence involves the speaker-hearer relationship in some way (for example, because the speaker feels strongly about a particular item, or considers that an event is unexpected (p. 52)). The Tyap particle *si* correlates with utterances that describe the major sequential events in a narrative, in other words, those that have thematic prominence. *sii* is used not only when there is an "action discontinuity" (Givón 1983:8) because there is a significant temporal gap between major events in a narrative, but also to give focus prominence to individual events. Finally, *sisi* indicates that the speaker is emphasizing the event concerned, for example, because it is of a pivotal nature or otherwise important to bear in mind.

1 Thematic development

An utterance marked for thematic development is viewed by the author as building on the previous context, and also as introducing a new development in the narrative (Levinsohn 1992:31). This section discusses the functions of two Tyap preverbal particles, *kan* and *kin*. *kan* indicates that a proposition is viewed by the author as representing a new development in the storyline. Its contextual effect[3] is to indicate that the proposition is independently relevant with respect to the preceding proposition(s). On the other hand, *kin* indicates that a proposition is viewed as closely affiliated with the preceding utterances such that it adds information but

---

[3]"Contextual effects" occur when information fits the hearer's assumptions about the world and best fits the immediate context (Blass 1990:44; Morgan this volume).

does not indicate a new development. Its contextual effect is to strengthen the previous utterances.

The absence of *kan* and *kin* implies that the proposition is viewed as neither a significant development in the thematic flow of events nor as an addition to a previous utterance. *kan* and *kin* can function as links both between individual propositions and between groupings of utterances. They also tend to occur with greater frequency at peaks in the narrative.

A summary of the functions of *kan* and *kin* is given in (1). By definition, the features + additive and + developmental do not occur together, as the function of the additive is to avoid a new development but rather to associate the proposition tightly with the preceding context. This is supported by the fact that *kan* and *kin* never occur together (i.e., they are in complementary distribution).

(1)   Discourse function

	+ additive	− additive
+ developmental	—	*kan*
− developmental	*kin*	∅ (default)

A summary of the contextual effects of *kan* and *kin* is given in (2). These particles function to guide the hearer's interpretation of the relationship between two propositions, to both optimize relevance and decrease misunderstanding between them (Blakemore 1987:123; Blass 1990:127). In the classification below, the relationship between two propositions is the basis for stating the contextual effects of *kan* and *kin.* It will be seen, however, that these particles can be related not only to the previous proposition, but also to larger sections of discourse in the same way as they relate to a single proposition.

(2)   Contextual effects

Proposition is relevant in its own right: *kan*
Proposition strengthens the previous one: *kin*

1.1 Thematic developmental particle *kan*

This section discusses the discourse function and contextual effects of the particle *kan.* First, the occurrence of *kan* is contrasted with its absence. Second, *kan* is discussed with respect to its contextual effects.

The utterances of a narrative are linked together in various ways. Many present events in natural sequence, i.e., there is action continuity between them (see Levinsohn's article "Discontinuities in Coherent Texts," this volume). An utterance marked as developmental does not present an event which is merely in natural sequence with a previous one. Rather, it is viewed by the author as building on the previous context and introducing a new development in the narrative (Levinsohn 1992:31). The author determines what is a new development or not, depending on the purpose for communicating.

There are various devices which languages use to indicate developmental relationships between utterances. In Tyap, one such device is the preverbal particle *kan*.[4] At this point, the contexts in which *kan* occurs are compared to those in which it does not.

Example (3) is drawn from a traditional story in which a woman, Bashila, discovers that her husband is a wizard when she comes back home from grinding and hears what he is singing to their child. The story continues (the absence of *kan* is marked by Ø):[5]

(3) a. She *si* Ø returned, she *si* Ø kept quiet.

    b. He *si* Ø took the child, he *si* Ø gave it to Bashila.

    c. Morning Ø dawned, he *si* Ø got up, he *si* Ø got up.

    d. When he Ø got up, he *si* Ø left, he *si* Ø again went to eat people.

    e. When he Ø went to eat people, Bashila *si kan* got up as well . . .

In (3), the absence of *kan* occurs in connection with sequential events which do not represent a new development in the story. Events such as

---

[4]In C. Follingstad (1991), *kan* was defined as having the basic meaning of 'now' or 'at this time', but not so much with a focus on the immediate action as on the reaction with respect to the rest of the discourse (i.e., at this point in the story). It was concluded that the function of the particle may well be more closely related to discourse pragmatics than that of some of the other particles. This article refines the above definition. See also A. Follingstad 1991:97–98.

[5]In the following examples, where extended amounts of discourse illustrate a particular feature, only the particles under consideration are highlighted unless otherwise noted. The particle *si* is the default coordinating conjunction 'and'. The absence of the particles or conjunctions discussed in this paper is not marked in complements, infinitival constructions, cleft constructions, and quotations in which they typically do not occur. 'Ø' indicates the absence of *si* unless otherwise noted.

the handing over of the child and the man's awakening and departure the next morning to go practice magic are either of a routine nature or have already been described in the preceding material as having occurred a number of times. Bashila's actions in (3e), however, are viewed by the storyteller as a new development in the story, arising from discovering that her husband is a wizard, and so she embarks on a stratagem to put an end to his activities, as the ongoing narration indicates. This use of *kan* is also consistent with the author's overall purpose in telling the story, namely, to show how somebody who practices evil on another will get his or her just desserts.

A longer passage is now presented to better illustrate where an author marks a new development. Example (4) is drawn from a personal account told by an Ətyap woman to this author. *kan* occurs in (4d, i, j, l).

(4) a. The person that I went to see, she Ø is a relative.

   b. During the time that the Hausa were taking the Ətyap, the Hausa *si* Ø took one Jju child [a nearby tribe]—my mother Ø is Jju.

   c. They *si* Ø took this one child, they *si* Ø brought it to Zango town [the Hausa enclave] when it was still small.

   d. They *si* Ø converted it, it *si* **kan** became a Hausa child.

   e. It *si* Ø lived there with the Hausa, it *si* Ø grew up.

   f. With respect to the thoughts that she had about the mother who bore her and her father, they (the parents) Ø were different.

   g. It did not Ø look like the Hausa were the ones who bore her.

   h. She *si* Ø grew up, she *si* Ø married, she *si* Ø said to her father that she was a Jju child, that they should take her to her own place, she would be able to ask how to find the place where her birth mother and father were.

   i. They *si* **kan** began asking to find the relatives whom she had.

   j. They *si* **kan** began to keep in touch with one another and Ø were friends with each other.

k. When they bore children, they Ø took their children, they Ø went out [from Zango] to see their [Jju] relatives, the relatives Ø did the same.

l. That is why we *si kan* knew each other, we *si kan* followed each other . . .

The significant developments in the account above as reflected by the occurrence of *kan* are: the captured child losing her identity and becoming Hausa (4d); her seeking after her true relatives (4i); the beginning of friendship with those relatives (4j); and the final development of knowing each other and developing friendship with respect to the narrator in particular (4l). The use of the developmental marker thus reflects the narrator's purpose, which was to explain her unusual activity of visiting Hausa people in a Hausa enclave. Those propositions lacking *kan* are not new developments, as far as the speaker is concerned.

It is interesting to note the frequency of the new developments in (4). The developmental marker can occur in consecutive propositions, if that is consistent with the author's purpose (4l). In contrast, it does not occur between (4d) and (4i), although a significant lapse of time has taken place.

Context is obviously vital for the interpretation of utterances. The hearer will try to interpret an utterance in a way that fits the context best. Particles such as *kan* (and *kin*) help to guide the hearer's optimum processing of the utterance. They place "constraints on relevance" (Blakemore 1987:122). *kan* guides the hearer to process the proposition in which it occurs as having relevance in its own right because it represents a new development in the storyline and neither contradicts nor strengthens the previous utterances.

1.2–1.6 The additive particle *kin*

These sections discuss the additive particle *kin*. First, examples are given of the typical discourse functions of *kin* in various contexts. Typically, *kin* links utterances that are closely associated in some way. It marks a natural response to a stimulus (intentional or unintentional), an atypical response to a stimulus which is nevertheless closely associated to the stimulus in a previous context, constituent parts of one main event, and conjoined dissimilar events which have been previously joined together in the discourse. Second, the basic pragmatic motivation for using *kin* is considered. *kin* is used to strengthen previous utterances in the light of other events in a story. Two other motivations for the use of *kin* are: to act as the specific lead-in to a series of resulting events in the storyline; and to disambiguate the relationship between two potentially confusing utterances. Finally, *kan* and *kin* occurring at peaks in the narrative are illustrated.

As noted above, *kan* indicates that an utterance has a developmental relationship with the previous utterances. Utterances can also be marked to indicate a close relationship with each other. No new development is introduced. Instead, an addition is made to the previous utterances. This type of marked relationship, then, can be thought of as nondevelopmental and is sometimes referred to as an "additive" relationship (Winer 1882:542). Levinsohn notes that such a conjunction "indicates a 'close affinity' between the utterances it links (because the events described are similar . . . or even the same)" (Levinsohn 1987:122).

1.2 *kin* and close affinity

kin adds a proposition to previous utterances. The propositions are typically not viewed as developmental because they do not represent events which are relevant in their own right. Rather, they are predictable responses to the previous utterance(s) and so have a natural affinity towards each other.

kin is used to link utterances in which the proposition marked by *kin* is the immediate and desired response to an intentional stimulus, typically a command or suggestion. A response to a command (5b) is marked by *kin,* as is a predictable response to a taunt in (6c). (The *kin* in (6b) is discussed in §1.4.)

(5) a. He *∅* said the woman should pass.

    b. The woman *si kin* passed.

(6) a. The woman *∅* stood on that side.

    b. She *∅ kin* began saying to the wizard, "It's your wife, it's your wife!"

    c. The wizard *si kin* twisted around, he *∅* returned.

kin is used to link utterances in which the utterance marked by *kin* is a predictable response to a nonintentional stimulus. This type of occurrence is by far the most frequent in the texts examined in this paper. In (7), the discovery of the trees provides the stimulus for eating the mangos (7b).

(7) a. They found the trees.

   b. They *kin* began to eat the mangos.

Examples (5)–(7) show *kin* functioning between propositions. In (8), *kin* marks a proposition as a response to a whole series of events that the narrator had been describing up to that point (more than thirty propositions). The immediate context (8a–b) consists of summary statements subsequent to those events. The topicalized 'there' in proposition (8c) is also characteristic of a larger unit.

(8) a. The soup Ø spilled over, the stirring spoon Ø burnt.

   b. Second, the meeting—if I would do another cooking of tuwo, I would have to cook another soup.

   c. There I *si kin* remembered a Tyap proverb,

   d. "If you put two irons on the fire, one will burn."

kin is used to link utterances in which the response utterance marked by *kin* has no obvious affinity with the stimulus, but which has been previously associated in a previous context. In (9), two events are mentioned in a stimulus-response relationship in (9a). The next mention of the two associated actions (9f) is marked by *kin*.[6] The 'cooking' and 'going out' are associated together four propositions before they occur again in conjunction with *kin*.

(9) a. Every time the wife COOKED food, the husband WENT OUT, he *si* called his friend to come eat with him.

   b. The wife Ø never wanted him to always be coming and eating food with her husband.

   c. The husband himself, he Ø did not stop (doing that).

   d. One day he *si* found money, he *si* went to the place where chickens were sold, he *si* bought two chickens.

---

[6]I am indebted to Stephen Levinsohn (p.c.) for drawing my attention to this example.

   e. He *si* gave (them) to his wife saying she should prepare them for
    him.

   f. The wife Ø was in the process of COOKING these two chickens, the
    husband *si kin* WENT OUT to get his friend to eat together ...

Sometimes *kin* is used to link utterances in which the utterance marked
by *kin* represents an event that is closely associated with the previous
event(s) in some way.[7] The events are typically constituent parts of a
macro-event or, as in (9), are dissimilar events which are nevertheless
closely associated together in the previous context. The pragmatic motivation for this association is discussed in §1.4.

In (10), the act of cooking (in Tyap culture) often involves putting
powder into the mixture. These two constituent parts of the act of cooking
are associated together in (10d).

(10) a. You Ø will see the water looking black.

   b. If you do not sieve the water, Ø throw the dregs away,

   c. you *si* cook (it),

   d. you *si kin* put things (powder) in there,

   e. when you eat it, it Ø will bring a stomachache.

In (11b), *kan* indicates that the storyteller views the woman's crossing of
the river as a new development in the storyline. *kin* in (11c) indicates that
the event concerned is perceived by the storyteller not as a new development and relevant in its own right, but as closely associated with (11b).
Example (11c) is part of the macro-event of 'getting to the other side of
the river' which includes crossing and passing through the river.

(11) a. The woman *si* Ø reached the river.

   b. The woman *si kan* crossed the river.

   c. She *si kin* passed through the river.

---

[7]This function is similar to one of the functions of the Koine Greek additive particle
te (see Levinsohn 1992:55).

In (12), two clusters of propositions represent the totality of the response to the question and are separate aspects of that response (looking-saying and turning to point). The second aspect of that response is marked by *kin* (12c).

(12) a.   We *si* asked him, "Where is this palm nut found?"

   b.   He *si* looked, he *si* said, "The tree that is very tall."

   c.   He *si kin* turned near there, he *si* saw, he *si* pointed . . .

1.3 *kin* and strengthening

The basic pragmatic motivation for associating two propositions closely together is so that the second can strengthen the first. When marking the second of two utterances, *kin* has the contextual effect of strengthening the previous utterance or the assumption behind it. For example, in (11b–c), proposition (11c) strengthens (11b) by describing the completion of the event begun in (11b). The presence of *kin* constrains the relevance of the two utterances by guiding the hearer to interpret (11c) as a support or confirmation of (11b).

As a particle which indicates relevance by strengthening the previous proposition, *kin* often interacts in interesting ways with negation. The occurrence of the negative in (13b) shows that, though (13a) and (13b) contrast semantically, *kin* indicates that (13b) really supports (13a). In particular, (13a) is strengthened by the negation of *kin* in (13b); in other words, the fact that sandy soil is good for yams is strengthened by saying the opposite about the other type of soil. The presence of *kin* in (13b) guides the hearer to interpret (13b) as strengthening (13a), rather than contrasting with it.

(13) a.   He Ø said the sandy soil usually is good for yams.

   b.   The one of mud, it usually Ø *kin* is not good for yams.

The next example, on the other hand, is a straightforward semantic contrast in which the default coordinating conjunction *si* (§2.1) links the two propositions. Because *kin* is absent in (14b), the hearer is not constrained to interpret (14b) as a confirmation of (14a).

(14) a. If you want to drink palm oil soup,

   b. you *si* find draw soup,

   c. you Ø drink Ø be satisfied.

kin can strengthen implicit assumptions behind previous propositions. In (15), *kin* strengthens some expectation that lies behind the proposition in (15d). The evidence (an immature tuber) seemed to have contradicted some expectation in the context, so the expectation needed to be reinforced, perhaps in order to avoid misunderstanding (see §1.4 on *kin* and disambiguation). In this case, two possible contextual implications are that matured yam tubers do not look like the one dug up, or that one does not normally uproot a yam tuber so early in the season and expect it to have matured.

(15) a. We *si* went to the yam farm.

   b. He *si* looked at one particular yam stem.

   c. He *si* dug, we *si* saw the yam.

   d. It Ø had already germinated, it Ø produced a tuber.

   e. The tuber, it Ø was **kin** not matured.

kin is also used to strengthen a previous contradiction. The implied assumption behind the question in (16a) is that ridges should be farmed high. Example (16c) states a contradiction of that implied assumption (i.e., the ridges which are used for transplanting should be wide). *kin* in (16d) strengthens the contradictory proposition (16c).

(16) a. They *si* asked why these (millet) ridges looked so wide.

   b. I *si* said to them,

   c. "We usually do not want to farm the transplanting ridges very high.

   d. That is why we usually **kin** farm them so they look wide.

   e. If not, we will have to throw away the millet because it will have grown too big."

1.4 Other pragmatic motivations for using *kin*

As noted in §1.3, a basic pragmatic motivation for using an additive particle like *kin* is to strengthen the previous utterance(s). This contextual effect is part of the basic function of the additive particle.

There are, however, other motivations for using *kin*. First, *kin* can indicate that the utterance concerned is a specific lead-in to other events. Second, *kin* helps disambiguate the two participants or items to which it relates.

kin as a specific lead-in to other events. Levinsohn notes that the Koine Greek additive particle *te* sometimes plays a highlighting role in acting as the "specific lead-in" event to subsequent events (1992:55). *kin* also seems to indicate that an utterance is a specific lead-in to other events. In particular, *kin* marks the final part of a collection of events as important for what follows.

In (17), the act of cooking involves boiling water and adding a powdered substance. The presence of *kin* marks (17d) as significant because it is specifically when you eat those things cooked in that spoiled water that you will get a stomachache. The constituent part of the main event of cooking is marked by *kin* because it serves as the specific lead-in to another event (i.e., getting a stomachache).

(17) a. You Ø will see the water looking black.

b. If you do not sieve the water, Ø throw the dregs away,

c. you *si* cook (it),

d. you *si kin* put things (powder) in there,

e. when you eat it, it Ø will bring a stomachache.

kin also marks the lead-in in (18e). Lifting a brick, which is part of the general activity of packing bricks, becomes the key event for the rest of the account. (Supplementary material is joined together to hasten the reading of the example.)

(18) a. There Ø was a certain man at the place where I was working, his name Ø was X. He Ø said that, from his point of view, he would be unable to pay money for an injection. Instead, he would use it to drink wine which would be better for him. As he himself was

near death (from old age), why should he take money and buy an injection with it?

b. I Ø said, "If you see death, will you stand around?"

c. He Ø said he would stand because he was unable to run away from death.

d. We Ø were in the process of packing bricks.

e. He *si kin* lifted up a brick.

f. I Ø said that a snake was under the brick.

g. He *si* dropped the brick, he *si* Ø ran away.

h. I Ø said, "I thought you said that if you saw death you would refuse to run? Why is it that you dropped the block and ran away ... You're Ø lying and you will pay for the brick!"

Example (19b) is the second part of the macro-event of 'getting across to the other side' (see discussion of (11)), and confirms the fact that the woman did indeed cross the river. The pragmatic motivation for marking (19b) with *kin* is probably that, seven propositions later, the wizard finds himself unable to cross the same river. Thus, *kin* marks (19b) as significant, albeit not a new development, because of what follows.

(19) a. The woman *si kan* crossed the river.

b. She *si kin* passed through the river.

c. (seven propositions later)
Everytime he Ø tried to cross the river, the water Ø overflowed.

d. Everytime he Ø tried to cross the river, the water Ø overflowed.

e. The wizard *si* became tired with that, he *si* Ø returned ...

kin and disambiguation. Blass notes that particles which guide the hearer into what is relevant in the communication occur particularly when there is a possibility of misinterpretation (1990:126–27). A proposition marked as independently relevant, as strengthening, or as contradicting guides the hearer in interpreting the relationship between two or more propositions. The speaker wants to ensure that the hearer overcomes the potential ambiguity and often adds a particle to assist him or her in doing so.

In (20), two participants perform the same action. The presence of *kin* in (20b) indicates that the proposition concerned is added to (20a); in other words, it cannot be the same action as (20a). This has the effect of underlining the fact that there are two wives in the story and it is necessary to keep them distinct.

(20) a. There the disliked wife *si* got up, she *si* went to the river.

    b. The beloved wife *si kin* got up, she *si* took her daughter ...

In (21), the presence of *kin* constrains the second, parallel proposition to be interpreted as strengthening the first, not as contrasting with it (see §1.3).

(21) a. He Ø said the sandy soil usually is good for yams.

    b. The one of mud, it usually Ø *kin* is not good for yams.

1.5 *kan* and *kin* at peak

Longacre makes the following comment: "The Peak of narrative discourse may also be marked by ... an increase in the incidence of particles found earlier in the discourse" (1976:38). Both *kan* and *kin* occur with greater frequency at peaks in the narrative. This is illustrated in passages (22) and (23), which are both taken from the same story. Whereas, in other parts of this narrative, *kan* and *kin* occur approximately once every twenty propositions, they are found in nearly every proposition in these passages.[8]

In (22), tension builds to a peak as the woman gets closer and closer to her husband, the wizard: Will he recognize her or not?

(22) a. She *si* caught the road, she Ø caught the road, she Ø went, she Ø went, she Ø went.

    b. She *si kan* took a look, she *si* saw the wizard.

    c. The wizard *si kan* saw her too.

---

[8]Other peak marking features include repetition of propositions, a shift to direct quotations, and unusually full reference to participants.

d. The wizard Ø said to himself, "What kind of woman is looking like this?"

e. She Ø walked, she Ø walked, she Ø walked.

f. The woman Ø was nearing him,

g. she *si kan* rubbed the ashes on her face.

h. She *si kan* put the chicken egg in her mouth.

i. She Ø reached him, she *si kan* bit down on the egg.

j. She *si* bit down in her mouth.

k. The egg *si kan* burst.

l. There he Ø said that she is not his wife, that she should pass.

m. The woman *si kin* passed.

n. The woman *si* reached the river, the woman *si kan* crossed the river.

o. She *si kin* passed through the river.

p. She *si* left the wizard on this side, the woman *si* was on that side.

q. The woman Ø stood on that side, she Ø *kin* began saying to the wizard, "It's your wife, it's your wife!"

r. The wizard *si kin* twisted around, he Ø returned.

s. Everytime he Ø tried to cross the river, the water Ø overflowed.

t. Everytime he Ø tried to cross the river, the water Ø overflowed.

u. The wizard *si* became tired with that, he *si* returned, he *sisi* left for home.

In this passage, each step the woman takes to disguise herself from her husband is marked by *kan* as a new development (22g, h, i, k). In contrast, once the peak is passed, with the husband telling his wife to pass (22l) and her crossing the river (22n) (another new development), the different events that subsequently occur, not being new developments, are introduced by *kin* (23o, q, r) (see discussion in §§1.2 and 1.3).

Preceding the passage in (23), the woman told her relatives that her husband is a wizard and they filled a hole with burning chaff to capture him. Tension builds to a peak as they seek to trick him into the hole.

(23) a. The wizard *si* woke up the next morning.

b. He *si* caught a road, he *si* came, he *si* went to the home of his wife.

c. He Ø came Ø was coming,—

d. the hole which they dug and into which they put the chaff and the fire—

e. they *si kin* took a mat,

f. they *sisi kin* spread it for him on the place,

g. they *si kan* spread it for him Ø saying he should come sit there.

h. The wizard, he *si kin* walked Ø walked Ø walked,

i. he Ø was sitting on the seat,

j. the mat *sii kan* fell into the hole with him.

k. The mat *si kan* fell into the hole with him.

l. The fire *si kin* burned him up there.

In this passage, which includes the overall peak of the story, the frequent interchange of *kan* and *kin* gives a staccato effect, as each new development is followed by the appropriate response. *kin* is used in connection with the final two parts of the preparations intended to catch the wizard (23e, f). Their invitation to him to sit is marked by *kan* as a new development (23g), whereas his response (spread out over several propositions (23h–i)) is marked by *kin* as consistent with the invitation. In (23j–k) the result of his sitting down is treated as a new development, while (23l) is

viewed as a second part to the macro-event of his destruction and serves
as the lead-in to the next section of the story, which deals with what the
relatives do with his ashes.

1.6 Concluding comments

This section has demonstrated that *kin* as an additive marker implies a
close affinity between the propositions it connects.[9] A common relationship
is stimulus-response. Such a stimulus-response effect conforms neatly with
the additive nature of *kin*. The response proposition is marked by *kin*. It
is not a new development *(kan)* because it is anticipated by the stimulus,
fulfills the conditions of the stimulus, or is closely associated with the
stimulus. The other relationship between propositions associated with *kin*
is that of constituent parts of a single event. This relationship also conforms to the additive nature of *kin,* as the events are joined together as
part of one event rather than one developing out of the other.

The contextual effect of the additive *kin* is to strengthen the preceding
utterance or assumption behind it. There are two other pragmatic motivations for using *kin* as well. *kin* often serves as the lead-in to a further series
of events and helps disambiguate potentially confusing relationships between propositions. The contextual effect of *kan,* on the other hand, does
not strengthen the previous utterance but, instead, indicates the relevance
of the utterance in its own right and, specifically, communicates that it
represents a development from the previous proposition(s). When two
propositions are joined by neither *kin* nor *kan,* their relationship is
deduced from the context, though in narrative they typically are in natural
sequence (see discussion of the conjunction *si* in §2.1).

2 Thematic prominence

In this section three mutually exclusive Tyap discourse particles are discussed with reference to the three kinds of prominence distinguished by
Callow (1974). Thematic prominence is "what I am talking about"; focus

---

[9]The discourse functions of *kin* and *kan* are supported by iconicity; that is, "a
selection of a point along the linguistic dimension determines and signals a certain
point along a non-linguistic dimension" (Haiman 1985:5). Haiman claims that, typically,
the high front vowel *i* is associated with proximity to the speaker. By analogy, *kin,*
which has a high front *i,* indicates that two propositions have close affinity with each
other. Low and open vowels, such as *a,* typically indicate distances farther away from
the speaker. This corresponds with the *a* of *kan* whose function is to indicate a new
development away from (though building on) the previous proposition.

prominence involves highlighting items of particular significance; emphasis prominence involves the speaker-hearer relationship in some way, for example, when the speaker feels strongly about a particular item or feels that an event is unexpected (1974:52). The Tyap discourse particles *si*, *sii*, and *sisi* are discussed, respectively, with reference to these types of prominence.

The default coordinating conjunction is *si*, which typically correlates with foreground events in narrative, in other words, those that have thematic prominence. The absence of *si* typically reflects the fact that the events concerned are preliminary to foreground events. *sii* is a temporal conjunction which preserves thematic continuity at points of action discontinuity in the discourse. Of relevance here is the fact that *sii* also indicates focus prominence on the events with which it occurs. The reduplicated form of *si* is *sisi*, which indicates that the speaker is emphasizing the event (e.g., as pivotal or otherwise important to keep in mind). All three particles are related phonologically and their phonological characteristics iconically reflect their discourse function.

The table in (24) illustrates the types of prominence which each conjunction indicates.

(24) Prominence

Thematic	Focus	Emphatic
si	*sii*	*sisi*

2.1 Thematic prominence

Thematic prominence as described above refers to that which the speaker is talking about, and occurs on the theme or event-line of a discourse, in contrast to background information which tends not to have such prominence (Callow 1974).

2.2–2.3 *si*

In the context of chronologically arranged material such as narratives and procedures, *si* is a coordinating conjunction which tends to imply temporal succession. As such, it tends to correlate with, but does not exclusively mark, prominent foreground events. These two uses of *si* are discussed in the next sections.

2.2 *si* as a coordinating conjunction

The default coordinating conjunction is *si*. Its primary use is to conjoin propositions, as shown in (25a, b). In this use, *si* indicates a relation of "coupling," where coupling refers to "a non-temporal underlying *and* relation" (Longacre 1985:241). Example (25c) is an instance in which the propositions coordinated by *si* may be interpreted as being in temporal succession.[10] It is in this way that *si* marks continuity in the discourse.

(25) a. *əbyiuk ənyiung yet   atsamyiə ənyiung si   yet   əjhyo*
          wife   one   was Chawai   one   and was Jju
          One wife was Chawai and one wife was Jju.

    b. *madaki byiə za   ə   si   byiə əbyit*
          Madaki has   tallness he and has   fatness
          Madaki is tall and fat.

    c. *əghyang ətuk bai   ənyuk-ba   si   nat   lyiai əbaan*
          another   day   came women-the and went selling milk
          One day came and the women went to sell the milk.

    d. *bə   si   tsot kura   bə   si   kai gu   ạwet*
          they and beat Hyena they and let   him go
          And they beat Hyena and let him go.

       kura   si   nat   ə   si   swan ə   tywei
          Hyena and went he and sat   he   crying
          And Hyena went and he sat down crying.

---

[10]Longacre states, "Succession is an underlying *and then* relation" (1985:244). While *si* is used to coordinate successive events in the discourse, it is *sii* which indicates the 'then' of a significant time lapse. Longacre's 'and then' relation could be ambiguous, as all of his examples could be interpreted as having a significant time lapse. In this discussion, *si* marks successive events and *sii* marks successive events with some time lapse between them.

2.3 *si* and foreground events

Passage (26) is an entire story which shows the correlation of *si* and foreground events.[11] The story is about a rat and an indigenous spice (in the form of a patty). Both the occurrence of *si* and its absence (∅) are marked before the verb. Quotations are indented. Implied information is supplied in parentheses. The occurrence of *sisi* as in (26q) is discussed in §2.9. *si* occurs in (26b, c, d, e, f, h, j, k, l, m, n, o, p, r). These are the main events.[12] The second occurrences of *si* in (26k) and (26l) do not imply sequential events in the story line, as the propositions concerned have not yet occurred. That is, 'he will go, he *si* [and] tell his mother' is in the future. However, the events are in succession with respect to each other and *si* serves to coordinate them.

(26) a. That Rat ∅ lived with Spice.

b. They *si* went plucking fruits.

c. That Rat *si* climbed up (the tree).

d. Rat *si* spoke to Spice ∅ saying, when he ∅ plucks an unripe fruit, Spice should eat it. If a ripe one, he ∅ should keep it for him (Rat).

e. Rat *si* was climbing down.

---

[11]It must be noted that the correlation, though a strong one, is a correlation only. *si* sometimes occurs (though rarely) in material not typically considered foreground (e.g., parenthetical comments). At times it can even occur with the imperfective aspect marker *bɔ*, as long as the event marked by *bɔ* is in sequence with the last. *bɔ* usually occurs without *si* when it is marking events which are the setting for other events at points of discontinuity and thus are not sequential with the preceding ones. This is in accordance with the prediction that imperfective aspect is used for background events (in this case, setting material). It could be, however, that the presence of *si* with parenthetical comments and the imperfective marker serves to foreground those typically background types of events (Levinsohn p.c.). In its extended function of indicating temporal succession, *si* might also be viewed as a type of narrative tense marker (see Longacre 1990). Thus *si* is not primarily a foreground event marker but correlates with sequential events in its coordinate function. The fact that *si* does not mark foreground events per se is consistent with the fact that most languages typically do not mark foreground events with a special marker.

[12]*si* occurs with speech events in (26d, f, h, k, l) but not in (26g, i), which are replies to the speech event initiated by *si*. Speech events sometimes occur with *si* and sometimes do not. Further investigation into speech events in Tyap discourse is yet to be done.

f. He *si* asked for his ripe fruits.

g. At that Spice Ø said it thought Rat was saying the unripe fruits were to be kept for him (Rat).

h. Rat *si* said, "If you Ø play with me, I'll Ø cut you to eat!"

i. At that Spice Ø said, "Ø Cut me then!"

j. Rat *si* cut Spice, he Ø ate.

k. Spice *si* began saying, he Ø will be going, he *si* tell his mother.

l. Rat *si* also began saying, he Ø will be going, he *si* tell his mother.

m. A fight *si kan* erupted between Rat's mother and Spice's mother.

n. Rat *si* also began a fight with Spice.

o. Rat's mother *si* beat Spice's mother to death.

p. Rat's mother *si* took the child Spice,

q. she *sisi* cooked gruel,

r. she *si* ate (it).

A comparison of the occurrences of *si* and its absence in the discourse supports the correlation of *si* and foreground events. First, *si* never occurs when a participant is first introduced at the beginning of a story, probably because there is nothing with which to conjoin at that point. Similarly, *si* never occurs with verbs in setting material such as topicalized time phrases and other points of departure, possibly due to the break in the flow of events, since the point of departure indicates a new beginning. Third, *si* typically does not occur with repetitive tail-head links. Fourth, *si* does not occur with simultaneous events or in serial verb constructions (e.g., He sat crying saying...). Fifth, *si* does not occur in a sequence of events which are of a preliminary, background nature.

Typically, *si* does not occur in events preliminary to the main events of the discourse even when they are in sequence. These preliminary events typically occur before the foreground events start up at the beginning of the story, though they can occur elsewhere as well (see (29)). Also, the preliminary events often describe habitual activities of which the foreground events are specific instances.

In (27), the preliminary events (27b–f) are characterized by the absence of *si*. When the corresponding foreground events take place, they occur with *si* in (27j, m, o, p). The sentence in (27a) has no *si* because it introduces the participant for the first time at the beginning of the story. The imperfective marker *bə* is marked in the utterance as well. The absence of *si* in (27j) after the initial *si* is indicative of a serial verb construction (see also (27k)).

(27) a. That Hare *bə* lived.

b. When Fulani women Ø went Ø sell milk,

c. he (Hare) Ø went in the hut.

d. He Ø opened the hut.

e. He Ø sat.

f. He Ø drank the milk.

g. That is how Hare Ø did.

h. He Ø drank the Fulani women's milk every day.

i. One day *bə* came,

j. the women *si* went Ø selling milk Ø leaving their husbands.

k. The husbands *si* hid Ø doing, they *si* see person who Ø walks Ø drinks their milk.

l. The small Hare *bə* coming this day,

m. he *si* opened the hut.

n. He *si* said, "These useless things have already left to sell milk!"

o. He *si* entered inside,

p. he *si* began Ø drinking.

In the next passage, (28a–j) represent the preliminary events and so do not occur with *si* even though they are sequential. The foreground events start in (28l). The presence of *si* in (28d) may indicate that the proposition is foregrounded. It does, however, occur in a subordinate proposition and links it with the other described preliminary events. It does not indicate that an actual event has taken place on the storyline. Note the correspondence between preliminary events (28e) and (28i) and foreground events (28p) and (28m), respectively.

(28) a. The pampered child only Ø sat Ø sat.

   b. The disliked child, he was Ø did all the work.

   c. The disliked child Ø lived quietly.

   d. Whenever the pampered child *si* did something,

   e. he Ø came, he Ø said it was the disliked child (who did it).

   f. They Ø caught him (the disliked child).

   g. They Ø beat him until he Ø cried.

   h. The chief Ø had a ram's skin that he lay on.

   i. The pampered child habitually Ø lay on it,

   j. when the chief Ø was not there.

   k. This day Ø came,

   l. the chief *si* went out.

   m. The pampered child *si* lay down on the ram's skin.

   n. He *si* urinated.

   o. Chief Ø *bə* returned.

   p. He (pampered child) *si* said, it Ø was the disliked child (who did it).

   q. Chief *si* said, "What will I Ø do with this stubborn child?"

In both (27) and (28), the preliminary events occur at the beginning of the story. Preliminary events can occur anywhere in a discourse, however. In the next passage, (29c–h) represent the preliminary events to (29i–l). In this example, the hare found that the man he was guarding had escaped and he now had to develop a stratagem to cover his mistake (so he cut himself to make it look like the man had done it). This section also may be leading up to a peak in the narrative.

(29) a. The man *si* ran away Ø left his thing (a flute).

b. He *si* left for home.

c. Hare Ø coming.

d. He Ø came.

e. He Ø *bə* found that the man Ø already ran away.

f. The rest (of the animals) Ø coming Ø saying, . . .

g. They Ø became quiet.

h. Hare Ø already had cried.

i. He *si* cried, he *si* cried.

j. He *si* dropped to the ground.

k. He *sisi* took thing (flute).

l. He *si bə* dragging on his head until blood Ø was seen . . .

2.4–2.6 *sii*

The particle *sii* is now discussed. First, the iconic relationship of *si* and *sii* is considered. Second, the typical function of *sii* as a conjunction that preserves continuity is illustrated with reference to three types of discourse contexts. Third, *sii* is shown to indicate that an event has focus prominence. *sii* and focus prominence are examined with reference to a concluding event in a series, to a delayed goal, and to Dik's (1981) selective focus.

2.4 The iconic relationship between *si* and *sii*

Lengthening is a productive phonological process in Tyap. It helps distinguish lexemes and also indicates grammatical tense distinctions (e.g., *nat* 'go', *naat* 'going'). The language also uses length to symbolize differences in discourse function.

The particle *sii* is a lengthened form of the coordinative conjunction *si*. Its primary meaning is 'then'. The relationship between *si* and *sii* and between their linguistic functions as 'and' and 'then' are iconic. The symbolic lengthening of *si* to *sii*[13] corresponds to the significant lapse of time in the linguistic dimension which *sii* indicates. That is, *si* (short) is noncommittal about a significant temporal lapse between two events. *sii* (long) indicates that a (greater) length of time has passed between the events. The length of the phonological unit in the linguistic dimension corresponds to the greater amount of time which has elapsed in the nonlinguistic one.

2.5 *sii* and preservation of coherence

The basic function of *sii* is to preserve coherence. When various action discontinuities occur in the discourse, *sii* can be used to maintain overall coherence: "It functions as a 'cohesive device' . . . indicating continuity of time between the parts that it links" (Levinsohn 1992:50). *sii*, in contrast with *si*, typically indicates that there has been a significant lapse of time between events. However, the function of *sii* is to maintain coherence despite the discontinuity. This lapse of time can be between successive events, between an intervening conversation and the resumption of the event line, and between a parenthetical comment and the event line. These are all points of discontinuity but *sii* is used to preserve the coherence. The above is not meant to be a classification, but rather examples of *sii* in different contexts.

It should be noted that *sii* occurs in a normal verb phrase position. It does not occur proposition initial. Levinsohn (1992:50) notes that 'then' in utterance-initial position can signal a discontinuity or point of departure. The Tyap word *əja* 'there, then', in contrast to *sii*, functions as this type of

---

[13]That *sii* is the lengthened form of *si* is not problematic when the entire phonology of the language is kept in perspective. Though all the other vowels can be lengthened, *i* cannot. It is also a phoneme with restricted occurrence. Finally, *i* and *i* are phonologically similar (i.e., high, close). Therefore, it is not strange that the lengthened form of *si* is *sii* and not *sii*. Indeed, it is possible that the *i* in *si* is really an *i* which is velarized in fast speech. Velarization as a productive process in the phonology is attested to in Jju, a closely related language to Tyap.

'then' utterance-initial introducer. The difference between *aja* and *sii* is reflected in the fact that the discontinuous pronoun *gu* 's/he' occurs after *aja*, whereas with *sii* the continuous pronoun *a* 's/he' occurs (C. Follingstadt 1993). *aja* indicates a discontinuity and reflects the nature of the break, whereas *sii* indicates a discontinuity but preserves coherence in spite of it. In one case, the author decides to indicate a point of departure; in another, s/he decides to note the discontinuity but desires to preserve coherence. This choice can be made regardless of the theoretical amount of time that has elapsed between events. The choice to start over or continue on from a potential discontinuity is up to the narrator.

In this way, *sii* acts in a way similar to what Levinsohn proposes for the Koine Greek conjunction *tóte* when he states that it "links narrative units that naturally cohere because of continuity of time and other factors, but between which there is some change or discontinuity, such as a partial change of cast or topic" (1992:52). (*sii*, however, does not occur sentence initially as noted previously.)

In (30), *sii* reflects a significant lapse of time in the events. The dialogue in (30) occurred between the author and a friend in the context of a car ride during which the friend's child vomited in the car. The child had been given a porridge called *akammu* about an hour or so before the event occurred. The use of *sii* indicates that a significant amount of time had passed with respect to the context and viewpoint of the one making the statement, but that the second event was not viewed as a new temporal point of departure.

(30) a. Why did she vomit?

    b. *n dyen ba' ka swuo akammu ka sii kwei*
        I know not she drank *akammu* she then vomited
        I do not know (exactly), she drank the *akammu* (some time ago)
        and then she vomited.

In (31), *sii* occurs in a relative proposition complex. The lapse of time between farming and uprooting/transplanting is a few months, yet the author chooses to view the stages of farming as continuous. (31b) continues directly after (31a).[14]

---

[14]The abbreviations used in the data are: FOC focus, IMPF imperfective, SUB subordinator.

(31) a. *si w*ent with them to the place of wide ridges where we usually
         farm our wide millet ridges,

   b. *zi sii bə   nga   zi chyim   əni*
       we then IMPF uproot we transplant SUB
       which then we uproot and transplant.

In another example of the basic use of *sii* (32), there is no contextual
indication of how much of a time lapse there was. The occurrence of *sii*
and the continuous pronoun *ə* indicate that the author perceives no
temporal discontinuity between the events.

(32) a. *əbyiuk wu nyiə ədidam   mə ədidam gu*
         wife   the did thoughts and thoughts her
         The wife was thinking and thinking,

   b. *ə   sii   nyiə kə n nat mə əbok*
       she then said if I go to wizard
       then she said, "If I go to the wizard ..."

sii also preserves coherence after a speech event when there is movement back to the foreground events. The occurrence of *sii* indicates that
there has been a lapse of time (viz., the speech event itself). In (33), the
narrator is relating how he taught someone to farm, and he digresses to
report some advice he gave to the prospective farmer. *sii* indicates movement from the reported speech back to the foreground events.

(33) a. *kə a   kwok nfang shansham ba'*
         if you pack stones well   not
         If you do not collect the stones into a pile well,

   b. *əghyang ətuk nə   na byiə ang əkhwu*
       another day they will have you death
       another day they will kill you (with work).

   c. *ə sii   doot khap   hu zi kap*
       he then began farming the we farmed
       Then he began farming, we farmed ...

sii is used also to preserve coherence after the interruption of a parenthetical comment. In (34), the foreground events (in this case, procedural
steps) are interrupted by a comment about how one knows if the harvest

was greater this year or last. After the comment, the procedure is continued. (34a) and (34c) represent the procedural steps, and (34b) represents the parenthetical comment.

(34) a. You will count the bundles.

b. If you got 30 bundles last year, and this year you got 40 bundles, you know that your harvest this year surpasses that of last year.

c. You *sii* pack those bundles...

2.6 *sii* and focus prominence

sii is also used to give focus prominence to certain events. First, *sii* can highlight the last in a series of events, even when the last event shows no apparent discontinuity with the preceding context. Second, *sii* can indicate that an obstacle to a desired state of events has been replaced by the event's fulfillment. Third, *sii* can indicate that a particular time is selected as opposed to other times; this usage would be a temporal analog to Dik's selective focus.

sii **and concluding events.** Levinsohn notes that one of the functions of 'then' is to highlight a concluding event to which a series of events has been building up, even if there is no apparent discontinuity involved (1992:52). The effect of this use of 'then' is to treat "the conclusion as though it were a separate narrative unit in order to highlight it." *sii* seems to function in a similar way at the climax of a story, as in the following excerpt. It marks the concluding event of the series, even though there does not appear to be any appreciable time lapse between the events.

(35) a. They *si kin* took a mat,

b. they *sisi kin* spread it for him over the place,

c. they *si kan* spread it for him Ø saying he should Ø come sit there.

d. The wizard he *si kin* walked Ø walked Ø walked,

e. he Ø was sitting on the seat,

f. the mat *sii kan* fell into the hole with him.

sii **and delayed goal.** Levinsohn notes another way in which 'then' is used: "Typically, conclusions introduced with *tóte* ['then'] attain the goal sought or predicted in earlier events ... Sometimes, realization of the goal which was sought or predicted is delayed by intervening speeches or events ... " (1992:52). In example (36), from a personal account narrative, the goal of getting the rats that had been killed is hindered until the obstacle (the snake in the rat hole) is removed.

(36) a. Soon the cobra Ø was feeling the medicine of the arrow catching it.

    b. It *si* turning, it *si* turning, it *si* tried, it *si* put *kpəu* (ideophone), it Ø go out.

    c. We *si* ran way Ø leaving the rats that we Ø had caught.

    d. We Ø were running away, we Ø said, "What shall we do?"

    e. God Ø gave fortune, the arrow Ø had poison.

    f. The poison Ø affected the cobra, it Ø was writhing around, it Ø was writhing around.

    g. We *si* went to find a stick,

    h. we *si* beat the cobra to death (with it).

    i. We *sii* went, we *si* gathered the rats that we Ø killed.

In (36), the blocking circumstance is overcome and the original goal, though delayed, is achieved. It is the 'delayed goal' proposition that is marked by *sii* in the discourse.

sii **and selective focus.** According to Dik (1981:63), selective focus occurs when "the Focus information selects one item from among a presupposed set of possible values ... it explicitly or implicitly excludes the other presupposed value(s) as the correct value for x." *sii* can be used in a way analogous to selective focus. One time is selected to the exclusion of other possible times. In (37) two possible options are offered. One option is to take crops and eat them at home. The other option is to take crops and eat them at the farm site. *sii* marks the selection of the latter option to the exclusion of the former.[15] Example (37c) could be paraphrased: '... and you roast it on the farm and THEN you eat (as opposed to eating it after taking it home), that is not stealing' (where THEN indicates primary stress).

(37) a. If you take something, you *si* bring it home (to eat), that is stealing,

b. but if you dig someone's things like coco yam, sweet potato, or yam,

c. you *si* roast it on the farm, you *sii* eat, that one is not stealing.

2.7–2.9 *sisi*

The Tyap particle *sisi* is now considered. First, the iconic relationship of *si* and *sisi* is discussed. Second, examples of *sisi* in context are given. Finally, *sisi* is related specifically to the author's purpose external to the story itself (versus set formulaic traditional story morals).

sisi indicates that an event is emphasized by the author in some way. Often the event is pivotal. Events which are pivotal typically are those involving participant interaction and stratagems. *sisi* also occurs near the end of a discourse. In this position it often indicates a summary of the author's purpose or main point of the story.

2.7 The iconic relationship of *si* and *sisi*

The particle *sisi* is a reduplicated form of the default coordinative conjunction *si*. The basic meaning of *sisi* is 'and!' where the exclamation point indicates author emphasis. It serves to indicate that the event with which it occurs has emphatic prominence; in other words, it reflects the speaker's strong feelings about the event. Specifically, it indicates that the event is pivotal or otherwise important in the whole discourse.

It is appropriate that *sisi* as an emphasis marker should be a reduplicated form of *si*. Reduplication is another productive phonological process in the grammar and always indicates intensity. For example, there is no adverb in Tyap for the intensifier 'very'. Instead, to emphasize an adjective, the stem is reduplicated to mean 'very x' (e.g., *byeibyɔk* 'watery', *byeibyɔk ɔbyɔk* 'very watery'). In fact, most adjectives constitute reduplicated forms even without intensification (e.g., *jun-jung* 'long', *gɔn-gɔng* 'tall'). The fact

---

[15]See Levinsohn (1992:50) for a similar example of a 'selective' use of the Koine Greek conjunction *tóte*.

that *si* is emphasized by the iconic process of reduplication is consistent with other processes in the language but, like *sii*, in this case the sound symbolism applies to particles with a discourse function.

2.8 *sisi* in context

sisi can occur anywhere in a discourse. Sometimes it is found near the beginning of a story, for instance, when key participants are brought together. At other times it can occur at the end, for example, marking a summary of the purpose of the narrative (as distinct from the formulaic moral of the story). It also can occur elsewhere in the story. It can but does not exclusively occur as the last event in a series of propositions marked by *si* (i.e., it can be followed by a proposition marked by *si*).

Since *sisi* is a particle indicating author emphasis, it occurs in a wide variety of contexts with different contextual effects.[16] Again, the following discussion is not meant as a classification of *sisi*, but rather to give some idea of the uses of this particle. Of course, the types of events that a speaker can emphasize are as varied as human experience. The following examples illustrate the occurrence of *sisi* to emphasize an event.[17] The presence of *si*, *sisi*, and *sii* and the absence of all of them (∅) are indicated in the text.

The most common use of *sisi* is to indicate that the emphasized event is pivotal to the plot of the discourse in some way. Pivotal events are those that change the direction of the story or set other events in motion (see footnote 18). In the following passage, the pivotal event (38b) is the accidental shooting of the dog.

(38) a.   One of us who ∅ had a bow, ∅ seeing the hare, he *si* shot at the hare.

     b.   Before the arrow hit the hare, it *sisi* hit the dog before the hare.

---

[16]*sisi* probably is a type of particle which "... is used in order to minimise processing effort by guiding the hearer to the most important information, i.e., information which is crucial to the main intended contextual effects. Such expressions should naturally arise in a framework where the speaker is constantly anxious to spare the hearer processing effort, and thus increase his willingness to go on listening" (Blass 1990:83).

[17]There are various ways to describe certain types of emphasized utterances. Terms used include "occasion" (Beekman, Callow, and Kopesec 1981:135), "inciting moment" (Longacre 1976:214f), "trigger" (Forster 1977:10), "complication" (Grimes 1975:241f), and "new initiative" (Levinsohn 1992:135). In this article, the term 'pivotal event' is used to include the idea of both "occasion" and "complication." It should be noted that particular examples of *sisi* in context are influenced by a variety of factors in the discourse; in other words, more than the particular factor cited in the text may influence the choice of *sisi*.

   c.   The dog *si* fell down.

   d.   We Ø caught the dog, we *si* pulled the arrow to remove it.

   e.   The arrow *si* remained inside.

   f.   The reason is, the barbs (of the arrow).

   g.   We *si* held the dog.

   h.   We *si* brought it home.

In (39), the wizard's healing of the headwife's boy in (39g) is the pivotal event that arouses the second wife's jealousy to such an extent that she causes her own child to fall just so that the wizard can heal him and make him better than before.

(39) a.   The child of the headwife *si* climbed the tree.

   b.   It *si* went to the top up there.

   c.   It *si* reached up for a dry branch.

   d.   It (the branch) *si* broke.

   e.   The small child *si* coming Ø fell.

   f.   She (headwife) *si* took it, she Ø went to the wizard.

   g.   The wizard *sisi* fixed it, it *si* became more beautiful than before.

   h.   The second wife *si* felt angry about how the headwife's child increased in beauty.

   i.   Morning Ø came, she *si* took her child.

   j.   She *si* forced it, it *si* climbed up . . .

In (40), the pivotal event is the donkey's stratagem (40e) to lie down so that eventually the hare would do the same thing, giving the donkey an opportunity to kick the hare. Although *sisi* occurs with the verb 'went', it effectively marks the whole proposition 'he Ø lay down' as the equivalent of an infinitival construction (i.e., 'Donkey went out to lie down').

(40) a. That hare lived, he *si* got up, he *si* said to the donkey that he Ø is better than the donkey.

   b. Donkey Ø said, "Nonsense, hare, I am better than you!"

   c. He (hare) *si* said, "Let's go and fight!"

   d. They *si* got up.

   e. Donkey *sisi* went out, he Ø lie down.

   f. Hare *si* jumped, he Ø stood on his head.

   g. When he Ø jumped, he Ø went up, he Ø again returned Ø fell back on his head.

   h. He *si* became tired.

   i. Donkey Ø said, "Are you tired?"

   j. To that hare Ø said, "Yes!"

   k. Donkey *si* said that hare should Ø lie down.

   l. Hare *si* went,

   m. hare *si* lay down.

   n. Donkey *si* got up,

   o. it *si* threw out a leg.

   p. The leg *si* kicked hare around (his body).

   q. Hare *si* cried out.

   r. He *si* put vooooooou (ideophone), he Ø fell into the bush.

   s. That is why hare Ø runs Ø goes into the bush.

There are many other examples from other traditional stories in which *sisi* marks the pivotal event. In one, the whole plot revolves around the question of which participant is really the chief, the present chief or a boy who is called 'chief'. *sisi* marks two propositions in which the chief's assistant hears the boy being called 'chief'. The hearing of the name sets two cycles of events in motion, the last of which includes the chief's attempt to kill the boy and his own demise. The formulaic closing moral of the story is the question, 'Now among the two, which one was the real "chief"?'

sisi often marks pivotal events which are emphasized particularly with respect to participant introductions and exits (from the discourse stage). In (41), the protagonist and antagonist are the hunter and snake, respectively. The presence of the stone is also a type of complication. Its removal and subsequent replacement forms the crux of the story.

(41) a. Hunter Ø lived.

    b. He *si* got up Ø going hunting one day.

    c. He *sisi* met with snake as it was lying down with a stone pressing it.

In (42), *sisi* in (42c) marks the proposition indicating a participant exit while (42e) introduces participants. Note also the occurrences of *kan* which indicate that the author sees (42e) and (42g–h) as new developments of the storyline (see §2.9 for the difference between *sisi* and *kan)*.

(42) a. The wizard *si* became tired with that,

    b. he *si* returned,

    c. he *sisi* left for home.

    d. The woman *si* also left, she Ø went.

    e. She *sisi kan* told her people at home.

    f. After she Ø told her people at home,

    g. those of home, they *si kan* got up,

    h. they *si kan* dug a hole . . .

Sometimes the emphasized pivotal event can specifically indicate the fulfillment of a major goal of one of the participants. In (43) (a personal account), the expressed desire of the narrator to see his relatives occurs approximately seventy-five propositions before he finally sees them. Before that goal is accomplished, the narrator faced a lack of transport, a car breakdown, an absent relative with whom he wanted to travel, and a failure to find his wife at the hospital. When he achieves the goal of seeing his relatives (43d), the proposition is marked with *sisi*. The reason *sisi* occurs here and not *sii*, which typically marks an event which fulfills a delayed goal, is that *sisi* indicates the event is pivotal to the rest of the narrative, whereas *sii* would only preserve coherence.

(43) a.   On Saturday I *si* left here, I *si* went to Zonkuwa, I *si* wanted to find a taxi to take me to Kaduna. I ∅ wanted when at Kaduna to pass to Zaria, I ∅ see my family who was there ∅ buying medicine (because the wife was ill).

    [Seventy-five propositions later]
  b.   I *si* entered a taxi.

  c.   I *si* went to the house of my brother-in-law.

  d.   I *sisi* found them at the time my child was napping.

  e.   I *si* felt very happy to see them . . .

2.9 *sisi* and the author's purpose

In all the examples so far, *sisi* has occurred at the beginning or middle of stories. When it occurs at the end of a story, it is emphasized not so much because it is a pivotal event with respect to those that follow, but because it is closely related to the overall purpose of the speaker in giving the story or account.[18] It has a summary function.

In (44), *sisi* emphasizes the next to last proposition of the story (44c). The reason for the emphasis is because one of the purposes of the story is to give a cultural explanation of how it came about that *Ǝtyap* women cook the particular gruel *ǝkǝti* with the particular spice mentioned in (44a–b).

---

[18]This is in contrast to *kan* which, though reflecting the author's purpose in signalling a thematic development, does not necessarily occur with emphasized events.

(44) a. Rat's mother *si* beat Spice's mother to death.

   b. Rat's mother *si* took the child Spice,

   c. she *sisi* cooked gruel,

   d. she *si* ate (it).

Sometimes the purpose for relating a narrative comes external to the narrative itself, and this external purpose can be reflected in the use of a proposition marked by *sisi*. For example, the author requested his language assistant to bring to language learning sessions various short stories. It was stressed that the stories should be humorous. In most of those texts, *sisi* occurs with the proposition marking the laughter of the participants in the story.

The humor in the following story comes from the fact that one man was boasting that he was not afraid to die, but when the narrator (the language assistant) said there was a deadly snake underneath one of the bricks he was lifting, the man ran away very quickly!

(45) a. I Ø said, "...You will pay for the brick!" (which the man had broken while running away from the snake).

   b. He Ø said that I was the cause of the destruction of the brick.

   c. I Ø said, "I wanted to test you, I Ø see whether, if you Ø really looked at death, you Ø would stand!"

   d. The people *sisi* started laughing.

It is interesting to note that, in long stretches of discourse, the propositions marked by *sisi* can give a type of summary of highlighted activities as far as the narrator is concerned. In one personal account which lasts some fifteen minutes on tape, the propositions in (46) were marked by *sisi*.

(46) a. I *sisi* showed them how we plant yams . . .

   b. I *sisi* showed them the ridges which had fertilizer and the ones that did not . . .

   c. We *sisi* saw a bee hive . . .

   d. We *sisi* entered his house . . .

Since the author of this article was one of the people being given the tour described in (46), the significance of the marked events was clear. This is especially so since there were many more things shown to the author during that time that were not marked by *sisi*. *sisi* indicates the events which the language helper thought pivotal or otherwise important. In (46a), the language assistant actually climbed on top of some huge yam heaps to illustrate how yams were planted. In (46b), he showed us the effect of the lack of fertilizer in the context of his own complaints about the high price of it. In (46c), my wife and I were asking many questions about the bee hive and the nature of beekeeping. In (46d), there was emotional significance in the act of giving and receiving hospitality.

3 Conclusion

This paper has shown that the concepts of thematic development and prominence contribute to a better understanding of various Tyap discourse features. The preverbal particle *kan* indicates that the author perceives a new development in the storyline. It has the contextual effect of being independently relevant with respect to the previous utterances. *kin*, on the other hand, indicates a close relationship between the utterances it links and adds to previous utterances, rather than indicating development from them. *kin* has the contextual effect of strengthening the previous utterances. *si, sii,* and *sisi* are conjunctions whose phonological relationship reflects differences in discourse function. *si* correlates with thematically prominent foreground events. *sii* can be used to indicate focus prominence on a particular event. *sisi* indicates that the author is emphasizing an event with respect to the speaker-hearer axis of communication.

References

Beekman, John, John Callow, and Michael Kopesec. 1981. The semantic structure of written communication. Dallas: Summer Institute of Linguistics.

Blakemore, Diane. 1987. Semantic constraints on relevance. Oxford: Basil Blackwell.

Blass, Regina. 1990. Relevance relations in discourse: A study with special reference to Sisaala. Cambridge: Cambridge University Press.

Callow, Kathleen. 1974. Discourse considerations in translating the Word of God. Grand Rapids: Zondervan.

Dik, Simon. 1981. On the typology of focus phenomena. In T. Hoekstra, H. van der Hulst, and M. Moortgat (eds.), Perspectives on functional grammar. Dordrecht: Foris Publications.

Follingstad, A. Joy. 1991. Aspects of Tyap syntax. M.A. thesis. University of Texas at Arlington.

Follingstad, Carl. 1991. Preliminary analysis of Tyap discourse particles. ms.

————. 1993. Tyap participant reference. ms.

Forster, Keith. 1977. The narrative folklore discourse in Border Cuna. In Robert E. Longacre and Frances Woods (eds.), Discourse grammar: Studies in indigenous languages of Colombia, Panama, and Ecuador 2, 1–23. Dallas: Summer Institute of Linguistics.

Gerhardt, Ludwig. 1989. Kainji and Platoid. In John T. Bendor-Samuel and Rhonda L. Hartell (eds.), The Niger-Congo languages: A classification and description of Africa's largest language family, 359–76. Lanham, MD: University Press of America.

Givón, Talmy, ed. 1983. Topic continuity in discourse. Philadelphia: Benjamins.

Grimes, Joseph E. 1975. The thread of discourse. The Hague: Mouton.

Haiman, John. 1985. Natural syntax. Cambridge: Cambridge University Press.

Haruna, D., Carl Follingstad, and A. Joy Follingstad. 1990. Learn to read and write Tyap. Jos: Nigeria Bible Translation Trust.

Levinsohn, Stephen H. 1987. Textual connections in Acts. Atlanta: Scholars Press.

————. 1992. Discourse features of New Testament Greek. Dallas: Summer Institute of Linguistics.

Longacre, Robert E. 1976. An anatomy of speech notions. Lisse: Peter de Ridder Press.

————. 1985. Sentences as combinations of clauses. In Timothy Shopen (ed.), Language typology and syntactic description 2, 235–86. Cambridge: Cambridge University Press.

————. 1990. Storyline concerns and word order typology in East and West Africa. Studies in African Linguistics, supplement 10. Los Angeles: University of California.

Winer, Gerald B. 1882. A treatise on the grammar of New Testament Greek. Edinburgh: T. and T. Clark.

Prominence in Bafut:
Syntactic and Pragmatic Devices

Joseph Ngwa Mfonyam

Abstract

Background information in Bafut narratives is marked by the presence of tense or aspect markers, a 'be' verb, indirect reported speech, and the insertion of a particle *aa* after repeated information. Material that follows *aa* is highlighted. Successive steps in the development of an author's purpose are marked by the verbal auxiliary *tigə,* while *kî* adds distinctive information when it does not constitute a new development. Highlighting of participants is achieved in direct reported speech by the use of a first-person singular pronoun, rather than a logophoric pronoun, and by the omission of the definite article, in connection with proper names. Devices to portray emphasis include phonological features, intensifiers, the pronoun *yi,* emphatic demonstratives and pronouns, and repetition.

Résumé

Dans les textes narratifs en bafut, les informations de second plan peuvent être signalées par la présence d'un marqueur de temps ou d'aspect, d'une copule ou d'un discours indirect, et/ou par l'insertion d'une particule *aa* après des informations qui sont répétées. Ce qui suit *aa* est mis en relief. Les étapes successives dans le développement de l'objectif d'un auteur sont marquées par

191

l'auxiliaire verbal *tigə* ; *kî,* pour sa part, s'il ne correspond pas à un nouvel
événement, ajoute des informations distinctives. Dans le discours direct, les
participants sont mis en relief par l'emploi du pronom exprimant la première
personne du singulier, plutôt que par l'utilisation d'un pronom logophorique,
ainsi que par l'omission de l'article défini se rapportant aux noms propres. Au
nombre des marqueurs de l'emphase, on trouve les caractéristiques
phonologiques, les intensifiants, le pronom *yi,* les démonstratifs et les pronoms
d'emphase et, enfin, la répétition.

This paper[1] describes some of the devices used to give prominence to
important information in narrative texts in Bafut.[2] Prominence is divided
by Callow (1974:53) into three categories: thematic significance, focus, and
emphasis. These terms are used in this paper in the sense given them by
Callow. Relevance Theory has also been used (Sperber and Wilson 1986)
to exemplify the "contextual implications" (Blass 1990:2) of a number of
verbal auxiliaries in Bafut narrative texts. The concept of a "developmental
marker" (Levinsohn 1992:32–37) has been used to show how one of them,
tigə, brings out the purpose of the author in narrating a story.

1 Thematic prominence

Thematic prominence, as defined by Callow, concerns the prominence
given to the information that constitutes the theme-line of a discourse.
Since such information is in contrast with material which is not so important, however, we must, by implication, deal also with nonthematic
material, which is, in essence, background information.

The sentences of a Bafut narrative are not all of equal importance with
regard to the author's purpose. Typically, theme-line events are unmarked
for prominence. Some of the sentences give background information while
others may be highlighted because they are important in view of the role
they play in accomplishing the purpose of the author.

---

[1]This paper was produced during a discourse workshop in Yaoundé, Cameroon,
directed by Stephen H. Levinsohn in the first quarter of 1993. The author is truly
thankful for all the help received from Dr. Levinsohn, both in the analysis of texts and
in the writing of this paper. Above all, the author is grateful to God for all the wisdom
and insights He has given for the work.

[2]Bafut is a Grassfields Bantu language of the Benue-Congo group, spoken in the
North-West Province of Cameroon by about 80,000 people (Mfonyam 1989:23–27).

1.1 Backgrounding

Background information in narrative includes nonevents and secondary events. Nonevents include the settings of the story, explanations and evaluations of the author, and collateral and performative information (Grimes 1975:55–70).

Background information may be distributed throughout a narrative. Although the sentences that give the overall setting for a narrative typically precede the body of the narrative, the settings normally change as the story progresses, with the result that both background and foreground information occur in the body of the text. Since the body of the text generally is unmarked for prominence, it is important to determine how to recognize background and foreground information.

In the Bafut texts so far studied, certain information is clearly marked for background. Thus, in narrative texts, the presence of past-tense markers such as P3³ *(lɛ)* and P0 *(mɔ̂)*, of aspect markers such as perfect *(lɛɛ̂)* and imperfective *(sì, nî)*, and of a 'be' verb *(bə)*, all signal that the information concerned is of a background nature. (See Longacre (1990:109) on the correlation of aspect markers with backgrounding in some languages.)

Background information is illustrated in (1)–(4), which establish settings for the story of Paa Yacob. The first sentence begins the story; the others are sentences (36)–(38) of the extract which appears in the appendix.

(1)   *à lɛ m-bə noò yî mɔʔɔ*
       3s P3 SS-be time PFX one
       (It was) some time ago . . .

(2)   *à sìgɔ̀   mɔ̂ ǹ-zi   aa*
       3s come^down P0 SS-come ANA
       (It was) when he came down . . .

---

³The writing system adopted for the examples of this paper is based on the phonological description found in Mfonyam (1989:31–47). The abbreviations used in the paper are: ADD additive *(kî)*, ADV adverb, ANA anaphoric *(aa)*, C noun class, DEM demonstrative, DM developmental marker *(tìgɔ̀)*, EMP emphasis, IMPF imperfective, LOC locative, LOG logophoric pronoun, PERF perfect, PFX prefix, P plural, POSS possessive pronoun, PREP preposition, P0 immediate past tense, P3 remote past tense, REL relative pronoun, RFX reflexive pronoun *(yi)*, S singular, SS same subject marker, 1, 2, 3 first-, second-, third-person.

(3) *mûmbâŋnə̀ yìi mə à lɛ sɨ   kwɛtə nî   yiʔi ɨkûm yi ɨ*
     boy   REL REL 3s P3 IMPF help IMPF 1p   name his C7

     bə joshua
     be Joshua
     A boy who was helping us, his name was Joshua.

(4) *à lɛ̀ɛ̂   m̀-bə a   njwi yì mɔ́ʔɔ a   noò ŋkwêfɔ̂*
     3s PERF SS-be PREP day PFX one   PREP time evening
     One day, in the evening...

If information is anaphoric in Bafut, it will usually be backgrounded. This
is illustrated in (5), taken from the story 'Soonjoo and Philip'.

(5) a. *à lɛ n-tswe nɨ   bàŋgyê   bi   bi tarə̀*
       3s P3 SS-have with PL^woman POSS PFX three
       He had three wives.

   b. *à tswè mə̂ nɨ   bàŋgyê   bi   bya bi tarə (l)aa*
      3s have P0 with PL^woman POSS DEM PFX three   ANA
      As he had his three wives,

   c. *ŋù   yì mɔ́ʔɔ a kɨ̂ ǹ-tswe ghu*
      person PFX one 3s also SS-sit there
      there was another person,

   d. *ɨkŭm yì   ɨ   bə philibo ŋ̀gwà*
      name POSS C7 be Philip Ngwa
      whose name was Philip Ngwa.

   e. *a ghɛ̀ɛ̂ ǹ-saʔa   ŋgwɛ philibo wâ*
      3s go   SS-seize wife Philip DEM
      He went and seized the wife of Philip.

   f. *à sà̀ʔà mə ŋgwɛ philibo wa   aa*
      3s seize P0 wife Philip DEM ANA
      When he seized the wife of Philip,

   g. *philibo wa   a ghaà*
      Philip DEM 3s speak
      Philip protested;

In clauses (5b) and (5f), the particle *aa* separates the background information which has been repeated from the rest of the sentence. The effect of this repetition is to highlight what follows because of its importance for the story. Thus, the clauses following (5b) introduce the second protagonist, without whom there would be no story. Similarly, the clause following (5f) indicates that the second protagonist protested; without this protest, there would have been no conflict. The presence of *aa* thus marks the boundary between the preceding background information, which is of an anaphoric nature, and the following highlighted information. More will be said about the sentences in (5) in connection with progression along the theme line in §1.2.

Another means by which background information is marked in Bafut is by indirect reported speech. In Babungo, a neighboring language, "3rd person pronouns are used for both the speaker and the person addressed" (Schaub 1985:2). Bafut does this also. However, in direct reported speech, second-person pronouns are used to refer to the addressee.

The contrast between indirect and direct speech in Bafut correlates with their functions as conveyors of background and foreground information, respectively. At the beginning of the story of Paa Yacob, for instance, the proposal in (6) (appendix (38b)) is in indirect speech.

(6)   *a swoŋ mə à lɔgə yi   bo   yu ghantə tâ   yu   yə*
       3s say   that 3s take him with LOG visit   that LOG see

       idigə   ajàŋ mə yaoundɔ̀ a kərə
       PL^place how that Yaoundé C1 look
       He said that he should take him out so that they could go out so that he could see what Yaoundé looked like.

In other stories and folktales studied, indirect speech is used for habitual acts, descriptions, and comments, all these being of a background nature.

1.2 Progression along the theme line

Background material sets the scene for the foreground events or theme line of a narrative. The theme line, or "time line," as Callow (1974:52) calls it, extends throughout a narrative.

Thematic information is characterized by the absence of the tense and aspect markers described in §1.1. Each new sentence which lacks a tense or aspect marker presents the next event on the theme line.

In (5), for instance, two clauses lacked tense-aspect markers. The first is (5e) ('He went and seized the wife of Philip'). The next, following the anaphoric background information of (5f), is (5g) ('Philip protested'), which is highlighted. These clauses describe the first foreground events of the story, and the theme line may be said to progress from the event of (5e) to that of (5g).

1.3–1.4 Thematic development

Levinsohn (1992:32), talking about the Greek developmental conjunction *dɛ*, says that this particle "is employed when the information associated with it is considered to develop from what preceded it." Levinsohn goes on to say that development relates to the purpose of the story, and that the marker indicates a new development in the story from the author's point of view.

Levinsohn's concept of development describes how the presence in Bafut of the verbal auxiliary *tigə* reflects the author's purpose in narrating a story. *tigə*, usually translated as 'then', marks new developments. The additive auxiliary *kî*, translated as 'also', is used to add events to other information within a developmental unit.

The extract for 'Paa Yacob' in the appendix will be used to illustrate how these auxiliaries are distributed.

1.3 The developmental marker *tigə*

The story of 'Paa Yacob' starts with an introduction of four sentences describing where the author lived and how Paa Yacob, an elderly civil servant, came to stay with them to settle some business in Yaoundé. A second protagonist, Joshua, is also introduced to the story in these sentences. *tigə* is not used in the introduction.

Although Joshua is one of the main protagonists in the story, *tigə* is never used in connection with actions that he performs. Rather, the author orients the story around Paa Yacob and the exclusive 'we' which includes herself. The story generally develops only as 'we' perform actions or as Paa Yacob performs actions that affect 'us'.

Thus, *tigə* first occurs in appendix (37a), in connection with the first action performed by 'us'. Paa Yacob comes to stay with 'us', but cannot stay in the family house because the house has only two bedrooms, with the result shown in (7).

(7)   *bǐʔì tìgà ǹ-lìgà   ìkuu wa   nda   mà mu wa   a lɛ sɨ*
      1p   DM SS-put^up bed DEM house REL boy DEM 3s P3 IMPF

      tswe ghu
      sit   there
      We then put up a bed in the house where the boy was living ...

The second significant development follows immediately (appendix (37b)).

(8)   *bo   yu   tìgà ǹ-lɛ   ghu*
      with him DM SS-stay^night there
      and both of them (were sleeping) there.

This sentence is marked with *tìgà* because it is the fact that they share the same room that prompts Paa Yacob to invite Joshua to go out with him (appendix (38b)).

Other developments in the story are marked by *tìgà*; they are listed in (9).

(9)   (39d) Paa Yacob and Joshua are drinking at the night club; Paa Yacob refuses to go home with Joshua and is locked out.

      (45b) Paa Yacob finally finds his way back to 'our' house.

      (47d)–(50) Paa Yacob comes back home annoyed and is banging at Joshua's door, which is just behind 'our' house.

      (53) Paa Yacob is scolding in 'our' hearing.

      (57b) 'We' are awakened and have to listen to Paa Yacob as he performs all these disgraceful acts.

      (59), (60) Paa Yacob stands there saying nothing because he is ashamed of his bad bahavior.

      (61) 'We' teach Paa Yacob a lesson in good behavior—"We plead with you, never do that kind of thing again"—which Paa Yacob docilely accepts.

      (63) (a final series of *tìgà*) Paa Yacob stays and finishes his business, then goes back home to the village.

The presence of *tigə* reveals the purpose of the author. The information marked by *tigə*, on the one hand, shows how 'we' behaved properly by extending hospitality to Paa Yacob and being concerned with this safety. On the other hand, it shows how Paa Yacob behaved badly in ways that abused 'our' hospitality. By means of *tigə*, the author succeeds in contrasting 'our' behavior with Paa Yacob's.

Finally, if an event which is repeated represents a new development and goes on and on, the whole verb phrase is repeated, including *tigə*, and not just the main verb. This is illustrated in (10).

(10)   *n-tigə ŋ-ghaantə n-tigə ŋ-ghaantə*
       SS-DM SS-scold   SS-DM SS-scold
       He then was scolding and scolding.

For further examples, see appendix (47d) and (49), which refer to an initial act of knocking which is then repeated and goes on and on. If just the verb had been repeated *(n-tigə ŋ-ghaantə ŋ-ghaantə)*, this would have given the meaning, 'he really scolded' (see appendix (53)).

1.4 The additive auxiliary *kî*

The additive *kî* is mutually exclusive with *tigə* and is used to associate information together within a developmental unit. In the texts examined for this paper, this information always involves a different subject. Three contexts in which *kî* is used are now described.

First, *kî* occurs in (11), where its function is to add a second participant to an existing scene (appendix (35a)).

(11)   *bìʔì kî   ǹ-tswe a   nda   nì   mûmbâŋnɔ̀ yìi   mɔ   à lɛ*
       we   ADD SS-have PREP house with boy   REL REL 3s P3

       sì   kwɛtə nî   yiʔi
       IMPF help   IMPF 1p
       We also had a boy who was helping us in our house.

kî is used in a similar situation in the story of 'Soonjoo and Philip', as shown in (12).

(12)   He (Soonjoo) had two wives. Another man *kî* was there called Philip.

kî is thus used in connection with the introduction of additional participants whose actions are significant in the story.

Second, *kî* occurs in the following sentences from the appendix.

(13)   (40) Joshua tells the elderly man, 'Paa, let's go!' (41a) He *kî* stayed.

(50) Paa Yacob is banging at Joshua's door. (51a) Joshua *kî* slept.

(53) Paa Yacob is scolding. (54) Joshua *kî* slept.

In these sentences, the function of *kî* is to add a second event to a preceding one, when it is the combination of the actions of the two participants that forms the basis for the next development. Thus, the fact that Paa Yacob stayed and did not want to go home with Joshua, caused Joshua to be annoyed and then to abandon him there. The fact that Joshua 'only slept', when Paa Yacob was knocking at the door, caused Paa Yacob to be furious, thus making him misbehave more.

Typically, when *kî* is used in this way, the primary relationship between the two events is not that of chronological sequence. In the case of appendix (41a), it is one of contrast; in appendix (51a) and (54), it is one of simultaneity. The presence of *kî* guides the hearer away from a relation of chronological sequence.

When two theme line events are described in successive sentences of a Bafut narrative and neither *tigə* nor *kî* occurs, the default interpretation is that they are in chronological sequence. To prevent that interpretation, *kî* is used. The effect of *kî* is to communicate that the events are not in chronological sequence.

The third usage of *kî* is shown in appendix (62), where Paa Yacob is told never to behave as badly as he had done the previous night and he says, "Yes, I shall never do it again." The answer of Paa Yacob strengthens the exhortation given in the first utterance by conforming to it. Here the role of the auxiliary is that of "backward confirmation" (Blass 1990:140).

We thus see that the additive auxiliary *kî* is used in connection with the development of the theme line to add participants to an existing scene: to add events by different participants which are not necessarily in chronological sequence (it is the combination of the actions of Paa Yacob and Joshua that contribute to each new development marked by *tigə*), and to indicate that the event concerned conforms to the intention of a previous exhortation and thus strengthens it.

2 Focus

Callow (1974:52, 60) defines focus in terms of highlighting thematic material that is of particular significance. Tamanji (1991:100), in his treatment of focus in Bafut, limits himself to cleft sentences with the dummy subject *a* which he calls the focus marker. Rather than repeat Tamanji's conclusions, this section concentrates on devices used to highlight participants and to highlight particularly important information.

2.1 Highlighting participants

Highlighting participants is achieved by means of two devices: (1) the use of the first-person singular pronoun, rather than a logophoric pronoun, in reported speech; and (2) the omission of the demonstrative, when referring by name to a specific, known participant.

Semi-direct and direct reported speech. As already mentioned, indirect speech marks background information (see §1.1), while direct reported speech is by default foreground. Direct speech, in turn, may be divided into two types: direct with the first-person singular pronoun, and direct with a logophoric pronoun, called "semidirect speech" by Perrin (1974) and "combined speech" by Hedinger (1984). Default encoding of reported speech in Bafut is direct with a logophoric pronoun. Marked encoding, that is, direct speech with the first-person singular pronoun, has the effect of highlighting participants.[4]

This contrast between the two types of direct reported speech is exemplified in the story of Paa Yacob. Example (14) is a direct quotation but with the logophoric pronoun (appendix (62)).

(14) *a kî   n̂-swoŋ mə n̂ŋə kaa m-bə yu   yi waʔà bù   ŋ̂-ghirə*
      3s ADD SS-say that yes NEG SS-can LOG F3 NEG again SS-do
      And he said, "Yes, I (LOG) will not do it again."

In this speech, no particular attention is being drawn to the participant. Paa Yacob is agreeing that he has misbehaved. There is no reason why he should be highlighted, consequently, the logophoric pronoun is used.

The situation in (15) is different. Paa Yacob is furious with Joshua because the latter not only left him at the night club, but also locked him

---

[4]This claim differs somewhat from that made by Wiesemann et al. for Babungo. They state (1984:155) that quotations with first-person singular pronouns are used for "personification: point culminant."

out. The use of the direct speech with first-person singular has the effect of highlighting himself, as he contrasts his own generosity with Joshua's ingratitude (appendix (52)).

(15) *a swoŋ mə yↄ̂ yə mûntsirə̀ mu   ghu   mə mə̀ lↄ̀gə*
      3s say   that see see little   child there REL I   take

      m-fɛ̀ʔɛ̀   ŋ̀-ghɛɛ nɨ   ghu   a   abɛɛ   a   zî   m̀-miʔi
      SS-go^out SS-go with there PREP outside 3s come SS-throw

      gha a abɛɛ   n-tsya zì   ǹ-nↄŋə   a   nda   ŋ-kuu
      1s 3s outside SS-pass come SS-sleep PREP house SS-enter

      ŋ-kuu   m-fɨ̈   ŋkya m-fɨ̈   abà̀ʔà mə tâ   mə̀ baŋnə
      SS-enter SS-lock gate SS-lock door   REL that 1s   instead

      n-lɛ   a   abɛɛ   mə̀ tuu aa   bə boŋ à ghɛ̀ɛ
      SS-stay^night PREP outside 1s not ANA be then 3s go

      a   abɛɛ
      PREP outside
He said, "See! See this little boy that I have taken out, and he has gone and abandoned me outside, and he has come and gone and slept in the house; he came, came and locked the gate and again locked the door so that I should have to sleep outside! Were it not for me, would he have gone out?"

Examples (16)–(18) from 'Soonjoo and Philip' further illustrate the contrast between the use of the logophoric and first-person singular pronouns in reported speech.

(16) *ǹ-swoŋ mə yu   lↄ̀ↄ   m-fɛ̀ʔɛ   n-yə   a   abɛɛ*
      SS-say that LOG want SS-go^out SS-see LOC outside
      And he said, "I want to go out and see."

(17) *ǹ-swoŋ mə wa philibo wa   à tùmə yi*
      SS-say that FOC Philibo DEM 3s shoot LOG
      And he said, "Philip has shot me."

(18)   *ǹ-swoŋ mə philibo à zǐ   waʔà bə̂ gha ləənsə̀ a ləənsə̀ bə̂*
       SS-say that Philibo 3s come NEG be 1s   wound 3s wound be

       gho
       you
       And she said, "Why did Philibo not hurt ME? Instead he hurts you."

In (16) and (17), the logophoric pronoun is used because the first-person singular (I and me) is not highlighted. Thus, in the context of (16), there is no suggestion that someone else wants to go out. Similarly, in (17), the speaker's concern is with being shot by Philip, rather than suggesting that it was 'me' who had been shot, and not someone else. In (18), however, the speaker wants to bring out the contrast between ME and you; consequently, direct speech with a first-person singular pronoun is used.

Proper names and the definite article. When a previously introduced participant is referred to by name in Bafut, the norm is for the name to be followed by the demonstrative appropriate to the noun class (unless there is a unique referent for the name, such as 'Jesus Christ' or, within the confines of an individual family, 'Paa Yacob'). (See (17) *(philibo wa)* as well as (5e–g).) If the participant is highlighted, however, the demonstrative is omitted. This occurs in various situations, three of which are now discussed.

First, the demonstrative is omitted, in connection with a proper name, when the referent is spotlighted because that person is in contrast with someone else. For example, in (19) attention switches from Paa Yacob to Joshua, as their behavior is contrasted (appendix (49)–(51); see also appendix (53)–(54)).

(19)   *ǹ-tigə ŋ-kwenə ǹ-tigə ŋ-kwenə joshua a kî   ǹ-nɔŋ*
       SS-DM SS-hit SS-DM SS-hit Joshua 3s ADD SS-sleep
       He then went on hitting and hitting (the door). Joshua just slept . . .

Second, the demonstrative is omitted when the referent is highlighted to act as a "foil" (Levinsohn 1992:84) for the main protagonist.[5] For example, in (20) Joshua is brought into temporary focus, before attention switches to what Paa Yacob did, after Joshua left him (appendix (43)).

---

[5]A foil, according to Levinsohn, is a constituent that is brought temporarily into focus for the purpose of being contrasted. The highlighting of a foil creates the impression that something important is to follow.

(20)   ǹtɔ̀ŋ joshua i̠ lwî   a lô   m̀-maʔatə paa yacob
       neck Joshua C7 bitter 3s go^away SS-leave   Paa Yacob
       Joshua got annoyed. He went away and left Paa Yacob...

The third situation in which the demonstrative is omitted occurs when the event performed by the referent is of particular importance. For example, the action described in (21), that of making spear handles, is important for the plot of the story.

(21)   bi̠ kà   mə aa fu   aa n-yə philibo a tswê ŋ̂-kɔɔ
       3p IMPF P0 ANA go^field ANA SS-see Philip 3s sit SS-make

       ni̠   mìmfaa
       IMPF handles
       While they were going (to the fields), they saw Philip sitting and making handles...

This omission of demonstratives with proper names in Bafut is particularly noteworthy, because a similar phenomenon occurs in Koine Greek. In the book of Acts, references by name to known participants lack the definite article when the referent is salient (Levinsohn 1992:98). In all three of the situations described for Bafut, the definite article would be omitted in the Greek of Acts.

2.2 Highlighting information

Some speeches and events in Bafut narrative are highlighted. One way that this is done is by repeating information from an earlier sentence. The information to be highlighted is separated from the background information by *aa*.

This use of *aa* has already been described in §1.1 (see the discussion of (5)). *aa* also occurs in (21), again with the effect of indicating that what follows is more important than what precedes.

To summarize this section, three devices for highlighting have been described: the use of a first-person singular pronoun, rather than a logophoric one, in reported speech; the omission of the demonstrative in connection with the use of a proper name to refer to a participant; and the repetition of information given earlier, followed by *aa*, to highlight what follows.

3 Emphasis

Callow (1974:52) says that emphasis has to do with the speaker's feelings or emotions. The speaker is strongly involved in what s/he is saying.

Bafut uses various devices to portray emphasis: various phonological features, intensifiers, the pronoun *yi*, emphatic demonstratives and pronouns, and repetition. These are now discussed in turn.

3.1 Phonological features associated with emphasis

Bafut uses some speech features for emphasis. This section mentions only two: heavy stress and pitch range.

The tape of the story of Paa Yacob reveals that some of the syllables and words are heavily stressed. This is particulary noticeable in the speech recorded in appendix (52).

In the same tape recording, the pitch range exhibits a number of changes to convey the emotions of the speaker. The voice pitch is particularly high in appendix (51a) and (54), given in (22).

(22)   *joshua a kî   ǹ-nɔŋ*
       Joshua 3s ADD SS-sleep
       Joshua just slept!

3.2 Intensifiers

Bafut makes use of various verbal auxiliaries and adverbs to reinforce and intensify an action or state. The equivalent of the auxiliaries in English would be an adverb or adjective. Examples (23) and (24) illustrate two intensifiers: the auxiliary *naŋsə* 'fix' and the adverb *tsiʔǐ* 'just, only'.

(23)   *n-naŋsə m-bə ŋù   yìi mə à lɛ n-tswe nî   ŋkabə*
       SS-fix   SS-be person REL REL 3s P3 SS-have IMPF money
       He was a person who was really (very) rich.

(24)   *ǹ-naŋsə n-no   mǐlùʔù tsiʔǐ nî   m̀-bə̂ ànnù*
       SS-fix   SS-drink wine   only IMPF SS-be matter
       They really drink wine, and drank it indeed.

3.3 The pronoun *yi*

yi is a reflexive object pronoun used with transitive verbs. It may, however, occur with intransitive verbs. In this marked usage, it conveys special effects, such as feelings of irritation, regret, or surprise, on the part of the speaker. Alternatively, it underlines the irreversibility of a state. It often occurs at the end of an episode.

The presence of *yi* in (25) and (26) suggests, respectively, surprise and regret that the person left unexpectedly.

(25)   *m-bɨɨ*   *yi*
       SS-return RFX
       and then returned

(26)   *ǹ-lo*   *ŋ-ghὲὲ* *yi*
       SS-go^away SS-go RFX
       and he left and went away

In (27) and (28), the presence of *yi* underlines the fact that the state described was irreversible:

(27)   *bɨ kà*   *mə aa* *ŋ-ghεε a*   *mânjì a kwô yi*
       3p IMPF P0 ANA SS-go PREP road 3s die RFX
       When they were on the way, she died.

(28)   *a fəʔə* *yi*
       3s blind RFX
       He became blind.

3.4 Emphatic pronouns and demonstratives

The use of emphatic pronouns and demonstratives is very common in Bafut narratives. The example in (29) is taken from a folkstory about Tortoise and Deer, and draws attention to the addressee (Deer) and the speaker (Tortoise) in turn, as Tortoise plays a trick on Deer and then makes fun of him.

(29)   *wò wa* *mə* *ò ghə mə* *mìkàʔa mo* *mɨ saʔakə aa*   *mɔ̀*
       2s EMP REL 2s say REL PL^leg POSS C6 long   ANA 1s

       ghulà   *mə*
       DEM^EMP REL
       You who say that your legs are long . . . look at me . . . ! (literally, here am I!)

3.5 Repetition

Repetition is one of the most common devices used for highlighting in Bafut narrative. Examples have already been given (see (5)) of the repetition of whole clauses, in connection with the highlighting of the information that follows. The examples in (30)–(32) illustrate the repetition of verbs and auxiliaries to emphasize the action or state described.

(30)   a yə̀ʔə n-yəʔə
        3s cry   SS-cry
        He cries a lot.

(31)   a ghaantə̀ ŋ-ghaantə
        3s scold   SS-scold
        He really scolded.

(32)   a bɔŋ   bɔ̀ŋ
        3s good good
        It is very good.

4 Conclusion

This paper has shown that Bafut uses a variety of devices to give prominence to significant information in texts. By means of them, an author directs the audience's attention to particular utterances and constrains their interpretation. The importance of discourse analysis becomes more and more apparent as texts, such as that which appears in the appendix, are studied.

Appendix

Extract from 'Paa Yacob and Joshua'

(33) a	A certain	
	elderly man	came down,
b	his name	was Paa Yacob.
(34)	He	had come to follow up his files.

(35) a			We	*kî*	had a boy who was helping us in our house,
b			his name		was Joshua.
(36) a	When	he came down,	we		had only two rooms in our house;
b			our children		were sleeping in one,
c			we		were sleeping in the other.
(37) a			We	*tigə*	put up a bed in the house where the boy was living and helping us
b		and	both of them	*tigə*	were sleeping there.
(38) a	One day, in the evening,		the boy		finished his work in the house,
b			he		said that he should take him out so that they could go out and see what Yaoundé looked like.
(39) a			The boy		took him;
b			Joshua DEM		took him
c		and	they		went to Kondongo,
			they		went to a certain night club and stayed there
d		and	were	*tigə*	drinking and passing time there.
(40)	At midnight,		Joshua Ø		told him that, "Paa, let's go home!"
(41) a			He	*kî*	stayed (only so) there
b		and			said that he should wait.
(42) a	Each time		he		told him the time that they should go home,
b			he		would tell him to wait a bit.
(43) a			Joshua Ø		got annoyed
b		and	he		went home
		and			left Paa Yacob at that place.
(44) a	When he came back,		he		unlocked the gate and went (him) in;
b			he		locked the gate and again went
c		and			entered the house where he was sleeping
d		and			again locked the door.

(45) a When the elderly
        man had stayed and
        stayed there (for long
        time)   he   stood up and went out
     b   and   *tigɔ*   tried very hard and found
                                                          the way (home).
(46)   When he came   he   had locked the gate.
(47) a   He   crawled up the gate, went
                                                          up,
     b   jumped and fell in [the yard];
     c   got up, went and stood at
                                                          the door of Joshua DEM
     d   *tigɔ*   was hitting (knocking hard
                                                          at) it.
(48)   The door   was just behind our house.
(49)   And   *tigɔ*   was hitting the door.
(50)   And   *tigɔ*   was hitting it.
(51) a   Joshua Ø   *kî*   slept (him) like a log of
                                                          wood
     b   and   was saying nothing (not
                                                          coughing him).
(52)   He   said that, "See! See this
                                                          little boy I took out: he has
                                                          gone and abandoned me
                                                          outside; he has come and
                                                          gone and slept in the house;
                                                          he came in, locked the gate
                                                          and also locked the door so
                                                          that I should have to sleep
                                                          outside! Were it not for me,
                                                          would he have gone out?"
(53) a   And   *tigɔ*   was scolding
     b   and   *tigɔ*   was scolding.
(54)   Joshua Ø   *kî*   slept [he slept on, unmoved]!
(55)   And when it pleased
        him   he   stood up and opened the
                                                          door.
(56)   The
                             elderly man   went in at that time.
(57) a While he had been
        talking   we   slept
     b   and   *tigɔ*   were listening.

(58)	When we woke up in the morning	we		asked him, "You went and came back and were climbing the gate, if these Gendarmes, who are here, saw you and hurt (pierced) you, what would you have done?"
(59)		He	*tigə*	stood there, saying nothing (without coughing).
(60)		He	*tigə*	was also ashamed.
(61)		We	*tigə*	told him that, "We plead with you, never do that kind of thing again."
(62)	And	he	*kî*	said, "Yes, I will not do it again."
(63) a	And		*tigə*	stayed
b	and		*tigə*	was following up his files until the day he finished
c	and		*tigə,*	left and went him back home.

References

Blass, Regina. 1990. Relevance relations in discourse: A study with special reference to Sissala. Cambridge: Cambridge University Press.

Callow, Kathleen. 1974. Discourse considerations in translating the Word of God. Grand Rapids: Zondervan.

Grimes, Joseph E. 1975. The thread of discourse. The Hague: Mouton.

Hedinger, Robert. 1984. Reported speech in Akɔɔse. Journal of West African Languages 14(1):81–102.

Levinsohn, Stephen H. 1992. Discourse features of New Testament Greek. Dallas: Summer Institute of Linguistics.

Longacre, Robert E. 1990. Storyline concerns and word order typologies in East and West Africa. Studies in African Linguistics, supplement 10. Los Angeles: University of California.

Mfonyam, Joseph N. 1989. Tone in orthography: The case of Bafut and related languages. Yaoundé: University of Yaoundé.

Perrin, Mona. 1974. Direct and indirect speech in Mambila. Journal of Linguistics 10:27–37.

Schaub, Willi. 1985. Babungo. London: Croom Helm.

Sperber, Dan and Deirdre Wilson. 1986. Relevance: Communication and cognition. Oxford: Blackwell.

Tamanji, Pius. 1991. Focus and relativization in Bafut. ms.

Wiesemann, Ursula, Cledor Nseme, and René Vallette. 1984. Manuel d'analyse du discours. Yaoundé: Société Internationale de Linguistique.

Further Thoughts on Four Discourse Particles in Mandara

Annie Whaley Pohlig and James N. Pohlig

Abstract

Four particles in Mandara indicate the relevance to the context of the information that follows. They constrain the hearer to interpret what follows as: relevant in its own right *(wa)*, strengthening a previous expectation *(ma)*, countering a previous expectation *(ni)*, or strengthening a counter-expectation *(mu)*.

Résumé

En mandara on rencontre quatre particules qui indiquent la pertinence de l'information qui les suivent par rapport au contexte. Elles obligent l'auditeur à interpréter la phrase qui suit la particule de la manière suivante: *wa* indique qu'il faut recevoir l'information telle quelle; *ma* renforce une information à laquelle on s'attendait; *ni* contrecarre une information à laquelle on s'attendait; *mu* renforce une information contre toute attente.

In Fluckiger and Whaley (1983), four particles in Mandara[1] were presented from a viewpoint of speaker perspective. The particles, all of them serving primarily as conjoiners, were characterized as follows in (1).

(1)   *wa*   what follows is important
       ma   what follows is fully expected
       ni   what follows is unexpected
       mu   what follows is perplexing, annoying, or astonishing

In the light of the development of Relevance Theory, these particles can be more profitably viewed as providing constraints on relevance. This paper shows that they are among those particles which, as described by Blass (1990a), do not impinge upon the semantic value of the propositions themselves. Instead, they guide the hearer in relating the propositions to each other and in drawing the intended inferences from them.

1 *wa:* Information which is relevant in its own right

Blass (1990a:16) asserts that particles such as those treated in this paper "are guides to processing, and that their processing 'tasks' determine their semantic content." Bearing this in mind, the particle *wa* may be defined as constraining the hearer to interpret the information which it introduces as "relevant in its own right" (Blass 1990b:256–57). That is to say, the hearer, in searching for the relevance which he assumes the speaker assigns to the new information, finds no signal that he should interpret the new information as either strengthening or countering what has gone before. The relevance of the new information is that it represents a new development with respect to what precedes.

---

[1]Mandara is a Chadic language spoken in and around the town of Mora, in the Far North Province of the Republic of Cameroon. The authors acknowledge their debt to Mr. Haman Oumaté, a Mandara speaker, who gave his time to discuss much of the data used for this paper. Thanks also go to Stephen H. Levinsohn and Mona Perrin for insight into the approach to take with this material; also to David Morgan for much valuable criticism of this paper. All deficiencies in it remain, of course, our own responsibility. All Mandara citations in the paper omit marking for high and low tones, generally following current orthographic practice.

wa exerts the effect of backgrounding the preceding information and of highlighting the new information, as in (2) and (3).[2]

(2)   *daaci daga ba   vacitu   **wa** itare keni jammeka elva-aatare*
      so   from EMP day^that   3p   ADD meet^NEG word-their

       dekideki tara indale antara yayye
       never   and Hyena and   Squirrel
       So from that day on, this is why Squirrel and Hyena never have any dealings together.

(3)   *am dunya **wa** hayre a pelava   aba an   hayre mandzawire*
      in life   good 3s rewarded EMP with good evil

       a pelava   aba an   mandzawire
       3s rewarded EMP with evil
       In life, good is rewarded with good, and evil with evil.

In (2), 'so from that day on' is backgrounded, while the current relationship between Squirrel and Hyena is described and highlighted. In (3), 'in life' is backgrounded as the framework for the highlighted expression which follows.

Within the effects discussed above, *wa* may also function as a spacer with a topicalizing effect, as in (4)–(6).

(4)   *palle **wa** zara palle **wa** fadi palle na   keni salata*
      one   Zara one   Fadi one this ADD Salata
      One was named Zara, one was named Fadi, and one was named Salata.

(5)   *malire **wa** sleksire   ka*
      old^age   sultanship NEG
      Old age does not confer wisdom.

---

[2]The abbreviations used in this paper are: ADD additive marker, ASS associative marker, DEV developmental marker, EMP emphasis marker, FUT future marker, NEG negative marker, OBL obligation marker, POS possessive, 1s, 2s, 3s first-, second-, third-person singular pronoun, 3p third-person plural pronoun.

(6)   *tsattse*   *mashagwali patem mani ŋane wa egdze a*
       3s^stood^up Mashagwali Patem Mani 3s   child ASS

      dawale a baka eŋye
      youth 3s hunts game
      Once upon a time, there was a certain Mashagwali Patem Mani. As
      for him, he was a young hunter.

In every case in (4)–(6), *wa* constrains the hearer to access what follows
as information which is relevant in its own right.

2 *ma:* Strengthening expectation

The particle *ma* functions to add a "proposition or property... [to
another] in an identical or similar context" (Blass 1990a:13). It is useful to
think of this in terms of strengthening expectation, i.e., in terms of confirming assumptions held by the hearer. Like *wa, ma* creates the effect of
backgrounding the preceding information in order to highlight what follows. At the same time, however, *ma* places the BACKGROUND +
FOREGROUND ensemble into a strengthening relationship with an element
of expectation which comes before it.

ma is observed in four kinds of situations, which are presented in the
next subsections.

2.1 Phrasal elements separated by *ma*

The hearer is constrained to interpret an ensemble of two phrasal
elements separated by *ma* as strengthening the expectation produced by a
preceding element. In (7), for instance, Panther spends three days learning
from Monkey how to swing about in trees.

(7)   *a mbansembe a mbansembe hare buwa ate keyire **ma** mazlaara*
       3s learn^it 3s learn^it   day two on third   now

      ka ademe-aaŋa aga   kina vatena say ya zakza
      2s go-2s^POS   friend now today OBL 1s eat^2s
      Panther learned and learned. He learned [Monkey's tricks] for two
      days and, on the third, [he said], "Now go wherever you like,
      friend... But today is the day I will eat you."

In (7), *ma* has the effect of backgrounding the phrase which it terminates and of highlighting the following reported speech. At the same time, it places the backgrounded information into an additive relationship with the first clause. This particular additive relationship is in the nature of a script: 'on the third' naturally follows from 'two days'.

2.2 Clauses separated by *ma*

The hearer is constrained to interpret an ensemble of two clauses separated by *ma* as strengthening the expectation produced by a preceding element. In (8), for instance, Lion, Squirrel, and Hyena decide to build a granary together.

(8)   *ay   ta maga elva-a-ndera   kuvere ta ndera kuvere   ma ekka*
      DEV 3p make word-ASS-build granary 3p build granary   2s

      akiye   ta elvan ge indale wa ekka wa ka hala haha
      it^is^said 3p speak to Hyena   2s   2s draw water
      They discussed building a granary and, (when) they built the granary, "You," they said to Hyena, "as for you, draw water!"

In (8), as in (7), *ma* has the effect of backgrounding the clause which it terminates and of highlighting the following reported speech. The backgrounded information is again in a script relationship with the first clause: 'they built the granary' follows naturally from 'they discussed building a granary'.

2.3 Sentences separated by *ma*

The hearer is constrained to interpret an ensemble of sentences separated by *ma* as strengthening the expectation produced by a preceding element. In the reported speech of (9), for instance, three workers are assigned their respective tasks.

(9)   *ekka wa ka hala haha iraa ka ka   yawe ay   yayye   ma*
      2s   2s fetch earth and 2s draw water DEV Squirrel

      a effa   ervare ma a takwara haha
      3s build^it Lion   3s roll^up earth
      As for you, you fetch earth and draw water; and as for Squirrel, he will build it; and as for Lion, he will make the balls of mud.

In (9), *wa* backgrounds the addressee with the phrase *ekka wa* 'as for you'. However, the other two workers, Squirrel and Lion, are backgrounded with *ma* as their various jobs are assigned. Each ensemble, Squirrel + task and Lion + task, stands in an additive relationship to the preceding ensemble.

Example (10) contrasts how a mule, a donkey, and a camel fared on a long journey in a dry region.

(10)   *tara ezzeŋwa an   tara nalpaadere tsarattse nawa aba ndera*
        and donkey with and mule   3p^stop here EMP thirst

        nawa aba kazlaŋa ate iga-aatare   ay   ezlgwame ma an
        here EMP things on backs-3p^POS DEV camel   not

        nja a tsaahe ka ba ekslya zlala ekslyanaa ka
        even 3s stop   NEG EMP tire go   3s^tire   NEG
        The donkey and the mule ... stopped because of thirst and their
        burdens. And the camel neither stopped nor tired of going.

The BACKGROUND + FOREGROUND ensemble of sentence (10) is added to what goes before: the camel and its performance are contrasted with the donkey and mule.

ma may follow a repetition of the information of the previous clause. In other words, the linkage between the sentences is that of tail-head. Such linkage may be considered to be a logical outgrowth of the additive role of *ma,* as in (11).

(11)   *daaci ta zlala ta zlala zlaɓe   ma ta beya guwe*
        so   3p go   3p go   further   3p find elephant
        So they went. As they went on, they found an elephant.

2.4 *ma* may imply something left unsaid

ma sometimes occurs in sentences which may be considered to be formally unfinished, when what is left unsaid has the effect of strengthening an expectation. In one story, Squirrel and Dove plant groundnuts. Those of Squirrel sprout, but none of Dove's come up (because Squirrel secretly ate them all when they were planted). Dove then speaks in (12).

(12)   *yayye   sasseka   naza-aaruwa   ma*
        Squirrel come^up^NEG groundnuts-1s^POS
        Squirrel, my groundnuts haven't come up and ... ?

Here, Dove asks a question which, according to our Mandara language assistant, is a very forceful request for an explanation of a surprising event. When asked if the *ma* in (12) would suggest to the hearer that any following phrase is implied, the assistant replied that one could easily add, 'What has happened?' Thus, *ma* in (12) can be considered to imply something left unsaid in line with the astonishment expressed in what precedes it.

3 *ni:* Countering of expectation

ni functions as a marker of countering expectation—the opposite role to that of *ma*. Blass (1990a:13) characterizes this function as "contradiction, which may lead to the erasure of assumptions in memory."

Like the other markers, *ni* creates the effect of backgrounding preceding information. In addition, it highlights what follows, treating it as something which counters an expectation that has been previously enunciated or implied. In (13), Squirrel counters the suggestion that he be sent somewhere by suggesting that the proposal is unreasonable.

(13) *iya ya egdzere **ni** ka 6ela iya a duwa indale*
     1s 1s child   2s send 1s 3s go   Hyena
     I, a child—you're sending me? Let Hyena go!

In (14), Hyena teaches Squirrel a song, who then promptly forgets it. Hyena says:

(14) *ekka **ni** ka viya   lahe-aaruwa tsawe wa say ya jakja*
     2s   2s forget song-1s^POS really   OBL 1s kill^2s
     You, you've really forgotten my song? I'll have to kill you.

In (14), the presence of *ni* constrains the hearer to interpret what follows as countering an expectation; the information emerges as a protest.

Because of the semantic value denoted by its function, *ni* is employed in some expressions of fear, as in (15), drawn from a text which discusses unsettling conditions arising from the abundance of rain in the rainy season.

(15) *ta kuva   ba **ni** a gejapte ka pala a se   ebzlyaterarhe*
     3p be^afraid EMP   3s fall^on NEG rock 3s come fall^on^them
     They fear that rocks may fall on them.

In (15), *ni* constrains the hearer to interpret what follows as contrary to
expectation, i.e., to normal conditions, when rocks do NOT fall on people.

ni may also occur in the final position of a sentence, in which case it
backgrounds what goes before and highlights a following unspoken implication. In (16), for instance, Hyena, having fallen down a well, begs
Monkey to pull him out. Monkey responds:

(16)   *ekka malakaamba zladzlada elva   an   ekka ura   watse ma*
       2s   king^of^bush difficult   word with 2s   person FUT   if

       eksaksekse   watse ka ezza   ni
       take^out^2s FUT   2s   eat^3s
       You, king of the bush, your word cannot be trusted. Whoever pulls
       you out, you will eat.

In (16), *ni* backgrounds the preceding idea (that Hyena will eat anyone he
can catch, including a benefactor). At the same time, according to our
language assistant, *ni* constrains the hearer to understand the following
implication: 'given these conditions, who would help you out of the well?'
This implication counters Hyena's expectation that he will be helped out
of the well by Monkey.

4 *mu:* Strengthening a countering relation

mu constrains an interpretation that a relation of counter-expectation is
being strengthened. It achieves this by backgrounding a preceding element
that goes against expectation and by highlighting a following element,
usually a question. For example, in (17), Lion accuses Hyena of having
secretly stolen all the sorghum in their granary.

(17) a. *daaci a za   wada wallaahi tallaahi ya pusa   iya ka*
        then 3s eat oath by^God by^God 1s remove^it 1s   NEG

        hiya   na a bina
        sorghum this 3s say
        Then he [Hyena] swore, "In the name of God, in the name of God,
        I did not take that sorghum."

b. *ka pusa   ekka   ka   **mu** a pusa   ware kena ka*
   2s   remove^it 2s^EMP NEG   3s remove^it who then 2s

    tsaka wada ba   dai selle na wa ka pusa   ba   ekka
    make oath EMP for nothing   2s   remove^it EMP 2s
    [Lion answered,] "If you did not take it, then who did? You're
    making useless oaths, you DID take it."

In (17b), Lion presents a hypothesis which he himself does not believe—'if you did not remove it'—and backgrounds the hypothesis with *mu* in order to present a further hypothetical idea, in this case, a rhetorical question: 'who did remove it, then?' This further question equals a statement such as, 'no one else took it', and must be interpreted as strengthening the inviability of the previous proposition, 'if you did not take it'.

The proverb in (18) features the willow tree.

(18)   *ka gejigeja   **mu** ka geji   ge   uwe*
       2s touch^1s   2s touch^1s for what
       You touched me; why did you touch me?

The proverb's sense is 'do not start an argument with someone easily provoked!' Here again, *mu* pragmatically backgrounds a preceding phrase, 'you touched me', while casting it in a light of incredulity or astonishment, contrary to the expectation of anyone who knows the nature of this particular tree, which is said to break upon being touched. *mu* then highlights the rhetorical question which follows and which equals a statement such as, 'you should not have touched me'. The effect of this rhetorical question is to strengthen the unexpected quality of the previous statement.

ni and *mu* may occur in the same sentence, as in (19) in which Monkey has pulled Hyena out of a well with his tail. Hyena refuses to let go of Monkey's tail and it is clear that he proposes to eat Monkey. Squirrel comes to watch and remarks to Monkey:

(19)   *iva   ŋwanye   am suwa indale **ni** a danaaka   nyahe*
       years how^many in   well   Hyena   3s remove^NEG saliva

    *hare an   ekka **mu** a ta   gevge*
    sleep with 2s   3s may become
    Seeing how long a time Hyena was in the well, would he not remove his saliva of sleep [breakfast] with you? It is [not] possible [that he would not].

In (19), *ni* constrains the hearer to place an interpretation of counter-expectancy upon the notion that follows, namely, that Hyena would not want to satisfy his hunger by feeding upon Monkey. In the process, *ni* backgrounds what precedes it and highlights the following element, which is to be interpreted in the light of counter-expectancy. The speaker then employs *mu* in order to constrain an interpretation that the countering relation of what precedes is being strengthened. *mu* accomplishes this by backgrounding the element which is so interpreted and by then highlighting the following comment, literally 'it is possible', which clearly signifies 'it is not possible that he would not'.

When *mu* occurs in sentence-final position, it constrains the hearer to place a countering interpretation upon what it follows, and to assume that the speaker is implying a statement which further strengthens such a countering interpretation. *mu* achieves this effect while backgrounding the preceding idea and implying an unspoken thought in a highlighted position. In (20), for example, two speakers have an exchange.

(20) a. *ka ndaya   ba   ekka*
  2s speak^to^1s EMP 2s
  Is it really you speaking to me?

 b. *ya ndaka   ba   iya mu iya mu*
  1s speak^to^2s EMP 1s   1s
  It is I that am speaking to you, I, I.

In (20b), *mu* constrains the interpretation of a countering relationship between the previous phrase and what the first speaker has been thinking. At the same time, *mu* constrains the hearer to assume that an unspoken thought follows, one which, if understood correctly, strengthens the countering relation of the speaker's actual words. According to the reaction of a native speaker, the hearer is to assume an unspoken question on the order of 'who do you think I am?'

5 Summary

This paper has shown that Mandara employs four particles which oblige the hearer to place the interpretations upon the relevance of new information that (a) the information represents a new development to what has gone before and which is relevant in its own right *(wa)*, (b) the new information is being added to preceding information so as to strengthen an expectation concerning it *(ma)*, (c) the information stands in a countering relation to what precedes it *(ni)*, or (d) the information is meant to strengthen the countering relation in which preceding information stands with its context *(mu)*. Furthermore, these four particles function in an identical way, in that they always background preceding information and highlight what follows.

References

Blass, Regina. 1990a. Constraints on relevance: A key to particle typology. Notes on Linguistics, 48:8–20.

———. 1990b. Relevance relations in discourse: A study with special reference to Sissala. Cambridge: Cambridge University Press.

Fluckiger, Cheryl A. and Annie H. Whaley. 1983. Four discourse particles in Mandara. In Ekkehard Wolff and Hilke Meyer-Bahlburg (eds.), Studies in Chadic and Afroasiatic linguistics, 277–86. Hamburg: H. Buske Verlag.

Notes on Markers of
Parallelism in Meta'

Klaus W. Spreda

Abstract

Meta' uses three particles of repetition to mark parallel events in narrative. *yì* marks strict parallelism, in which the actor and the action remain the same between the clauses concerned. *wúrì* marks an action or situation as parallel to another when it involves the same actor but is the reverse or opposite of the first. *bɔ̀* marks an action as parallel to another when the action itself remains the same but the actor and/or some other significant constituent is different.

Résumé

En meta', trois particules de répétition servent à marquer des événements parallèles au sein des textes narratifs. La première particule, *yì*, permet de marquer un parallélisme strict dans lequel l'acteur et l'action restent les mêmes entre les propositions concernées. La deuxième particule, *wúrì*, indique qu'une action ou une situation donnée est parallèle à une autre action ou situation, lorsque le même acteur participe à cette action ou situation ou que l'action ou la situation en question est le contraire de la première action ou situation. Enfin, *bɔ̀* indique qu'une action est parallèle à une autre, quand l'action proprement dite reste la même mais que, soit l'acteur, soit un autre constituant important, ou bien encore les deux, est différent.

Three morphemes used in Meta'[1] to indicate parallelism between actions and situations are shown in (1).

(1)   *yì*   'add'
       wúrì ~ *wìrì*   '(back) again'
       bə̀   'also'

The morphemes *bə̀* and *yì* may also be combined in the same verb phrase. Each of the three morphemes and one combination are discussed in turn.

1 *yì* 'add'

The morpheme *yì*, which is a full verb, marks STRICT PARALLELISM in which actor and action are identical in the two clauses which form the parallel.

The background to (2) is that Tortoise has borrowed money from Pig. In (2a), Pig goes to Tortoise to ask for the return of the loan. Tortoise promises to pay it back after six months. So, in (2b), 'on the correct day' Pig goes again to Tortoise to ask for his money. Sentence (2a) contains the parallel action to which *yì* in (2b) refers.[2]

(2) a. *à sí   ə́ní ə́mɔ̀'ɔ kúŋə́ sɔ   ə̄kwɨ   kyímə́kɔ̀'*
       it then day some   Pig   go^out^early to^compound of^Tortoise
       Then one day, Pig went out early to the compound of Tortoise.

    b. *əní zé ə̄   kù'   kúŋə́ yì   wó*
       day ART SCON correct Pig   add go
       On the correct day Pig went again.

---

[1]Meta' is spoken by a population of approximately 30,000 in the Momo Division of the North West Province of Cameroon. The author has lived in the area and studied the language for several periods of four to eight months over the past eighteen years. Mr. John Mufu Takud of Bome has been the principal language teacher and source of language data during this period. Research has been conducted under authorization from the Ministry of Scientific and Technical Research.

[2]Examples are written in the orthography currently in use, which is described in Spreda (1991). Abbreviations used in this paper are: ART article, CON concord marker, DIR directional, F1 future tense (default), IMPF imperfective, INF infinitive marker, P2 past tense 2 (remote), PERF perfect, QM question marker, REL relative pronoun, SCON subject concord marker, 3s third-person singular pronoun.

The parallelism exhibited in this example is a very strict one, inasmuch as it involves the same actor and the same action, although it is not necessary that the same verb be used to describe the action. Instances in which *yì* occurs with *bɔ̀* are treated in §4.

2 *wúrì* '(back) again'

The particle *wúrì*, which freely fluctuates with *wírì*, also marks instances of a fairly strict parallelism, in that the same actor is involved and the actions must correspond to each other; they are, however, REVERSED or OPPOSITES.

The passage in (3) is taken from a short text describing the activities of a mother on the day before a market day.

(3) a. *wì nɔ̂   isɔsɔ wò ɔ̄ mbēŋ wī   tōŋ   īzō'*
     3s rise early go to farm go^to dig^out yams
     She rises early to go to the farm in order to dig out yams ...

   b. *à sí   ɔ́nī mìnyùm fàmì tì   ɔ̀bà wì wīrì   yè'e ɔ̄ nɔ̄b*
     it then at hours   eight and half 3s again come to house
     Then at half past eight she comes again to the house.

In (3b), *wúrì* occurs before the verb 'come', which is opposed to the verb 'go' in (3a). Both are verbs of movement; they are opposed in that the movement is in opposite directions, with respect to a spatial point of reference.

The background to (4) is that a child has died but the people have not told the parent.

(4)   *imbɔ̀'   ìghɔ̄m nì   mbī nyá'-ɔ̀ ghà-ɔ̀   ni   ìghɔ̄m mɔ̀'ɔ*
     because sake REL they P2-IMPF say-IMPF that time   some

     wán wē   wì bìrì wìrì   zwēmɔ̄ ɔ̄wí
     child ART 3s F1   again rise^up 3s
     ... because they said that maybe the child will rise up again.

The rising up would be the reverse process of dying and is thus marked by *wúrì*.

In light of the fact that *wúrì* indicates reversal or oppositeness, it is not surprising that this particle often occurs in utterances which negate a previously performed action as illustrated by (5).

The parallel in (5a) to which *wúrì* in (5b) points, occurs a number of sentences earlier in the text concerning Pig and Tortoise. The background to these sentences is that Pig approached Tortoise's compound in order to ask for the repayment of his loan, and Tortoise quickly slipped out. This happened a number of times, but then one day Tortoise's wife saw Pig coming, and (5b) describes how Tortoise was unable to play this trick again.

(5) a. *wì nì pè kyimàkɔ' fɔ cè jwì í*
3s before arrive tortoise PERF pass go^out 3s
Before he (Pig) arrived, Tortoise had already gone out.

b. *cɔ nya'a í ínɔ́njì ì nì tì kyimɔ̀kɔ̀ vì rì ɔ nɔ̄b*
not P2 it road it REL can Tortoise escape from CON house

wírì káa
again at^all
There was no way at all by which Tortoise could escape again.

wúrì marks a reverse parallelism in that a previous action by the same actor is not repeated.

In (6), a marauding leopard disrupts the everyday life of an area, so that the women can no longer go to their farms. The opposite action, i.e., that the women go to their farms, is not stated in the text. Nevertheless, since it is normally an everyday occurrence, *wúrì* may be used to indicate the reversal of such a custom.

(6) *ce í mɔyí ɔ wùrì wò-ɔ̀ ɔ̄ mbēŋ*
not it women SCON again go-IMPF DIR farm
The women were no longer going to their farms.

Pragmatically speaking, the reversal of the normal everyday happening strengthens the conclusion which the hearer is led to draw, namely that the leopard presented a menace that needed to be dealt with.

The use of *wúrì* in (7) differs from those considered heretofore in that what is reversed is not a single verb but a whole situation. The example is taken from a short text about a trader and a farmer, where the trader unsuccessfully tries to become a farmer himself instead of continuing to buy food from the farmer.

(7) a. ɔ́nɨ́ sɨ́   ɔ́nɨ́ əmɔ̀'ɔ wə̀d   ɨwɨ̌n   nɔ̂'   ɨ   wɨ̄   zōn
as then day one   person of^market leave to   go^to buy

tɨ̀jɨ̌g tɨ́   ə̄mbɨ̄ ɔ̄   wə̄d   ɨ̀   mbē̄ŋ
food from at   CON person of farm
One day the trader left to go and buy food from the farmer.

b. zɔ̄ nya'a wɨ̀rɨ   pè   ənɨ̄ ɔ̄   nyūmə̀ mɔ̀'ɔ ɨnyod ɨ̄   tɔ
it P2   again reach as   CON time   some body SCON pain

ə̄mbɨ̄ ɔ̄   wə̄d   ɨwɨ̌n   wɔ̂   ɨmbə̀'   ɨcɨ̄ nɨ   wɨ̀
to   CON person of^market that because way REL 3s

yè'-ɔ̂   zōn-ɔ̂   tɨ̀jɨ́g ɨ́ghə̂m ɨ̀jɨ̀m
come-IMPF buy-IMPF food times all
There (again) came a time when it annoyed the trader, because he
was always buying food.

In this text, there does not seem to be a parallel or counterpart verb in
any of the previous sentences, though the situations which are compared
involve both the same person and the action of buying food, and there is
a certain parallelism with regard to time between sentences (7a) and (7b).
The contrast comes in the attitude of the trader. Using *wúrɨ̀* in this case
alerts the audience to the fact that what is beginning at this point in time
is something opposed to what has been going on before.

Thus, in each example involving *wúrɨ̀,* the action or situation so marked
is to be understood as the reverse or opposite of that with which it is
associated.

3 *bɔ̀* 'also'

The particle *bɔ̀* marks a LOOSER PARALLELISM than *yɨ̀* or *wúrɨ̀.* This is
because, while the action described is the same or similar in the two
propositions connected through this particle, the actor or some other
constituent which is central is different.

For example, *bɔ̀* in (8b) indicates the proposition that the chief is
thinking about something that has a parallel antecedent. This can be
identified in (8a) as the proposition that the princes are thinking about
something. In the text, (8b) directly follows (8a).

(8) a. *mbī kɔn icî ni mbī bírí ghì mbī ɔ́fɔn   zé*
they think way REL they F1 do with leopard ART
They (the princes) pondered what to do with the leopard.

   b. *icî ni ifɔn nya'a fɔ̄   be ghà ni wì bɔ̄ si-ɔ̀*
way REL chief P2   PERF first say that 3s also then-IMPF

      kɔn-ɔ̂   ni tɔ̀ tɔ́ wī ghì riyè ni
think-IMPF that 3s QM go^to do how that
Since the chief had earlier said that . . . he was then also considering how he would do it that . . .

In (9b), *bɔ̀* marks a parallel action by the same actor in which the object
of the verb is different.

(9) a. *bɔ̂d   ī   kɔ́ ghàn-ɔ̂   nòr-ɔ̀   nyì-ɔ̂   mbēŋ*
people SCON begin go^about-IMPF flee-IMPF enter-IMPF bush
People began going about fleeing into the bush,

   b. *bɔ̀ nyì-ɔ̂   mìsûm*
also enter-IMPF caves
also entering into caves.

Sometimes the parallelism of action in the two clauses is not expressed
by the same verb; one clause uses a particular and narrowly-defined action
verb and the other clause uses a more generic expression. For example, in
(10), the generic 'do' refers to the same action as 'thrust'.

(10) a. *tɔ̄ bìrì sɔ́   īwùrì baghi ɔ̄tū   ɔ̄mɔ́d*
3s F1 thrust feather red   at^head his
He will thrust a red feather at his head,

   b. *ɔ́nī īcĭ ni mbī ɔ̄   bɔ̀ ghì-ɔ̀   iŋgā ɔ̄bèŋi   ɔ̄ghâ*
as way REL they SCON also do-IMPF inside of^country here
as they are habitually doing in the country here.

In (11), both the actor and the undergoer (i.e., the constituent which is
affected) of the parallel action are different.

(11) a. *à   mī nà' ìtí   tìté*
you if give stone of^pepper
If you give (back) the grindstone,

b. *mə bə̀ nà' té   ndə̀ŋ*
I   also give your brass
I will also give (back) your brass (rods).

It is to be expected that the investigation of a wider corpus will yield further contexts in which the particle *bə̀* functions to mark loose parallelism.

4 The combinations of *bə̀* and *yì*

It is quite common for *bə̀* to be followed by *yì* within the same verb phrase. In such instances, both indicate their particular type of parallelism. In (12), the two particles are seen in (12d).

(12) a. *mád zē   wì nɔ̄   rətɪ̄ə̄*
       spit ART 3s stand upright
       Soon he (Təghən Ngum) stood up.

b. *wátɔ̄' mɔ̀'ɔ a nɔ̀'   rətɪ̄ə̄   ghà*
   prince some P2 stand upright say
   A certain prince stood up and said . . .

c. *əmád rízómbí í təghán   ŋgŭm yɪ̄ nɔ̀'   rətɪ̄ə̄*
   spit not^long it Təghən Ngum add stand upright
   After a short while Təghən Ngum again stood up.

d. *wátɔ̄' mɔ̀'ɔ bə̀   yì   ghà ì̄ bɔ   ni*
   prince some also add say to him that
   A certain prince also again said to him that . . .

There is strict parallelism between (12b) and (12d) consistent with the function of *yì*, in that both the actor (a certain prince) and the action (say) are the same. In turn, the antecedent for the wider parallelism indicated by *bə̀* in (12d) may be identified as (12c); the two different participants did something again.

In (13), the sentence with the particles *bə̀* and *yì* is (13b).

(13) a. *əbéɲí   ɔ̄   nya'a jwì   əjìm*
        population SCON P2   come^out all
        All the population came out (to catch the leopard).

b. *ìtú'ú   nya'a cīg   mbī bə̀   yì   jwì*
daylight P2   dawn they also add come^out
The next day they (the population) also came out again.

yì indicates strict parallelism between (13a) and (13b); both have the same actor and the same action. The wider parallelism conveyed by *bə̀* consists of the same action (*jwì* 'come out'), together with a difference in a constituent, namely, the adverbial manifested by 'the next day', which implies that the action of sentence (13a) took place on an implicit first day.

Speakers of Meta' find it useful to employ the two particles indicating the two different types of parallelism in one proposition in order to point the audience to two different parallel circumstances. In this way, a speaker can doubly ensure that the intended conclusion is reached. The conclusion from (13), for instance, would be something like (14).

(14)   The population made a big effort to catch the leopard.

The devices available to Meta' speakers to indicate parallelism are, therefore, very rich, and enable them to guide their audience to the intended conclusion in an economical manner, thus achieving a fast-moving and action-oriented style.

Reference

Spreda, Klaus W. 1991. Alphabet and orthography statement for Meta'. Yaoundé: Société Internationale de Linguistique. ms.

Rheme and Focus in Mambila

Mona J. Perrin

Abstract

The rheme (most important piece of new information) of a Mambila sentence with "topic-comment articulation" (Andrews 1985:77) typically terminates the sentence. Highlighted (focused) constituents occur in the same place, with the exception of highlighted subjects and verbs, which are characterized by the presence, in final position, of an appropriate focus marker. Focused constituents may often be distinguished from rhemes by the left-shifting of other constituents of the comment. Focused quantifiers also terminate the sentence; if the noun they modify is stated, it remains in its default position. If a non-quantifier is focused, in contrast, it is separated from the noun it modifies by the possessive marker.

Résumé

En mambila, les phrases caractérisées par une "articulation topique-commentaire" (Andrews 1985:77) se terminent généralement par le rhème, c'est-à-dire, l'information nouvelle la plus importante. Les constituants focalisés se trouvent eux aussi à la fin de la phrase, à quelques exceptions près : soit les sujets et les verbes focalisés qui sont caractérisés par la présence, en position finale, d'un marqueur de focalisation approprié. Bien souvent, les constituants focalisés peuvent se distinguer des rhèmes par un déplacement vers la gauche d'autres constituants qui font partie du commentaire. Les quantifiés focalisés se

placent eux aussi à la fin de la phrase ; si le quantifiant est explicité, il reste
dans sa position normale. Si, par contre, un non-quantifié est focalisé, il est
séparé du nom qu'il modifie par le marqueur possessif.

Dik (1981:19) states that focus "presents what is relatively the most
important or salient information in the given setting." This definition
includes both rheme and focus as they are defined in this paper. The paper
claims that in Mambila[1] such information is placed at the end of the
sentence.

In a sentence with "topic-comment articulation" (Andrews 1985:77),[2] the
comment is arranged, as far as grammatical constraints allow, so that the
more important a part of its information is to the speaker, the further it
will be placed to the right. The end of the comment, therefore, tends to
contain the most salient information, subject to core-periphery require-
ments. The end of the sentence thus typically forms the RHEME (what
Crozier (1984:119) calls "unmarked focus"). FOCUS, as used in this paper,
refers to highlighting of new information when this is an item of particular
significance (Callow 1974:52; what Crozier (1984:141) calls "marked
focus").

The structures involved in Mambila are illustrated first with reference to
the object of the verb (§1). The place of left-shifting in focus constructions
is discussed in §2. This is followed by consideration of focused subjects
(§3), focus and emphasis on the verb (§4), and focus in content questions
and stative constructions (§§5 and 6). The paper terminates with examples
of focus on part of a clause constituent (§7).

1 Object focus, an illustration

Rheme and focus in Mambila are distinguished by constituent order.
Consider the pair of sentences in (1) and (2).[3]

---

[1]Mambila is spoken by about 80,000 people, living in the Mayo-Banyo Division of
Adamawa Province, Cameroon, and in Gongola State, Nigeria. It is a member of the
Mambiloid group of Northern Bantoid languages (Hedinger 1989:23–25). Mambila
examples cited in this paper are written in the practical orthography; for descriptions
of the phonology and tone system of Mambila, see Perrin and Hill 1969 and Perrin
1991.

[2]See also Levinsohn's article "Discontinuities in Coherent Texts" in this volume.

[3]Abbreviations used in this paper are: EMP emphasis, NEG negative, P1, P2, P3 past
time indicators (see footnote 5), PL plural, SFOC subject focus, VFOC verb focus, 1s, 2s, 3s
first-, second-, third-person singular.

(1) *mè ŋgeé naâ cɔ̀gɔ̀ léílé*
     1s buy PAST cloth yesterday
     I bought cloth yesterday.

(2) *mè léílé   ŋgeé naâ cɔ̀gɔ̀*
     1s yesterday buy PAST cloth
     It was cloth that I bought yesterday.

In (1), 'cloth' and 'yesterday' are both salient items of new information, with 'yesterday' being more salient, or rhematic, than 'cloth'. In (2), 'yesterday' is left-shifted, which has the effect of highlighting 'cloth', i.e., bringing 'cloth' into focus.

To highlight 'yesterday', 'cloth' is left-shifted, as in (3).

(3) *mè cɔ̀gɔ̀ ŋgeé naâ léílé*
     1s cloth buy PAST yesterday
     It was yesterday that I bought cloth.

Sentence (3) can be an example of contrastive focus. That is, it was not on some other day that I bought cloth. Givón (1990:727) says that the fronting of contrasted constituents is a pragmatic universal of human language. In Mambila, however, the focus position, whether contrastive or non-contrastive, is sentence final.

When the sentence contains only core elements, the order of constituents is the same, whether the most salient item of new information is rheme or is in focus, as in (4).[4]

(4) *mè ŋgeé naâ cɔ̀gɔ̀*
     1s buy PAST cloth
     I bought cloth. *or* It was cloth that I bought.

When the verb is the most salient item of new information but is not highlighted (i.e., it is rhematic), it is the final constituent of the sentence, as in (5).

(5) *mè naâ cɔ̀gɔ̀ ŋge*
     1s PAST cloth buy
     I bought cloth.

---

[4]It is possible that rheme and focus may be distinguished by intonation. This has not been verified.

2 Left-shifting

As has been suggested by (2) and (3), one of the devices involved in focus constructions is left-shifting of nonfocused constituents. Such constituents occur preceding the verb (and following the subject and time indicator[5] if present), as shown in (6).

(6)   mè lé cɔ̀gɔ̀ ŋgeé naâ ké tan
       1s P1 cloth buy PAST at market
       It was at the market that I bought cloth.

More than one element may be left-shifted in any given sentence. There are three potential post-verbal elements in (7) and (8): 'cloth', 'you', and 'yesterday'. The left-shifting of any one of them indicates that the remaining ones are in focus. If only one element follows the verb, it carries nuclear focus. If two elements follow the verb, the first bears subsidiary focus and the second, nuclear focus (for nuclear and subsidiary focus in English, see Delin 1989).[6]

(7)   mè wò cɔ̀gɔ̀ ŋge haá naâ léílé
       1s 2s cloth buy give PAST yesterday
       It was YESTERDAY I bought you cloth.

(8)   mè cɔ̀gɔ̀ ŋge haá naâ wò léílé
       1s cloth buy give PAST 2s yesterday
       It was YESTERDAY I bought *you* cloth.

3 Focus on the subject

Any complete clause constituent may be placed in focus. The focus construction for objects, indirect objects, and adverbials is as illustrated in §1 and only involves constituent order in the clause.

Because the subject normally occurs in sentence-initial position, focus on the subject is achieved by the placing of the subject-focus particle kɔɔ́ in

---

[5]Mambila has three past time indicators: recent past (today), more distant past (yesterday and previous to yesterday), and remote past. These are abbreviated to P1, P2, and P3 respectively.

[6]In the free translations, the element carrying nuclear focus is in small caps, i.e., 'yesterday' in (7). If an element bears subsidiary focus ('you' in (8)), it is in italics.

sentence-final position. No other element follows the verb (9), unless it carries subsidiary focus (10).

(9)   *mè cɔ̀gɔ̀ ŋgeé naâ kɔ́*
        1s   cloth buy PAST SFOC
        It was I who bought the cloth.

(10)   *mè ŋgeè naâ cɔ̀gɔ̀ kɔ́*
        1s buy PAST cloth SFOC
        It was I who bought the *cloth.*

The subsidiary focus on 'cloth' in (10) suggests that perhaps someone else had bought a different item. In English, the difference between (9) and (10) is carried by intonation. There would be a secondary accent on 'cloth' in (10), but not in (9).

An alternative structure for subject focus[7] exists, in which the subject does occur clause finally and there is therefore no subject-focus particle. This structure is used when a left-shifted construction begins the clause as topic and is given information. In (11), 'this cloth', the object of the verb, has been left-shifted as topic.

(11)   *cɔ̀gɔ̀ hên lé ŋgeé naâ mè*
        cloth this P2 buy PAST 1s
        This cloth, it is I who bought it.

4 Focus and emphasis on the verb

There are two ways of giving prominence to a verb when the clause is positive. The one is contrastive focus, contrasting the action of the verb with some other action, either explicit or implicit. The other emphasizes the reality or truth of the action. (See (5) for the verb as rheme, occurring as the final constituent of a sentence.)

Contrastive verbal focus uses a verb-focus particle which occurs in clause-final position. As stated for subject focus (§3), no other element follows the verb (12), unless it carries subsidiary focus (13).

---

[7]The author knows of no distinction between subject focus and subject as rheme in this construction.

(12)   *mè cɔ̀gɔ̀ hên ŋgeé naâ lòù*
       1s   cloth this buy PAST VFOC
       I BOUGHT this cloth.

(13)   *mè ŋgeé naâ cɔ̀gɔ̀ hên lòù*
       1s   buy PAST cloth this VFOC
       I BOUGHT *this cloth.*

Sentence (12) would be said in a context where I might alternatively have stolen the cloth or been given it. Sentence (13) suggests that I may have acquired some other cloth in a different way.

Emphasis on the reality or truth of an action is achieved by terminating the clause with the main verb, followed by the emphatic particle *bɔ̀n,* as in (14).

(14)   *mè né bú kɔ́ɔ́ bɔ̀n*
       1s be 3s know EMP
       Truly I know him.

Emphasis on the verb in the context of counter assertion is achieved by repeating the verb. The repeated verb bears a falling tone and occurs in clause-final position.

(15)   *mè kɔ bú kɔɔ̀*
       1s know 3s know
       I DO know him.

The statement in (15) might be spoken as a counter assertion to someone saying that I did not know the person.

When the verb is negative, there are again two constructions. The one is contrastive, as with the positive verb; the other is not. They are discussed in turn.

In negative constructions in Mambila, imperatives excepted, the negative particle normally occurs clause finally. In the case of contrastive verbal focus, this constraint takes precedence over the constraints of the focus construction, where the element in focus is normally the element in clause-final position. This is seen in (16).

(16)   *mè lòù ŋgè ná ŋgwêh*
       1s VFOC buy PAST NEG
       I did not BUY (it).

The statement in (16) might be spoken in a context where the speaker had been given the cloth. Similarly, one finds the construction in (17).

(17) *mè lòù   kɔ́   ŋgwéh*
     1s   VFOC know NEG
     I do not KNOW.

Here, the meaning might be 'I suspect something to be the case; I am not claiming to know'.

The second verbal focus construction uses the same verb-focus particle *lòù*, but it occurs clause finally, following the negative particle.

(18) *mè kɔ́   ŋgwéh lòù*
     1s know NEG   VFOC
     It is that I DO NOT KNOW.

In saying (18), I might be offering the excuse of ignorance for some action I should not have performed.

5 Content questions

The order of constituents in Mambila content questions is that which is used in focused constructions. The question word (the focused element) occurs in sentence-final position. The answer to a content question follows the same pattern. This is illustrated in (19) and (20).

(19) *wò nde né he*
     2s go be where
     Where are you going?

(20) *mè nde né kɛ́ tan*
     1s go be to market
     I am going to market.

When the content question word is the subject, that is, when the question is 'who', the same construction is used as for any subject focus.

(21) *neì ŋenè naâ wò kɔɔ́*
     who see PAST 2s SFOC
     Who saw you?

In certain contexts, where the fact of having been seen is the topic, one also finds the construction in (22).

(22) ŋenè naâ wò neì
      see PAST you who
      You were seen by whom?

For this construction, see (11).

6 Statives

As already indicated in §1, focused elements may be distinguished grammatically from rhematic ones by the presence versus absence of left-shifting. This option is generally absent in the case of stative constructions. Consequently, when the focus is on the complement of the 'be' verb, there is nothing to distinguish that focus grammatically from the rheme. This is seen in (23).

(23) à né ké gwò
      3s be at house
      He is in the house. *or* It is in the house that he is.

Here, 'in the house' is naturally the most salient piece of information and cannot be given additional prominence grammatically.

When the subject of the 'be' verb is in focus, left-shifting of the complement may occur, as in (24). The same ambiguity between focus and rheme exists in (24) as was noted concerning (11) (see footnote 7).

(24) mgbè né gèà
      chief be Gea
      It is Gea who is chief. *or* The chief is Gea.

Contrast the construction in (25).

(25) gèà né mgbè
      Gea be chief
      Gea is the chief.

As has been noted in §§3 and 5, this way of constructing subject focus is only possible when the resultant clause-initial element is the topic of a larger unit. Where this is not so, the subject-focus marker *kɔɔ́* is used and there is no left-shifting. This is illustrated in (26).

(26) *gèà né mgbè kɔɔ́*
      Gea be chief SFOC
      It is Gea who is chief.

7 Focus on part of a clause constituent

Givón (1990:704) points out that, in English, stress focus can be on verbal auxiliaries as well as on the subject, object, and verb. He gives as an example: 'Joe WILL milk the goat'. In a verb phrase in Mambila, focus may only be placed on the verb (§1.4).

It is possible, however, to focus on modifiers within the noun phrase, without focusing on the noun. There are two classes of modifier in this respect, quantifiers and non-quantifiers. The focus construction for each class is different.

The focus construction for quantifiers uses the clause-final position typical of focus constructions. This construction can be seen by comparing (27) and (28). In (27), the modifier 'many' occurs following the noun and 'there' is rhematic. In (28), 'many' is in focus, though no left-shifting occurs.

(27) *bɔ̀ huaán kókoó lé naâ   teèn*
      PL child   many   P2 PAST there
      Many children were there.

(28) *bɔ̀ huaán lé naâ   teèn kókoó*
      PL child   P2 PAST there many
      MANY children were there.

Absence of left-shifting is typical of this type of focus construction in Mambila. For this reason, sentence (29) is potentially ambiguous as to whether the quantifier 'two' is part of the rheme 'two children', or whether it is in focus.

(29) *mè ŋenè naâ   huaán fà*
      1s see   PAST child   two
      I saw two children.

If 'two' were in contrastive focus with some other number, however, 'children' would be given information and left implicit in order to focus on the quantifier. One can therefore say that 'two' in (30) is rhematic.

(30) mè ŋenè naâ fà
      1s see PAST two
      It was two (of them) that I saw.

The focus construction for non-quantifiers involves a change only within the noun phrase concerned. Sentence (31) shows the noun phrase 'small children' with no element focused. Sentence (32) shows the same noun phrase with focus on 'small'. In (32), perhaps the older children had stayed away. In both sentences, the verb is rhematic.

(31) bɔ huaán memaàn naâ waà
      PL child small   PAST arrive
      Small children arrived.

(32) bɔ huaán dé memaàn naâ waà
      PL child of small   PAST arrive
      The SMALL children arrived.

Thus, whereas quantifiers are focused in the same way as clause constituents (albeit, without the left-shifting of other constituents), nonquantifiers are focused by the insertion of dé between the noun and the modifier.

References

Andrews, Avery. 1985. The major functions of the noun phrase. In Timothy Shopen (ed.), Language typology and syntactic description 1, 62–154. Cambridge: Cambridge University Press.

Callow, Kathleen. 1974. Discourse considerations in translating the Word of God. Grand Rapids: Zondervan.

Crozier, David H. 1984. A study in the discourse grammar of Cishingini. Ph.D. dissertation. University of Ibadan.

Delin, Judy. 1989. The focus structure of it-clefts. Edinburgh: Centre for Cognitive Science.

Dik, Simon C. 1981. Functional grammar. Dordrecht: Foris Publications.

Givón, Talmy. 1990. Syntax: A functional-typological introduction 2. Amsterdam: Benjamins.

Hedinger, Robert. 1989. Northern Bantoid. In John Bendor-Samuel and
    Rhonda L. Hartell (eds.), The Niger-Congo languages, 421–29. Lan-
    ham, MD: University Press of America.
Perrin, Mona J. 1991. The tone system of Mambila: Some further com-
    ments. Yaoundé: Société Internationale de Linguistique.
——— and Margaret V. Hill. 1969. Mambila (parler d'Atta): Description
    phonologique. Yaoundé: Université Fédérale du Cameroun.

Summer Institute of Linguistics and
The University of Texas at Arlington
Publications in Linguistics

10. Verb studies in five New Guinea languages, ed. by Alan Pence. 1964.
15. Bolivian Indian tribes: Classification, bibliography and map of present language distribution, by Harold Key and Mary R. Key. 1967.
18. Tzotzil grammar, by Marion M. Cowan. 1969.
19. Aztec studies 1: Phonological and grammatical studies in modern Nahuatl dialects, ed. by Dow F. Robinson. 1969.
20. The phonology of Capanahua and its grammatical basis, by Eugene E. Loos. 1969.
21. Philippine languages: Discourse, paragraph and sentence structure, by Robert E. Longacre. 1970.
22. Aztec studies 2: Sierra Nahuat word structure, by Dow F. Robinson. 1970.
23. Tagmemic and matrix linguistics applied to selected African languages, by Kenneth L. Pike. 1970.
24. The grammar of Lamani, by Ronald L. Trail. 1970.
25. A linguistic sketch of Jicaltepec Mixtec, by C. Henry Bradley. 1970.
26. Major grammatical patterns of Western Bukidnon Manobo, by Richard E. Elkins. 1970.
27. Central Bontoc: Sentence, paragraph and discourse, by Lawrence A. Reid. 1970.
28. Identification of participants in discourse: A study of aspects of form and meaning in Nomatsiguenga, by Mary Ruth Wise. 1971.
29. Tupi studies 1, ed. by David Bendor-Samuel. 1971.
30. L'énoncé Toura (Côte d'Ivoire), by Thomas Bearth. 1971.
33. Two studies on the Lacandones of Mexico, by Phillip Baer and William R. Merrifield. 1971.
36. Tagmeme sequences in the English noun phrase, by Peter H. Fries. 1970.
37. Hierarchical structures in Guajajara, by David Bendor-Samuel. 1972.
38. Dialect intelligibility testing, by Eugene H. Casad. 1974.
39. Preliminary grammar of Auca, by M. Catherine Peeke. 1973.
40.1. Clause, sentence, and discourse patterns in selected languages of Nepal 1: General approach, ed. by Austin Hale. 1973.
40.2. Clause, sentence, and discourse patterns in selected languages of Nepal 2: Clause, ed. by Austin Hale and David Watters. 1973.
40.3. Clause, sentence, and discourse patterns in selected languages of Nepal 3: Texts, ed. by Austin Hale. 1973.
40.4. Clause, sentence, and discourse patterns in selected languages of Nepal 4: Word lists, ed. by Austin Hale. 1973.
41.1. Patterns in clause, sentence, and discourse in selected languages of India and Nepal 1: Sentence and discourse, ed. by Ronald L. Trail. 1973.
41.2. Patterns in clause, sentence, and discourse in selected languages of India and Nepal 2: Clause, ed. by Ronald L. Trail. 1973.
41.3. Patterns in clause, sentence, and discourse in selected languages of India and Nepal 3: Texts, ed. by Ronald L. Trail. 1973.
41.4. Patterns in clause, sentence, and discourse in selected languages of India and Nepal 4: Word lists, ed. by Ronald L. Trail. 1973.

42. A generative syntax of Peñoles Mixtec, by John P. Daly. 1973.
43. Daga grammar: From morpheme to discourse, by Elizabeth Murane. 1974.
44. A hierarchical sketch of Mixe as spoken in San José El Paraíso, by Julia D. Van Haitsma and Willard Van Haitsma. 1976.
45. Network grammars, ed. by Joseph E. Grimes. 1975.
46. A description of Hiligaynon syntax, by Elmer Wolfenden. 1975.
47. A grammar of Izi, an Igbo language, by Paul E. Meier, Inge Meier, and John T. Bendor-Samuel. 1975.
48. Semantic relationships of Gahuku verbs, by Ellis W. Deibler. 1976.
49. Sememic and grammatical structures in Gurung, by Warren W. Glover. 1974.
50. Clause structure: Surface structure and deep structure roles, by Shin Ja Joo Hwang. 1975.
51. Papers on discourse, ed. by Joseph E. Grimes. 1978.
52.1. Discourse grammar: Studies in indigenous languages of Colombia, Panama, and Ecuador 1, ed. by Robert E. Longacre and Frances Woods. 1976.
52.2. Discourse grammar: Studies in indigenous languages of Colombia, Panama, and Ecuador 2, ed. by Robert E. Longacre and Frances Woods. 1977.
52.3. Discourse grammar: Studies in indigenous languages of Colombia, Panama, and Ecuador 3, ed. by Robert E. Longacre and Frances Woods. 1977.
53. Grammatical analysis, by Kenneth L. Pike and Evelyn G. Pike. 1977.
54. Studies in Otomanguean phonology, ed. by William R. Merrifield. 1977.
55. Two studies in Middle American comparative linguistics, by David Oltrogge and Calvin R. Rensch. 1977.
56.1. An overview of Uto-Aztecan grammar: Studies in Uto-Aztecan grammar 1, by Ronald W. Langacker. 1977.
56.2. Modern Aztec grammatical sketches: Studies in Uto-Aztecan grammar 2, ed. by Ronald W. Langacker. 1979.
56.3. Uto-Aztecan grammatical sketches: Studies in Uto-Aztecan grammar 3, ed. by Ronald W. Langacker. 1982.
56.4. Southern Uto-Aztecan grammatical sketches: Studies in Uto-Aztecan grammar 4, ed. by Ronald W. Langacker. 1984.
57. The deep structure of the sentence in Sara-Ngambay dialogues, including a description of phrase, clause, and paragraph, by James Edward Thayer. 1978.
58.1. Discourse studies in Mesoamerican languages 1: Discussion, ed. by Linda K. Jones. 1979.
58.2. Discourse studies in Mesoamerican languages 2: Texts, ed. by Linda K. Jones. 1979.
59. The functions of reported speech in discourse, by Mildred L. Larson. 1978.
60. A grammatical description of the Engenni language, by Elaine Thomas. 1978.
61. Predicate and argument in Rengao grammar, by Kenneth J. Gregerson. 1979.
62. Nung grammar, by Janice E. Saul and Nancy F. Wilson. 1980.
63. Discourse grammar in Gaꞏdang, by Michael R. Walrod. 1979.
64. A framework for discourse analysis, by Wilbur N. Pickering. 1980.
65. A generative grammar of Afar, by Loren F. Bliese. 1981.
66. Phonology and morphology of Axininca Campa, by David L. Payne. 1981.
67. Pragmatic aspects of English text structure, by Larry B. Jones. 1983.
68. Syntactic change and syntactic reconstruction: A tagmemic approach, by John R. Costello. 1983.

98. **The structure of Thai narrative,** by Somsonge Burusphat. 1991.

99. **Tense and aspect in eight languages of Cameroon,** ed. by Stephen C. Anderson and Bernard Comrie. 1991.

100. **A reference grammar of Southeastern Tepehuan,** by Thomas L. Willett. 1991.

101. **Barasano syntax: Studies in the languages of Colombia 2,** by Wendell Jones and Paula Jones. 1991.

102. **Tone in five languages of Cameroon,** ed. by Stephen C. Anderson. 1991.

103. **An autosegmental approach to Shilluk phonology,** by Leoma G. Gilley. 1992.

104. **Sentence repetition testing for studies of community bilingualism,** by Carla F. Radloff. 1991.

105. **Studies in the syntax of Mixtecan languages 3,** ed. by C. Henry Bradley and Barbara E. Hollenbach. 1991.

106. **Tepetotutla Chinantec syntax: Studies in Chinantec languages 5,** by David Westley. 1991.

107. **Language in context: Essays for Robert E. Longacre,** ed. by Shin Ja J. Hwang and William R. Merrifield. 1992.

108. **Phonological studies in four languages of Maluku,** ed. by Donald A. Burquest and Wyn D. Laidig. 1992.

109. **Switch reference in Koasati discourse,** by David Rising. 1992.

110. **Windows on bilingualism,** by Eugene Casad. 1992.

111. **Studies in the syntax of Mixtecan languages 4,** ed. by C. Henry Bradley and Barbara E. Hollenbach. 1992.

112. **Retuará syntax: Studies in the languages of Colombia 3,** by Clay Strom. 1992.

113. **A pragmatic analysis of Norwegian modal particles,** by Erik E. Andvik. 1992.

114. **Proto Witotoan,** by Richard P. Aschmann. 1993.

115. **The function of verb prefixes in Southwestern Otomí,** by Henrietta Andrews. 1993.

116. **The French imparfait and passé simple in discourse,** by Sharon Rebecca Rand. 1993.

117. **Beyond the bilingual classroom: Literacy acquisition among Peruvian Amazon communities,** by Barbara Trudell. 1993.

118. **Epena Pedee syntax: Studies in the languages of Colombia 4,** by Phillip Lee Harms. 1994.

119. **Discourse features of ten languages of West-Central Africa,** ed. by Stephen H. Levensohn. 1994.

121. **The Doyayo language: Selected studies,** by Elisabeth Wiering and Marinus Wiering. 1994.

For further information or a catalog of SIL publications write to:

International Academic Bookstore
Summer Institute of Linguistics
7500 W. Camp Wisdom Road
Dallas, TX 75236